To my sister,
Darlene Gadley

CONTENTS AT A GLANCE

Create Your First Web Page

In a Weekend

Third Edition

STEVE CALLIHAN

A DIVISION OF PRIMA PUBLISHING

A Division of Prima Publishing

Prima Publishing and colophon are registered trademarks of Prima Communications, Inc. PRIMA TECH and In a Weekend are trademarks of Prima Communications, Inc., Rocklin, California 95765.

Publisher: Stacy L. Hiquet

Associate Publisher: Nancy Stevenson

Marketing Manager: Judi Taylor

Managing Editor: Sandy Doell

Associate Acquisitions Editor: Rebecca I. Fong

Senior Editors: Kim V. Benbow, Kevin Harreld

Project Editor: Lorraine Cooper

Technical Editor: Chris Aloia

Copy Editor: Martin Lasater

Interior Layout: Marian Hartsough

Cover Design: Prima Design Team

Indexer: Sherry Massey

Microsoft, Windows, Internet Explorer, and Notepad are trademarks or registered trademarks of Microsoft Corporation. Netscape is a registered trademark of Netscape Communications Corporation.

Important: Prima Publishing cannot provide software support. Please contact the appropriate software manufacturer's technical support line or Web site for assistance.

Prima Publishing and the author have attempted throughout this book to distinguish proprietary trademarks from descriptive terms by following the capitalization style used by the manufacturer.

Information contained in this book has been obtained by Prima Publishing from sources believed to be reliable. However, because of the possibility of human or mechanical error by our sources, Prima Publishing, or others, the Publisher does not guarantee the accuracy, adequacy, or completeness of any information and is not responsible for any errors or omissions or the results obtained from use of such information. Readers should be particularly aware of the fact that the Internet is an ever-changing entity. Some facts may have changed since this book went to press.

ISBN: 0-7615-2482-7

Library of Congress Catalog Card Number: 99-65817

Printed in the United States of America

00 01 02 03 BB 10 9 8 7 6 5 4 3 2

CONTENTS

SATURDAY MORNING
The Basic HTML Tutorial

SATURDAY EVENING
The Tables Tutorial (Bonus Session) 169

SUNDAY MORNING
Planning Your First Web Page 201

ACKNOWLEDGMENTS

The creating of any book is much more than just a one-person job. Any author owes a large debt to the many helpers who perform many of the necessary tasks required to produce a quality and, hopefully, successful book. Much appreciation is due to Lorraine Cooper (Project Editor), Rebecca Fong (Associate Acquisitions Editor), Chris Aloia (Technical Editor), Martin Lasater (Copy Editor), David Plotkin (CD-ROM Producer), and Marian Hartsough (Interior Layout) for their strong efforts and very real contributions to this new edition.

ABOUT THE AUTHOR

Steve Callihan is a freelance and technical writer from Seattle, Wash. He is the author of three other books, *Learn HTML In a Weekend (Revised Edition)*, *Create Your First Mac Web Page In a Weekend*, and *Create Web Animations with Microsoft Liquid Motion In a Weekend*, all published by Prima Tech. Steve is also co-author, with Lisa D. Wagner, of *Create Front-Page 2000 Web Pages In a Weekend*, also published by Prima Tech. He has had several articles published in major computer magazines, including *Internet World*, and has extensive experience writing and producing hardware and software user guides.

INTRODUCTION

You live in a busy world in which time is at a premium. You've surfed the Web and wondered what it would take to start creating your own Web pages, but it seemed as if you had to become an expert on HTML *(HyperText Markup Language)*, and somehow you just never managed to find the time. But you don't have to wait! Even if you know absolutely nothing about HTML, you can create your first Web page in just one weekend! You also don't have to become an HTML expert—the Saturday HTML tutorials tell you everything you need to know about HTML to create a wide variety of Web pages.

NOTE

This book is targeted to Windows users. Although many Macintosh users have successfully used previous editions of this book to create their first Web page, I have since written a book specifically targeted to Macintosh and iMac users, *Create Your First Mac Web Page In a Weekend*, also published by Prima Tech.

Anyone who has a basic understanding of HTML and a few easily available software tools can readily create the vast majority of the sites you see on the Web. That's exactly what this book is about. Everything you'll need to know is covered, including everything you need to know to put your page up on the Web.

Who Should Read This Book

What is so liberating about the Web is that you don't have to be a computer expert to take advantage of its benefits. Everyone has interests besides computers. Computers, the Web, and HTML are tools that enable people to do stuff, not ends in themselves. The Web, via HTML, should serve as an extension of your interests. People make the mistake of thinking HTML is for computer professionals, but HTML is actually for everybody. Consequently, this book, like the Web, is for everybody—or at least for anyone who wants to get a Web site up and running right away, without having to become an expert first.

HTML isn't something you learn first and do later. It's more like riding a bicycle. You learn by doing. Don't worry about making mistakes. Mistakes are just experimental results by another name. Play around with it and experiment. That's the only way you're going to truly learn.

What You Can Do in a Weekend

I'm not going to promise that you'll be able to learn HTML and develop a full-blown multipage Web site in a single weekend. That would be selling snake oil! But you can learn many of the most useful features of HTML and apply them in creating a wide variety of different types of attractive and effective Web pages.

This book uses a graduated fast-track approach to learning HTML and creating your first Web page. If this weekend you only complete the Basic HTML Tutorial, scheduled for Saturday morning, you'll learn *everything* you need to know to create a very credible Web page. Everything else is really frosting on the cake.

The point of this book is to get the learning of HTML out of the way so you can move on to what you really want to do. You might want, for instance, to create your own personal page so you can tell the world about yourself. You might want to create a page for your family, your fraternity or sorority, or your church or club. If you're looking for a job or want to advance your career, you might want to create an online version of your résumé. You might want to put up a page featuring a hobby, interest, or area of expertise that you have. If you have a business with products or services to offer, you might want to create an online brochure or a catalog, or put up a general description of your organization.

If you have information or expertise you want to share with others, you might want to create a glossary or an FAQ (*Frequently Asked Questions*) page. If you are helping to run a civic organization or a social club, you might want to create a calendar of upcoming events or publish the agenda for your next meeting. If you're creative, you could put up a page of your poetry, a short story, or a gallery of your drawings, paintings, or photographs. If you're a student, you might want to publish an online version of an abstract, book review, or thesis. Professors might publish course outlines, required reading lists, and assignment descriptions. You could publish your own page of movie reviews, or your own newsletter or journal. The list goes on and on—your options are unlimited!

You may not necessarily set up a whole Web site in just one weekend, but you could definitely get its development off to a substantial start. The idea isn't to create just one Web page but by the end of the weekend to have enough hands-on experience with HTML to be able to create any kind of page mentioned here, or any other type of page you might dream up.

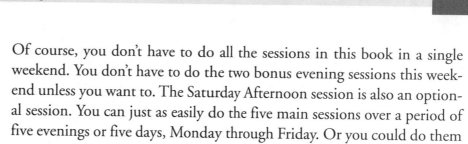

Of course, you don't have to do all the sessions in this book in a single weekend. You don't have to do the two bonus evening sessions this weekend unless you want to. The Saturday Afternoon session is also an optional session. You can just as easily do the five main sessions over a period of five evenings or five days, Monday through Friday. Or you could do them over a period of a week if you want to also do the bonus sessions. It's entirely up to you.

What You Need to Begin

You don't need to be a techie or computer nerd to use this book, but you should have a working knowledge of basic Windows operations, such as using File Manager or Windows Explorer to create, copy, move, and delete files or folders. You should also know how to switch between Windows applications (although the Saturday Morning session does provide a rundown on this activity).

This book is written under the assumption that you already know how to use a Web browser and navigate on the Web. It mentions quite a few resources available on the Web, so you should know how to download a file or program from the Web. Because many programs on the Web are in compressed format—ZIP or TAR, for instance—you should know how to decompress files using utilities such as WinZip or PKUnzip.

Although a CD-ROM does ship with this book, you don't need to have a CD-ROM drive to complete all the tasks. Web addresses (URLs) are provided for all the software programs, Web art, and reference materials included on the CD-ROM, so you can download them even if you can't use the disc. Sample Web pages and graphics created just for this book are available for downloading at this book's Web site at **http://www. callihan.com/create3/**.

You don't need any fancy software tools to create your own Web pages. At minimum, all you really need is a text editor to create your HTML files and a graphical Web browser so you can preview your work. If you want to create your own personalized graphics for your Web pages, you'll need an image editor capable of creating GIF or JPEG images. Finally, to transfer your Web page files up onto a Web server, you'll need an FTP program. Here's a rundown on some of your choices:

- **A text editor.** My recommendation is that you use a text editor and not a word processor to create HTML files. Windows Notepad is perfectly suitable for doing this. You'll also find some additional text editors and Notepad-like HTML editors on the CD-ROM.

- **A graphical Web browser.** To do the Basic HTML Tutorial and to create a basic Web page, you only need to have a fairly recent graphical Web browser installed. However, if you want to do most or all of the examples included in the Intermediate HTML Tutorial and the Tables Tutorial, you should have at least an HTML 3.2- or HTML 4.0-compliant Web browser installed, such as Microsoft Internet Explorer 4.0+ or Netscape Navigator 4.0+. (You can also install an evaluation version of the Opera browser from the CD-ROM that can be used to preview all of the HTML 3.2 examples in the Intermediate HTML Tutorial.)

- **An image editor.** To create personalized Web graphics, you'll need an image editor that can create GIF and JPEG images. You don't need a professional painting program, such as Adobe Photoshop or Corel PhotoPaint, just to be able to create your own Web graphics. In the Sunday Evening bonus session, "The Graphics Tutorial," you'll learn how to use Paint Shop Pro 5 (included on the CD-ROM) to create your own personalized Web images.

- **An FTP program.** Once you've created your first Web page, you'll want to be able to transfer it up onto the Web. Appendix D, "Putting It Up on the Web," covers using WS_FTP LE (included on the CD-ROM) to transfer your Web page files up onto a Web server.

How This Book Is Organized

The book is divided into five main sessions scheduled for Friday evening, Saturday morning, Saturday afternoon, Sunday morning, and Sunday afternoon and two bonus sessions scheduled for Saturday evening and Sunday evening that you can do if you have the time. Each of the main sessions should take no more than three or four hours to complete, and the bonus sessions should take no longer than a couple of hours. I've tried to take different learning styles into account and build in as much flexibility as I can. The whole Saturday Afternoon session plus both bonus sessions are optional, for instance, to be done only if you have the time (you can always come back and do them later). I've also included a number of appendixes, including a resource directory, the CD-ROM contents, a table of special characters, and instructions on how to put your Web page up on the Web. Here are some details of what's included in the book:

- **Friday Evening: Getting Started.** This session covers essential background information and the minimum requirements for doing the two Saturday HTML tutorials. It also includes an optional section on tools and resources that can help you create your Web page.

- **Saturday Morning: The Basic HTML Tutorial.** Here you have a step-by-step tutorial that covers the basic HTML codes most commonly used to create Web pages. It's organized according to function, to teach you what each code does and to give you an overall view of HTML and how it works. Although this tutorial is slated for Saturday morning, feel free to go ahead and take all day to do it.

- **Saturday Afternoon: The Intermediate HTML Tutorial.** This is an optional tutorial that you only need to do if you have the time and energy after completing the Basic HTML Tutorial. It primarily covers features of HTML that give you more control over the layout and appearance of your Web page.

- **Saturday Evening (Bonus Session): The Tables Tutorial.** Take on this optional tutorial only if you have the time and energy. It covers all the essentials you need to know to effectively use tables in your Web pages.

- **Sunday Morning: Planning Your First Web Page.** This is a hands-on session that guides you in planning your Web page, including defining an objective, doing an outline, writing some text, and assembling or creating the different pieces or components that will make up your page. It also furnishes models that you can follow in assembling or creating these components.

- **Sunday Afternoon: Creating Your First Web Page.** Here you actually create your first Web page based on the decision tree you designed during the morning's planning session. Depending upon the Web page model you use, you'll choose which options you want to implement for your page. Extra options are also provided for those who've completed the Intermediate HTML Tutorial.

- **Sunday Evening (Bonus Session): The Graphics Tutorial.** This optional tutorial can be done after you create your first Web page. It shows you how to use Paint Shop Pro 5 to create a banner graphic, as well as a 3-D button image, for your Web page.

Once you've planned and created your first Web page this weekend, you can check out the appendixes in this book for additional guidance and resources for further pursuing and enhancing your Web publishing efforts. Here's a rundown on what is in the appendixes:

- Pointers to where on the Web you can find lots of additional Web publishing resources, including HTML references, guides, tutorials, and software tools

- A chart of all of the HTML codes for special characters (characters not on your keyboard) that can be included in a Web page

- Pointers and tips on how to add background sounds, counters, guestbooks, Java applets, and other wish-list items

- Guidance in finding a Web presence provider to host your pages, as well as guidance in using an FTP program, WS_FTP LE, to transfer your Web page or pages up to your Web space folders on the Web

- A rundown on the past and future of HTML, including how HTML got to be what it is today and where it's headed

✿   Instructions on how to use the CD-ROM, as well as a rundown on its contents

What's New in the 3rd Edition

The 3rd Edition has been updated to reflect the very latest developments in HTML and Web publishing, including additional sections and examples for implementing HTML 4.0 and style sheets. A lot of great feedback from readers has gone into making this edition even easier to read and use.

On the CD-ROM, all of the software has been updated to the very latest available versions, and many new freeware, shareware, and evaluation software programs have been added to help enhance your Web publishing efforts. All of the HTML templates included on the CD-ROM have also been updated and improved.

In response to many reader queries, a new appendix, "Completing Your Wish List," has been added. As mentioned, it covers adding background sounds, hit counters, guestbooks, Java applets, and other wish-list items for your Web pages.

Special Features of This Book

This book uses a number of special text formats and icons to make your job easier as you work through the sessions. They are used to highlight and call your attention to notes, tips, cautions, buzzwords, additional resources located on the Web, and programs or other resources that are included on the CD-ROM.

NOTE   Notes are food for thought as you work through the tutorials. They will bring up points of interest or other relevant information you might find useful.

TIP

Tips offer helpful hints, tricks, and ideas to apply as you progress in the creation process.

CAUTION

Cautions warn you of possible hazards and point out pitfalls that typically plague beginners.

BUZZ WORD

Buzzwords are terms and acronyms that you should be familiar with and keep in mind as you develop and expand your skills.

ON THE

CD

The CD-ROM icon marks resources or tools located on the accompanying CD-ROM that may be helpful to you in your Web endeavors.

Visit This Book's Web Site

I have set up the *Create Your First Web Page In a Weekend (3rd Edition)* Web site at **http://www.callihan.com/create3/**. At the Web site, you will find a list of affordable Internet presence providers (IPPs) that you can use as a starting point in your search for a server to host your Web page, continually updated lists of Web publishing resources and tools, as well as a tip sheet on how to implement "seamless" offline browsing, links to readers' pages, additional Web page templates (as I develop them), and other information, advice, and feedback. All sample Web pages and graphics used in the book are available for download. You'll also find downloads that are not on the CD-ROM, including a Web art library and a collection of fonts. And if you run into any trouble that you can't resolve, you can use the e-mail link to query the author.

Getting Started

- ✪ What tools do you need?
- ✪ What are the Internet and the Web?
- ✪ What is a Web page?
- ✪ Browsing offline

It's Friday evening—at least if you're following the schedule. Yes, for the purposes of this book, Friday evening constitutes part of the weekend. Okay, maybe that is fudging a bit, but if you're going to create your first Web page in a weekend, you need to get this little reading assignment out of the way first.

The first part of this session provides a quick rundown on the tools you'll be using to complete the tutorials and to plan and create your first Web page. These include a text editor, a Web browser, and an image editor (optional for this weekend).

The middle part of the session includes general background information on the Internet, the World Wide Web, HTML, and Web pages. You really should have some grounding in the medium before you start the HTML tutorials on Saturday or begin to create your first Web page on Sunday. Of course, if you're already familiar with something covered in these sections, feel free to skip or merely skim it.

The last part of the session covers running your Web browser offline. It includes quick-and-dirty methods for running the latest versions of Netscape Navigator and Microsoft Internet Explorer offline, so you can preview your HTML files locally on your own hard drive.

What Tools Do You Need?

You don't need any special software tools just to create and edit your own HTML files. The only tools you really need, starting out, are a text editor and a graphical Web browser. If you want to create your own personalized Web art images, you'll also need an image editor that can save GIF and JPEG images. Additionally, once you get to the point where you want to put your Web page files up on the Web, you'll need an FTP program to transfer them. The following sections provide some details on the tools you'll need for your weekend.

Using a Text Editor to Edit HTML Files

You don't need anything fancy to create HTML files. Because HTML files are straight text files, any plain and ordinary text editor will do. My recommendation, at least for the purposes of doing the tutorials in this book and planning and creating your first Web page, is that you stick to using Windows Notepad, which comes with all versions of Windows, as your text editor.

Notepad has a number of advantages that make it the tool of choice for many professional Web publishers:

✿ You already have it.

✿ It's a small, efficient program, so it can easily remain in memory with your Web browser without hogging precious system resources. New Web browsers are known to be resource hogs.

✿ Because Notepad is a text editor rather than a word processor, you can have an HTML file open in both Notepad and your Web browser at the same time. You can't do that with Write, Word, WordPerfect, and most other word processing programs.

Using an HTML Editor

You can also use an HTML editor, if you wish, to do the HTML tutorials and create your first Web page. My recommendation, however, is that you don't get bogged down trying to learn the ins and outs of an HTML editing program when you need to focus on learning HTML itself (that is, if you want to get your first Web page created in a weekend). Learn HTML first, and then investigate what HTML editing programs can do for you.

It is also important, I believe, to gain a code-level familiarity with HTML. Only then can you stick your head under the hood if something doesn't work right. That means typing in your HTML codes the old-fashioned way, not just inserting them from a drop-down menu or toolbar.

Once you've done the HTML tutorials and planned and created your first Web page, feel free to experiment with some of the different HTML editors that are available. You'll find several HTML editors on the CD-ROM. For the time being, however, I recommend you stick with Windows Notepad.

If you do decide to use an HTML editor, I recommend that you use an editor that will allow you to work the same way you would using Notepad. You should avoid using WSYWYG HTML editors that won't allow you to type in your own HTML from scratch.

Using a Word Processor

I don't recommend that you use a word processing program for the tutorials in this book. That's because you cannot keep the same file open in both your word processor and your Web browser, which means you won't be able to dynamically debug your HTML files. Take it from me: Do yourself a favor and don't bother trying to use a word processor for creating HTML files. Stick to Notepad or one of the Notepad-like HTML editors.

Previewing Your HTML Files in Your Browser

You will need to use a Web browser to preview your work as you do the HTML tutorials and create your first Web page. In tomorrow morning's session, I'll show you how to hop back and forth between your text editor and your Web browser to be able to dynamically update your work as you go.

Any graphical Web browser you already have installed can be used to do the Basic HTML Tutorial, and then to help you plan and create your first Web page. For the Intermediate HTML Tutorial, you'll need to have an HTML 3.2-compliant Web browser installed. I recommend that you use either Internet Explorer 4.0+/5.0+ or Netscape Navigator 4.0+ to do the HTML tutorials in this book—at a minimum, you should have at least Netscape Navigator 2.0+ or Microsoft Internet Explorer 3.0+ installed. Other browsers, such as Opera 3.0 or Neoplanet 2.0, can also be used.

At the end of this session, under "Browsing Offline," I've included instructions for browsing offline in Netscape Navigator and Internet Explorer.

Do You Need a Connection to the Internet?

If you're using Windows 95, 98, NT, or 2000, it is not required that you have a connection to the Internet just to preview HTML files on your local computer. Windows 3.1 users, however, may need to be connected to the Internet to be able to browse HTML files on a local computer.

You'll need to have a connection to the Internet, of course, when you get around to publishing your Web pages to a Web server. For more information on getting Web space and transferring your Web pages up onto the Web, see Appendix D, "Putting It Up on the Web."

Using an Image Editor to Create Your Own Web Art

Creating your own personalized Web art images for your Web pages can add a lot of excitement and satisfaction to your Web publishing endeavors. If you don't get around to it this weekend, before too long you'll want to choose an image editor capable of creating GIF and JPEG images.

In the Sunday Evening bonus session, "The Graphics Tutorial," you'll learn how to use Paint Shop Pro 5 (included on the CD-ROM) to create Web page banners, transparent backgrounds, drop shadows, fill effects, 3-D buttons, and other Web image effects.

Many software tools can be used to create professional-looking and effective Web images, from more commercial, professional software tools, such as Adobe Photoshop, MetaCreations' Painter, and Corel PhotoPaint, to less expensive shareware and evaluation programs, such as Paint Shop Pro, LView Pro, Adobe Photoshop LE, and others. Several image-editing tools have been included on the CD-ROM. And see Appendix A, "Web Resources," for where you can find additional graphics tools on the Web.

You don't need a graphics editor to do the HTML tutorials that are scheduled for Saturday because I've already created all the graphics used in those tutorials for you. Optionally, if you don't already have a graphics editor installed that can create GIF and JPEG graphic files, you may want to install Paint Shop Pro 5 from the CD-ROM to create a custom banner graphic for your first Web page. But there is no need to install a graphics editor right now. The earliest you might need a graphics editor is for the Sunday Afternoon session, "Creating Your First Web Page," although even there I provide some sample graphics that you can use until you get around to creating your own custom graphics.

Using an FTP Program to Transfer Your Web Page Files

Once you've created and tested your Web page on your local computer, you'll want to put it up on the Web for all to see. I've included a special appendix, Appendix D, "Putting It Up on the Web," that covers finding a Web host for your Web page files and using an FTP program, WS_FTP LE (included on the CD-ROM), to transfer your Web page files up to your server folder. Other FTP programs, such as CuteFTP, for instance, can also be used.

A Little Background Information

Before you actually get around to creating your own Web pages, it is important and valuable for you to know something about the medium in which you'll be working. If you're already familiar with the questions covered in this section, please feel free to skim or skip it.

What Is the Internet?

It could be said that the Internet is the most valuable legacy left over from the Cold War. It originally came into being as the ARPANet, which was founded by the U.S. Department of Defense's Advanced Research Projects Agency (ARPA) to link academic research centers involved in military research.

BUZZ WORD

◄◄

An *internet* is a network of networks, a kind of meta-network. Simply put, the Internet is a set of protocols (rules) for transmitting and exchanging data between networks. In a broader sense, however, it is a worldwide community, a global village, and a repository of global information resources.

◄◄

Today's Internet has grown far beyond its original conception. Originally linking just four university research centers, it has become an international and global system consisting of hundreds of thousands of *nodes* (servers). In many ways, it has become what Marshall McLuhan called "the global village," in that every node is functionally right next door. You can just as easily communicate with someone in Australia as you can with someone two blocks down the street—and if the person down the street isn't on the Internet, it's actually easier to communicate with the bloke in Australia. That is the premise, even if the original founders didn't realize it, and today it has become an increasingly pervasive reality.

◄◄

A *client* is a computer that requests something from another computer. A *server* is a computer that responds to requests for service from clients.

◄◄

◄◄

TCP/IP *(Transmission Control Protocol/Internet Protocol)* is the standard rule set for Internet communication. The essence of the Internet is not the wire, but the means for sending and receiving information across the wire. It doesn't matter what type of systems are connected to the Internet, be they mainframes, minicomputers, or UNIX, Macintosh, or MS-DOS computers. All that matters is that they all use the same protocol, TCP/IP, to communicate with each other.

◄◄

What Is the World Wide Web?

The World Wide Web, also called the WWW, W3, or simply the Web, dates back to 1989, when Tim Berners-Lee, often called "the inventor of the World Wide Web," proposed it. Many others have been critically involved, but Berners-Lee gets the credit for originally proposing and evangelizing the idea as a way to facilitate collaboration between scientists and other academics over the Internet.

On the original Web page for the World Wide Web Project, posted on the CERN (the European Laboratory for Particle Physics, birthplace of the World Wide Web) server in 1992, Berners-Lee described the World Wide Web as "a wide-area hypermedia information retrieval initiative aiming to give universal access to a large universe of documents." Today, he is more likely to describe the Web as the "universal space of all network-accessible information." Ted Nelson, inventor of the concept of hypertext, wrapped all this up in a wonderfully apt term, describing the Word Wide Web as a "docuverse."

Like the Internet, the Web is essentially defined by a set of protocols:

- **HTTP (Hypertext Transfer Protocol).** Used to exchange Web documents across the Internet. When you request a Web document from a server, the protocol used for the request is HTTP.

- **HTML (Hypertext Markup Language).** Enables users to present information over the Web in a structured and uniform fashion. It is used to mark up documents so that a Web browser can interpret and then display them. See "What Is HTML?" later in this session for more information.

- **URLs (Uniform Resource Locators).** Addresses that identify a server, a directory, or a specific file. HTTP URLs, or Web addresses, are only one type of address on the Web. FTP, Gopher, and WAIS are other types of addresses you'll find fairly often on the Web as well. In fact, until fairly recently, there were still more FTP and Gopher servers on the Internet than HTTP servers. See "What Is a URL?" later in this session for additional information.

- **CGI (Common Gateway Interface).** Serves as an interface to execute local programs through a gateway between the HTTP server software and the host computer. Thus, you can include a hypertext link in a Web document that will run a server program or script, for example, to process input from a customer request form.

Although other mediums of exchange on the Internet share the same cyberspace, the Web has come to epitomize the new paradigm. In fact, Web browsers can access not only Web or HTML documents, but also the entirety of the Internet, including Gopher, FTP, Archie, Telnet, and WAIS, as well as Mail and News servers. The Web's tendency to embrace and incorporate all other mediums, in effect to operate as a universal medium, is its most revolutionary characteristic.

A LITTLE HISTORY

The beginnings of the Internet go back at least as far as 1957, to the founding of the U.S. Department of Defense's Advanced Research Projects Agency (ARPA) in response to the Soviet Union's launching *Sputnik*. In 1963, ARPA asked the Rand Corporation to ponder how to form a command-and-control network capable of surviving attack by atomic bombs. The Rand Corporation's response (made public in 1964) was that the network would "have no central authority" and would be "designed from the beginning to operate while in tatters." These two basic concepts became the defining characteristics of what would eventually become the Internet. The Internet was conceptualized as having no central authority and as being able to operate in a condition of assumed unreliability (bombed-out cities, downed telephone lines). In other words, it would have maximum redundancy. All nodes would be coequal in status, each with authority to originate, relay, and receive messages.

What happened between this first military initiative and the Internet we know today? Here are some of the highlights:

1965: Ted Nelson invents the concept of and coins the term *hypertext*.

1969: ARPANet, the forerunner of the Internet, is commissioned by the U.S. Department of Defense. Nodes at UCLA, Stanford, UC Santa Barbara, and the University of Utah are linked.

1971: Number of nodes on the Internet increases to fifteen (twenty-three hosts). New nodes include MIT, RAND, Harvard, and NASA/Ames.

1972: Telnet is introduced.

1973: The first international connections to the ARPANet occur from England and Norway. FTP (*File Transfer Protocol*) is introduced.

1977: E-mail is introduced.

1979: Usenet newsgroups are introduced.

1982: ARPANet adopts TCP/IP (Transmission Control Protocol/Internet Protocol), the real beginning of the Internet.

1984: DNS (*Domain Name Server*) is implemented, allocating addresses among six basic domain types: gov, mil, edu, net, com, and org (for government, military, educational, network, commercial, and noncommercial hosts, respectively). One thousand hosts (computer systems each identified by a unique IP address) are present on the Internet.

1985: First registered domain name is assigned.

1986: NSFNet is formed by the NSF (*National Science Foundation*) using five supercomputing centers. Unlike ARPANet, which is focused on military and government research, NSFNet is available for all forms of academic research.

1988: The Web backbone is upgraded to T1 (1.544 Mbps).

1989: Tim Berners-Lee proposes the creation of the World Wide Web. Australia (AU), Germany (DE), Israel (IL), Italy (IT), Japan (JP), Mexico (MX), Netherlands (NL), New Zealand (NZ), Puerto Rico (PR), and the United Kingdom (UK) join the Internet. One hundred thousand hosts are on the Internet.

1990: ARPANet closes down. Archie is introduced. The first commercial provider of dial-up access to the Internet opens shop. Eleven more countries, from Europe, South America, and Asia, join the Internet.

1991: Gopher is introduced. The World Wide Web is released by CERN (European Laboratory for Particle Physics) in Switzerland. The Web's backbone is upgraded to T3 (44.736 Mbps).

1992: The Internet Society (ISOC) is formed. Viola, the first English-language graphical Web browser, is released. Jean Amour Polly coins the phrase "Surfing the Internet." One million hosts are on the Internet.

1993: Marc Andreesen's Mosaic browser is released by NCSA. The White House goes online.

1994: Mosaic Communications, later to become Netscape Communications, is formed by Marc Andreesen and James Clark, former president of Silicon Graphics. The first meeting of the World Wide Web Consortium, or W3C, is held at MIT. The first cybermalls form.

1995: Netscape goes public. WWW traffic on the Internet outstrips FTP, with the Web becoming the most popular form of accessing the Internet. RealAudio is introduced. InterNIC starts charging for registering domain names.

1996: Bill Gates and Microsoft jump into the game with the Internet Explorer browser. Ten million hosts are on the Internet.

1997: HTML 3.2 is released in January. The Justice Department files an antitrust complaint against Microsoft. HTML 4.0 is released in December.

1998: Two million domain names are registered. XML 1.0 (*Extensible Markup Language*) is released by the W3C. Netscape is purchased by AOL. The number of users on the Web is estimated at between thirty-five and fifty million.

1999: Draft specification for XHTML 1.0 (*Extensible HTML*), a reformulation of HTML 4.0 in XML, is announced by W3C. Web Content Accessibility Guidelines, which improve access to Web sites for people with disabilities, are published. Over forty million hosts are on the Internet.

What Is Hypertext?

You could say the Web is a graphical, platform-independent, distributed, decentralized, multi-formatted, interactive, dynamic, nonlinear, immediate, two-way communication medium. The basic mechanism that enables all of it is actually quite simple—the *hypertext link,* a kind of "jump point" that allows a visitor to jump from a place in a Web page to any other Web page, document, or binary data-object (a script, graphic, video, etc.) on the Web. Not only can you jump to another Web page, but you can also jump to another place, either in the same Web page or another Web page. If you've ever clicked on a link, then jumped to a place in the middle of either the same or another Web page, you've seen this capability in action. A link can connect anything anywhere that has an address or URL on the Net. When Ted Nelson coined the term "hypertext" in 1965, he conceptualized it simply as "non-sequential writing." In other words, any link can go to any object anywhere (anything with an address) within the "docuverse," or "universal space of all network-accessible information," as Tim Berners-Lee puts it. See Figure 1.1 for a general representation of how hypertext links work.

Figure 1.1

Using hypertext links, you can jump from one Web page to another, or to another place in another (or the same) Web page.

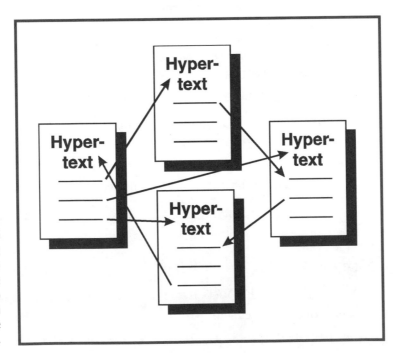

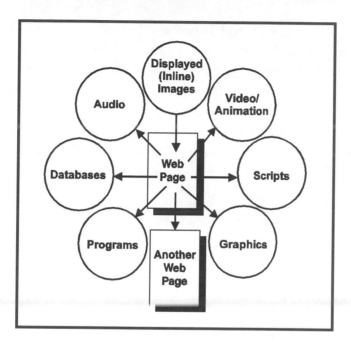

Figure 1.2

A Web page can link to many kinds of data objects.

Figure 1.2 illustrates some of the different kinds of data objects to which you can link from a Web page. Note the difference here between an inline image, which appears as part of the Web page, and other graphics, which your browser or viewer can link to and display separately.

A hypertext link, also referred to as an *anchor,* actually works much like a cross-reference in a book, except that you can immediately go to it simply by clicking on the link, whether it's a link within the same document or to a page or document halfway around the world. You don't have to thumb through the book or go down to the local library to find the reference. Anything that has an address on the Web can be linked, including Gopher documents, FTP files, and newsgroup articles.

What Is Hypermedia?

Given that hypertext linking occurs within and between documents, it makes sense that hypermedia (a term also coined by Ted Nelson) refers to connecting with and between other nontext (binary) media such as graphics, audio, animation, video, or software programs. Many pages on the Web are now generated on the fly from scripts, programs, or database queries. Increasingly, Java applets are being used to generate dynamically interactive Web sites. Over time, the Web will naturally evolve from a system predominantly composed of primarily static hypertext Web pages to one predominantly composed of dynamically interlinked hypermedia, within which text is just another medium.

For now, though, the Web still mainly consists of documents, or pages, and you can still think of hypermedia as a subcategory of hypertext.

What Is HTML?

HTML is a subset of SGML *(Standard Generalized Markup Language)*. SGML was developed to standardize the *markup,* or preparation for typesetting, of computer-generated documents. HTML, on the other hand, was specifically developed to mark up, or encode, hypertext documents for display on the World Wide Web.

An HTML document is a plain text file with codes (called *tags*) inserted in the text to define elements in the document. HTML tags generally have two parts, an on-code and an off-code, which contain the text to be defined. A few tags don't require an off-code, and I'll note those when we cover them. You can represent a tag in the following way, where the ellipsis (. . .) represents the text you want to tag:

```
<Tagname> . . . </Tagname>
```

For instance, the following is the tag for a level-one heading in a Web document:

```
<H1>This is a level-one heading</H1>
```

The most important thing to keep in mind about HTML is that its purpose isn't necessarily to specify the exact formatting or layout of a Web page but to define and specify the specific elements that make up a page—the body of the text, headings, paragraphs, line breaks, text elements, and so on. You use HTML primarily to define the composition of a Web page, and much less to determine its appearance. The particular Web browser you use to view the page controls the display of the Web page. For instance, you can define a line using the <H1> . . . </H1> tag, but the browser defines the appearance of a first-level heading line. One browser might show H1 lines as 18-point Times Roman text, and another might show H1 lines in a totally different font and size.

How HTML and Browsers Work Together

To understand why HTML works the way it does, you need to understand how HTML-coded Web pages and Web browsers work together. To display a Web page on your computer, a Web browser must first download it and any graphics displayed on the page to your computer. If the Web page were to specify all the formatting and display details, it would increase the amount of data to be transmitted, the size of the file, and the amount of time it takes to transfer. Leaving all the formatting and display details to the Web browser means that the size of HTML documents sent over the Web can remain relatively small—they're just regular ASCII text files. It's rare to have an HTML file that exceeds 30KB (not counting any graphics that it may contain).

However, this means that every Web browser has its own idea about how to best display a particular Web page. Your Web page may look different in Netscape Navigator than it does in NCSA Mosaic. That's why you may want to test your completed page on more than just one browser. Features that have been incorporated into HTML only relatively recently (in HTML 3.2 and 4.0) may not display in older browsers (tables, for instance). Both Netscape and Microsoft support extensions to HTML that may not display in other browsers.

Most current graphical Web browsers—not just Navigator and Internet Explorer—should now fully support HTML 3.2. In the Intermediate HTML Tutorial scheduled for Saturday afternoon, I'll show you how to effectively incorporate HTML 3.2 features into your Web pages.

Browsers Playing Catch-Up

The advent of the new HTML 4.0 specification adds more complications to the mix. The current versions, at the time of this writing, of Netscape Navigator and Internet Explorer already support parts of, but by no means all of, what is included in HTML 4.0. Additionally, though the latest version of Internet Explorer seems to be almost completely compliant with the Cascading Style Sheets, level 1, standard, the latest version of Navigator is somewhat lagging behind in this area. Neither browser has yet to fully support the latest proposed standard, Cascading Style Sheets, level 2. Add into that the other recent developments such as DOM (Document Object Model), XML (Extensible Markup Language), XHTML (Extensible HyperText Markup Language), and MathML (Mathematical Markup Language), and it is clear that the two major browsers are currently playing catch-up.

Most of HTML 4.0 should be supported fairly quickly, as well as most of the new Cascading Style Sheets standards (CSS1 and CSS2), especially where competitive pressures between the two main browsers dictate that they be entirely up-to-date. But other aspects of HTML 4.0 for which there may not be the same degree of competitive demand may not be implemented as quickly. The "sexier" features, such as full support for Cascading Style Sheets, should be implemented first, and less eye-catching features, such as some of the new Form elements and attributes, may have to wait their turn. Anyway, trying to predict the future of HTML is like trying to predict the weather. Stay tuned for the nightly report, because that is exactly how fast things are changing. Remember also, however, the old adage that the more things change the more they stay the same—most of what is being added to HTML now is frosting on the cake. The body of the cake is still composed almost entirely of HTML 2.0 and HTML 3.2 elements and attributes.

If you are concerned with compatibility with the vast majority of current graphical Web browsers, it may be wise for the time being to stick with HTML 3.2 elements and attributes, at least until HTML 4.0 is more fully supported. If you want to incorporate any of the new HTML 4.0

features, you should thoroughly check your pages in both of the main Web browsers. Although other Web browsers, or earlier versions of Navigator and Internet Explorer, simply ignore unrecognized tags, you should be aware that a Web page that looks fantastic in a Web browser supporting HTML 4.0 may look pretty crummy in one that doesn't. Thus, it's probably not a bad idea to keep an older Web browser installed on your system so you can make sure your pages display acceptably in browsers that don't support HTML 4.0. Saturday's sessions, "The Basic HTML Tutorial" and "The Intermediate HTML Tutorial," include several examples of how the same HTML coding can have quite different results depending on the Web browser used to view it.

NOTE As HTML has evolved, both officially and in an ad hoc manner (by browsers having their own extensions), it has become more descriptive, allowing you more freedom to "design" your page rather than simply schematicize it. The more you design your page to have a particular appearance, however, the less likely it is that all browsers will display your page consistently and accurately. The Basic and Intermediate HTML Tutorials show you how different browsers can display the same element. Also, many of the "designer" features that have been added to HTML require a Web browser that is up-to-date enough to display them.

In this book, the discussion of HTML falls into three categories: basic HTML, intermediate HTML, and advanced HTML. These divisions are in no way official—they're just an attempt to pare down the material into more serviceable chunks.

Basic HTML encompasses most, but not all, of what was HTML 2.0 (the HTML standard prior to HTML 3.2). I cover this level of HTML in the Saturday Morning session, "The Basic HTML Tutorial." Most graphical Web browsers, new or old, should support this level of HTML.

Intermediate HTML encompasses most of what is included in HTML 3.2, as well as a few tidbits from HTML 4.0. I cover this level of HTML in the Saturday Afternoon and Saturday Evening sessions, "The Intermediate

HTML Tutorial" and "The Tables Tutorial." Most current graphical Web browsers should fully support HTML 3.2, although support from earlier browser versions may be quite sketchy. (HTML 3.2 is largely a pastiche of what were previously called "Netscape extensions" and elements that were intended to be part of the failed HTML 3.0 proposal.)

Advanced HTML includes HTML 2.0, HTML 3.2, and HTML 4.0 tags, as well as other advanced features such as Cascading Style Sheets and Dynamic HTML. These features require considerably more space and time to properly explain than is available in this book. For instance, this book doesn't cover creating input forms or image maps, even though they're included in HTML 2.0, simply because they're too advanced for a beginning Web publisher to jump into right away. Similarly, this book doesn't deal directly with creating frames or using CGI or other scripts. However, Appendix A, "Web Resources," provides links to where on the Web you can find many resources, tutorials, and tools for including these advanced features in your Web pages. I've also included HTML templates on the CD-ROM to assist you in creating two- and three-frame Web sites, as well as a template for including an image map navigation bar on your Web pages. For more information on the Web page templates included on the CD-ROM, see Appendix F, "What's on the CD-ROM."

Take a Break?

You might welcome an opportunity at this juncture to take a break. Relax and stretch a bit. Fix a cup of tea or get yourself a glass of juice. I'll see you back in five minutes or so for the remainder of this session.

What Is a URL?

A URL (*Uniform Resource Locator*) identifies the address, or location, of a resource on the Internet. Every Web page has its own unique URL. If you know the URL of a Web page and access is not restricted, you can connect to it and view it in your browser. Resources other than Web pages also have URLs, including FTP, Telnet, WAIS, Gopher, and newsgroups.

A URL may consist of the following parts:

- **Service.** The service designator specifies the service being accessed: `http` (for WWW), `ftp`, `gopher`, `wais`, `telnet`, or `news`.

- **Host.** The host designator specifies the domain name of the server being accessed, such as `www.myserver.com`.

- **Port number.** The port number only needs to be specified if it is a nonstandard port number for the service being accessed—most URLs don't require port numbers. (The default port number is 80 for Web servers and 21 for FTP servers, for instance.)

- **Resource path.** The resource path specifies the directory path and often the file name of the resource being accessed. At minimum, you should probably include a "/" here to indicate the root directory of a domain (although most Web browsers let you get away with leaving this off following a domain name): `http://anywhere.com/` rather than `http://anywhere.com`, for instance. You can exclude the file name here if you use the default file name for index files specified by the server, which may be `index.html`, `index.htm`, or `default.htm`, depending on the actual server. If you don't use the default file name for index files, then you must include the actual file path and name of the Web page, for instance: `http://anywhere.com/myfolder/mypage.html`.

Figure 1.3 shows a diagram of a URL. Because most Web addresses don't use port numbers, this illustration leaves out the port number.

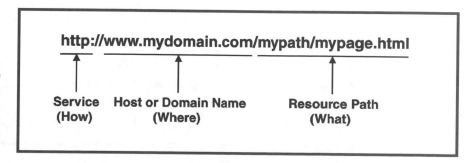

Figure 1.3

A Uniform Resource Locator (URL) is the address of a resource on the Internet.

A URL is actually an instruction or request from an agent such as a Web browser to a server on the Internet that specifies the following three things:

- **How?** This is the protocol for the transaction. For Web pages, this is HTTP. Essentially, it tells the server what software it needs to run to manage the transaction. More than one server can reside on the same computer—for instance, a single computer can function both as an FTP server and as an HTTP (or Web) server.

- **Where?** This is the address where the transaction is to take place. For instance, `www.mydomain.com/mypath/` would specify the domain name and location within that domain of what is to be transacted.

- **What?** This is the name of what is to be transacted. For instance, `mypage.html` would specify the actual HTML document, or Web page, that is the subject of the transaction.

NOTE If you link to a file or data object that resides within the same directory structure as the referring page, you don't have to supply the full URL for it, just as you don't have to dial the area code for a local phone call. When a link is local and uses abbreviated information, it's known as a *relative URL*; standard (full) URLs are known as *absolute URLs*. The advantage of using relative rather than absolute URLs to reference local files is that if you later want to move your Web pages and their attendant files, you don't have to redo your local URLs as long as the directories in which they reside retain the same names and relations. See "Using Relative URLs" in the Saturday Afternoon session for a more complete explanation of this concept.

CAUTION Most Web pages reside on UNIX servers. Unlike MS-DOS and Windows systems, UNIX systems use case-sensitive file paths and file names. So if you see a path and file name like **MySite/HOMEPAGE.html**, you should type it exactly as it appears.

What Is a Domain Name?

Every Internet server has a numerical IP *(Internet Protocol)* address, which usually consists of four numbers from 0 to 255 separated by periods (something like 185.35.117.0, for instance). Computers prefer numeric addresses of this type because they're precise. Unfortunately, humans have trouble remembering numbers—they prefer meaningful text addresses, like www.mysite.com. That's what a domain name is: a text alternative to an IP address. You can usually use the two interchangeably. The point is that if you know the domain name, you don't have to know anything about the IP address. You will, however, sometimes run into an odd URL on the Web that specifies the IP address rather than the domain name (and nothing forbids a server from having an IP address but no domain name).

The registration of domain names has in the past been handled exclusively by InterNIC (the *Internet Network Information Center*), which was run by Network Solutions, Inc., under contract to the U.S. government. If you wanted a domain name, you had to register it with Network Solutions, Inc. However, a new, nonprofit, international organization, ICANN (*Internet Corporation for Assigned Names and Numbers*), has been formed to take over from the U.S. government the responsibility for "coordinating domain name system management, IP address space allocation, protocol parameter assignment coordination, and root server system management." These responsibilities had been handled by IANA (*Internet Assigned Numbers Authority*) under the auspices of the U.S. government. Part of ICANN's responsibilities is the accreditation of domain registrars that will handle the registration of domain names for the .com, .net, and .org domains. ICANN initially accredited five domain registrars to participate in its test-bed program. At some point following the completion of the test-bed program, you'll be able to register a domain name through any accredited domain registrar of your choice. Due to the introduction of competition in this process, the price of registering and renewing a domain name is expected to decrease from the current $70 to register and $35 to renew.

Most servers have applied for and received a domain name. As long as your Web pages are located on a server that has a domain name, you can use that domain name in the addresses, or URLs, for those Web pages. You don't have to have your own server to have your own domain name. You can also set up a Web site on someone else's server and use your own domain name in what is often referred to as a *virtual host* arrangement: to the outside world, you appear to have your own server (www.yourname.com, for instance).

NOTE Registering domain names used to be free, but this led to a free-for-all somewhat similar to the Oklahoma Land Rush, as companies and individuals scrambled to grab up domain names before anyone else could claim them. Because an organization or individual could claim an unlimited number of domain names, speculative trading (in other words, scalping) in domain names evolved. For these reasons, as well as to help fund the costs of registering rapidly increasing domain-name requests, as of September 1995, InterNIC started charging a fee for registering and maintaining a domain name. Initially, these fees were $100 for the first two years and $50 a year thereafter, although the cost has since been reduced to $70 for the first two years and $35 a year thereafter. Even so, one company still forked out the $70 to grab up as many last names (smith.com, jones.com, etc.) as possible so it could resell them for Web-based e-mail addresses. (Luckily, I got mine, callihan.com, before they started doing this.)

TIP To check for the availability of any domain name you might like to get, you can use Network Solutions' "Register a Web Address" form at **www.networksolutions.com/**. You may have to try several variations or alternatives before you'll find a domain name available that you want. Don't try to use Network Solutions' form to actually register the domain name you want—you should have the ISP or Web hosting service that will be hosting your Web site do this for you (see Appendix D, "Putting It Up on the Web," for information on finding a Web host for your pages). However, if you're not planning on finding a Web host for your pages for some time, you can use the form to reserve a domain name (at a cost of $119 to reserve a domain name for up to two years).

A domain name represents a hierarchy, starting with the most general word on the right and moving to the most specific on the left. It can include a country code, an organization code, and a site name. For instance, `myname.com.au`, reading from right to left, specifies the name of a site in Australia ("au") in the commercial (com) subcategory called "myname." Every country connected to the Internet has its own code, such as "uk" (United Kingdom), "ca" (Canada), "fr" (France), "nz" (New Zealand), and so forth. The country code for the United States is "us." Most sites in the United States don't include the country code, however, because the Internet began in the United States and the country codes were created later, after the Internet went international. The organization codes are:

- **EDU for "education."** Schools and universities, for instance, use the EDU organization code.
- **GOV for "government."** Various governmental departments and agencies use the GOV organization code.
- **MIL for "military."** The Internet was, after all, originally a U.S. Department of Defense initiative (the ARPANet).
- **NET for "network."** NET can refer to a network connected to the Internet. In practice, you usually run into NETs with ISPs (Internet Service Providers) that are offering public access to the Internet.
- **COM for "commercial."** This code was created to accommodate commercial usage of the Internet by business enterprises.
- **ORG for "organization."** This code is for noncommercial, non-profit organizations.

Figure 1.4 gives you a graphical representation of the domain-name system.

NOTE For quite some time, there has been a proposal for seven new top-level domain-name categories: ".firm," ".shop," ".web," ".arts," ".rec," ".info," and ".nom." It is fairly certain that these new domain-name categories (or close variants of them) will be added, but exactly how soon is entirely up in the air.

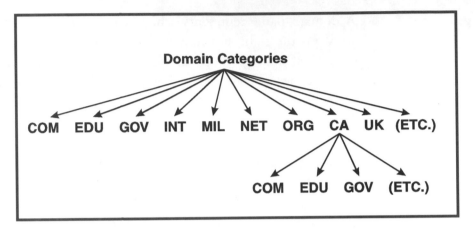

What Is a Web Page?

A Web page is a hypertext (HTML) document contained in a single file. To have more than one Web page, you must have more than one file. Despite the connotation of the word *page,* a Web page can be any length, although most Web pages display no more than two or three screens of data.

A Web page is simply a plain text document. All codes are entered into the document as ordinary text, with none of the binary-level formatting a word processor would embed in it. When you mark text as italic in a word processing document, you don't see the actual computer code that causes the text to appear or print in italics. In HTML, you have to do it all yourself. There's no underlying program code to translate what you type as you go. You type in <I> where you want the browser to turn on italics and </I> where you want it to turn off italics. This cuts down on the computer overhead, allowing Web pages to remain small but still pack quite a punch.

When a browser displays a Web page, the page may appear to contain special graphical elements like logos or buttons. These graphics don't reside in the HTML file itself; they're separate files that the HTML file references. For instance, you might see a line like this in the HTML file:

```
<IMG SRC="mylogo.gif">
```

This code instructs a browser to open the specified graphic, `mylogo.gif`, and display it "inline" (in the middle of a text paragraph, for instance, if that is where it is placed) in place of the code. You can include a banner or logo, buttons, icons, separator bars, navigational icons, and more. See Figure 1.5 for a graphical representation of a Web page that contains these different kinds of elements.

What Is a Web Site?

The term *Web site* has a couple of different, although analogous, meanings. Servers often are called Web sites (sites on the Web), but any grouping of related and linked Web pages sharing a common theme or subject matter may also be called a Web site. To avoid confusion, in this book I'll always refer to a collection of related Web pages as a "Web site," and I'll

Figure 1.5

Graphic elements, such as banners or logos, images, icon bullets, horizontal rules, and navigational buttons, are actually separate files linked to and displayed as part of your Web page.

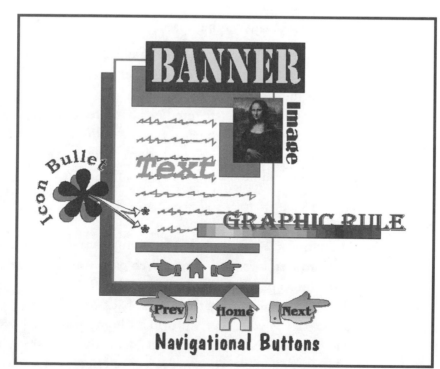

refer to a Web server as simply that, a "Web server," or alternatively as a "Web host" (a Web server that "hosts" Web sites).

Your service provider (the company or organization that provides you access to the Internet) may give you space for a personal, noncommercial Web site at little or no cost. If you're a student, you may be able to have your pages hosted by your school's server. Many online services, such as CompuServe or America Online, also host Web pages at little or no cost. If you want to create a commercial Web site that offers a product or service, or if you want to create a more sophisticated Web site that requires more space, higher traffic allowances, more technical support, and a wider range of features than your ISP will give you, you may need an *Internet Presence Provider (IPP)*—a company that focuses on or specializes in Web space and can offer a fuller menu of services aimed specifically at Web publishers. A presence provider also can register and maintain a domain name for you, usually at a reasonable cost, making it look to the outside world as if you own your own server—rather than merely as a tenant renting space.

A Web site is simply a collection of allied Web pages, similar to the chapters in a book, tied and linked together, usually through a home page that serves as the directory to the rest of the Web site. The different Web pages that compose the site are interlinked and related to each other as parts of a whole. Dissimilar Web pages that are unlinked—that is, unrelated—to each other, on the other hand, don't form a Web site even if they are stored in the same directory on the same server.

What Is a Home Page?

The term *home page* can have a number of meanings. When you start your browser, it loads whatever Web page you designate as its home page (including a page on your own hard drive). Most browsers have a Home button or command that takes you back to the home page. Usually, this home page is your access provider's home page, or possibly Netscape's, Microsoft's, or NCSA's home page, depending on which browser you use. A browser's home page sometimes is referred to as a start page.

A home page can serve as an entry point (or front door) to a Web site, or group of linked and related Web pages. The term *home page* serves to designate any Web page that stands on its own (in keeping with the front-door comparison, you could think of a stand-alone Web page as a one-room shack). The diagram in Figure 1.6 shows the relationship between home and Web pages.

Most servers let you create a default home page, most often `index.html`, that loads automatically without having to specify the file name in the URL. (Other default home page file names may also be allowed—`index.htm`, `welcome.html`, and so on—depending on how the server is configured.) This allows you, for instance, to have `http://www.myserver.com/mydirectory/` as your URL rather than `http://www.myserver.com/mydirectory/index.html`.

Home pages used as entryways are often kept small, often serving simply as menus or directories to the Web pages that make up the rest of the Web

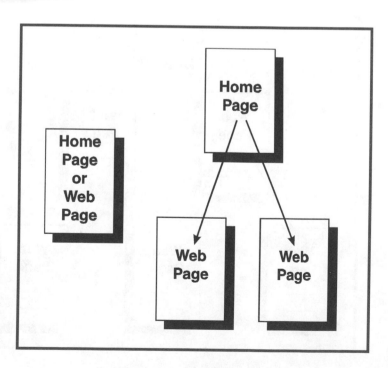

Figure 1.6

A home page can be either a stand-alone Web page or an entry point (index file) or front door to a Web site.

site. The idea here is that a viewer need only display the home page, which is relatively small, and then decide what else to see in the remainder of the Web site.

Having a Web site go deeper than three or four levels is rare, but the number of levels of Web pages you might want to have appended as subpages off of your home page is technically unlimited. The deeper a Web page is (a subpage of a subpage of a subpage of a subpage of your home page), the less accessible it will be to visitors to your site. See Figure 1.7 for an illustration of a multilevel Web site.

You can also create a home page that links multiple home pages. You might, for instance, have a series of Web sites that are relatively autonomous, share

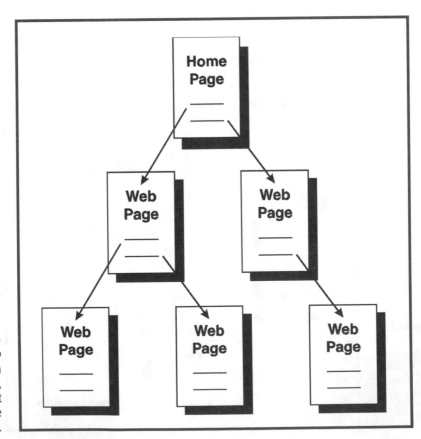

Figure 1.7

A Web site can have several levels, although it is best to keep it to three or fewer levels.

a common theme, are produced by the same department, or are part of a larger project. Or you may simply want to link pages to share traffic between them.

Browsing Offline

Browsing offline means using your Web browser to view HTML files located on your local computer without being connected to the Internet. In Windows 95, 98, NT, and 2000, this is relatively simple and easy. (Although this book does not directly support Windows 3.1, I've included some tips on browsing offline in Windows 3.1 at the Web site for this book at **www.callihan.com/create3/**. Just click the "Offline Browsing" link in the sidebar.)

NOTE If you have a connection that is always on, such as one through a cable modem, or through your network at work, you won't be able to work offline. You can skip ahead to the Wrapping Up section at the end of this session. If you're an AOL user and are using their default browser, you also won't be able to work offline. You can, however, download Netscape Communicator (which includes Navigator) from NetCenter (http://home.netcenter.com) and use it to browse local HTML files offline. Just click the Download button, and then click the Netscape Browsers link in the sidebar.

Browsing Offline in Netscape Navigator

The following is the quick-and-dirty way to run Navigator 4.0+ offline. It's a bit clunky, but it's pretty simple, and it works:

NOTE After you insert text in Paint Shop Pro, the text is selected. If your "Headline" text is no longer selected (no dashed line around the letters), you won't be able to add the drop shadow effect without reselecting your text (or starting over and reinserting your text). You can use the Magic Wand tool to reselect your text: just select the Magic Wand tool from the Tool Palette, click on the first letter of your text, then hold down the Shift key and click on the remaining letters, as well as on the dot on the "i".

1. Run Netscape Navigator 4.0+. At the Connect To dialog box, which prompts you to make a dial-up connection to the Internet, click on the Cancel button (to avoid connecting to the Internet).

2. You'll get an error message that reads "Netscape is unable to locate the server . . ." This is just Navigator trying to tell you it tried to connect to the Internet but couldn't. Click on the OK button.

3. Navigator will display a copy of its default home page if it can be loaded from the cache. Otherwise, it will display a blank page.

4. To open and display a local Web page (HTML file) from your hard drive, choose File, Open Page, and Choose File.

5. Change to the folder where your HTML file is saved and double-click on the file name to open it.

6. Make sure the Navigator (and not the Composer) radio button is selected. Click on Open.

Browsing Offline in Microsoft Internet Explorer

The following is the quick-and-dirty way to run Internet Explorer 4.0+/5.0+ offline. As with Netscape, it's a bit clunky, but it's simple and it works:

1. Run Microsoft Internet Explorer 4.0+ or 5.0+.

2. At the Connect To dialog box, which prompts you to make a dial-up connection to the Internet: in Version 4.0, click on the Cancel button; in Version 4.01 or greater, click on the Work Offline button.

3. If Internet Explorer can't retrieve your default start page from its cache, Internet Explorer 4.0 will display a pop-up message, and

later versions will display a Web page, telling you that Internet Explorer can't open the page. If using Version 4.0, just click on OK to clear the pop-up message.

4. In all versions, to open and display a local Web page (HTML file) from your hard drive, select File, Open, and Browse. Go to a folder where a local HTML file you want to use is stored and then double-click on it to open it. Click on OK to load the file into Internet Explorer.

NOTE Unlike Netscape Navigator, Microsoft Internet Explorer does not conveniently create a bookmark file in HTML format that you can use to test the loading of a local HTML file. You can use Find (click on the Start button and on Find) to search for any HTML files that may be on your hard drive (just search for "*.htm" or "*.html"). If you also have Netscape Navigator installed, you can open its bookmark file (`bookmark.htm`) in Internet Explorer to test this. Otherwise, you'll have to wait to actually test this until you do the Basic HTML Tutorial tomorrow morning, which will walk you through creating and saving an HTML file.

TIP You can also open a local HTML file using Windows Explorer or the Start menu's Run option. Just go to its folder and double-click on its file name—it'll be opened in your default browser. You may also be able to reopen a Web page that was recently accessed by clicking on its file name in the Start menu's Document menu.

Browsing Offline in Other Browsers

The methods for browsing offline in other browsers will be quite similar to what was described for Netscape Navigator and Internet Explorer. Just run your browser and then choose not to connect to the Internet. The specific steps, of course, will vary from browser to browser.

If you're using an online service, such as AOL or CompuServe, you may not be able to run its default Web browser offline. If that is the case, you should just connect to the Internet to be able to use your browser to browse offline and do this book's tutorials and work sessions. Later, nothing says that you can't download and install one of the regular versions of Internet Explorer or Netscape Navigator and then use it to browse offline. You can also install the evaluation version of the Opera browser from the CD-ROM and use it to browse offline.

Seamless Offline Browsing

The previous sections covered quick-and-dirty methods for browsing offline in Netscape Navigator and Internet Explorer. To make your offline browsing experience more "seamless," you can specify either a blank or a local start page for your browser, so you won't be prompted to connect to the Internet when you run your browser. I recommend that, for the time being, you stick to the quick-and-dirty method described in the previous sections to browse offline in Navigator and Internet Explorer. Later, after you've finished your weekend, you can experiment with setting up your browser for more seamless offline browsing. At the Web site for this book, **www.callihan.com/create3/**, I've included a page, "Tips for Offline Browsing," that describes in more detail what you need to do to set your browser up for more seamless offline browsing. To view it, just click on "Offline Browsing" in the sidebar.

Wrapping Up

You should now have a good grounding in the basics of the Internet and the World Wide Web. You should have a good grasp of URLs, hypertext, HTML, and Web pages. You should also have a good idea what tools you'll need to use (just Windows Notepad and a graphical Web browser are all that are required) to do the HTML tutorials and plan and create your first Web page, as well an understanding of what you need to do to run your browser offline. So, get a good night's sleep, and be ready for the Basic HTML Tutorial tomorrow morning.

SATURDAY MORNING

The Basic HTML Tutorial

- ⚙ Anatomy of an HTML tag
- ⚙ Creating headings, paragraphs, and line breaks
- ⚙ Adding bold, italic, and monospaced text
- ⚙ Creating lists, hypertext links, and link lists
- ⚙ Inserting inline images

Last night you read up on the Internet, the Web, hypertext, HTML fundamentals, and Web pages. You should now have some idea of what Web publishing is all about.

You also reviewed the software tools you'll be using to do this book's HTML tutorials and create your first Web page. My recommendation is that you stick for now with using Windows Notepad to create and edit your HTML files. For doing this tutorial, any graphical Web browser can be used—there is no need at this point to download a more recent browser if you haven't upgraded your browser in a while. No other tools are required to do this tutorial.

This morning's tutorial walks you through a top-down approach to learning HTML, organized according to function. Just start from the beginning and continue to the end, and by then you'll know enough HTML to create a wide range of different kinds of Web pages.

HTML contains many more tags and attributes for defining document elements than most people could learn in an entire week, let alone in a weekend, let alone on a Saturday morning. But fear not. This book cuts it down to size. This tutorial covers "basic" HTML, which includes the most useful of the HTML 2.0 tags. All graphical Web browsers should fully support HTML 2.0, which until fairly recently was the standard for HTML.

Actually, HTML 2.0 continues on as the core of the later versions of HTML (HTML 3.2 and 4.0), so you don't need to be concerned that it will ever go out of style or become outmoded. As long as HTML exists, what counts for "basic" HTML will remain largely the same and unchanged. The lessons learned in this tutorial will remain good as long as there is such a thing as HTML.

The optional Intermediate HTML Tutorial that is scheduled for this afternoon covers many of the HTML 3.2 tags, along with a few of the new HTML 4.0 tags as well.

Everyone has his or her own learning style and speed. Although the Basic HTML Tutorial is designed to be completed in a single morning, you may take more or less time to complete it. The most important thing is to work at your own speed without feeling rushed. If you want to take the whole day to do this one tutorial, do so. It covers everything that you'll need to know when you get around to planning and creating your first Web page tomorrow. So relax, sit back, and have some fun.

NOTE   By default, Windows hides the file extensions for known file types, showing only the file-type icon to help identify the file type. In this book, I'll be including the file extension for all file names. It is easy to turn on the display of file-type extensions (highly recommended). In Windows 98, just click on the Start button, select Settings and Folder Options, and then click on the View tab. Under Files and Folders, make sure that the check box, Hide file extensions for known file types, is unchecked. In Windows 95, double-click on the My Computer icon on your Desktop and select View and Options from the menu bar; click on the View tab and make sure the check box, Hide MS-DOS file extensions for the file types that are registered, is unchecked.

Installing the Example Files

On the CD-ROM, I've included example files for you to use in this tutorial, as well as in the two other HTML tutorials scheduled for today. You can use the interface on the CD-ROM to create your working folder (C:\HTML) and install the example files to it:

1. Insert the CD-ROM in your CD-ROM drive.

2. If Prima Tech's user interface doesn't automatically run, do the following:

   a) Click on the Start button, and then select Run.

   b) In the Open text box, type *d*:\CDInstaller.exe (where *d* is your CD-ROM's drive letter), and then click on OK.

3. Read the license agreement and click on I Accept to accept its terms. (When the CD user interface is displayed, the Install and Help buttons are grayed out.)

4. In the left windowpane, expand the contents (click on the "+" button to the left) of Create Your First Web Page In a Weekend.

5. Expand the contents of Book Examples, and then click on Tutorial Example Files. Click on the Install button.

6. At the WinZip Self-Extractor window, click Unzip to automatically unzip the example files to C:\HTML. (Note: Do not change the Unzip to Folder content.)

7. Click on OK when the example files have been unzipped, and then click on the Close button. (To exit the CD interface, click on the Close button (the "x" button).

A Quick Word about HTML

Before you begin to do the tutorial, a quick reminder about the nature of HTML might save some unnecessary confusion. The philosophy behind HTML is to specify the framework of a page, not its actual appearance or display. Remember: The onscreen appearance of a Web page is determined by the browser used to view it.

Actually, you do have a good deal of control over how most browsers present your page. Today's graphical Web browsers allow you to include not only inline graphics but also interlaced and transparent graphics, background images and colors, image maps, forms, tables, font size and color changes, animations, streaming audio and animation, and more.

Although most current graphical Web browsers now support most of these enhancements, HTML 2.0 specifies only some of them. Many features that give you more complete control over how your Web page will be displayed have been incorporated into HTML 3.2 and HTML 4.0, the latest versions of HTML. You should remember, however, that many people still use older browsers that do not support the latest HTML developments, including those who are still using text-based browsers such as Lynx.

NOTE

A very real concern in HTML is backward compatibility and universal access to one's documents. Old Web pages need to be displayed properly in new Web browsers, just as new Web pages, in most cases, should be coded in such a fashion that they won't break old browsers. (The word "break" here in the world of HTML means that the browser will fail to display your page.)

Old browsers never go away but just keep getting used. Every visitor is precious, in other words. Obviously, if you are creating a page, say "Internet Explorer 5.0 Tips and Tricks," you need only be concerned about people using Internet Explorer 5.0. If, however, you are putting up a page, "Genealogy Tips and Tricks," you would not want to exclude someone from viewing your page simply because his or her choice of browser is not the same as yours. Even if someone were using Lynx, a text-based browser that is more like an HTML 1.0 browser, you would still want him or her to be able to access and read your page. In this afternoon's Intermediate HTML Tutorial, I'll be showing you how to use many of the new HTML 3.2 and HTML 4.0 features without breaking older browsers. Where a feature is liable to have a deleterious effect on earlier browsers, I'll let you know.

Anatomy of a Tag

The words *tag* or *tag element* refer to the HTML codes that define the elements in an HTML file—the headings, images, paragraphs, lists, and whatnot. There are two kinds of tags: *container tags*, which bracket or contain text or other tag elements, and *empty tags*, which stand alone. A container tag element actually consists of two tags, a start tag and an end tag, which bracket the text they affect. An empty tag functions as a single stand-alone element within an HTML document, and thus doesn't bracket or contain anything else.

HTML tags are inserted into a document between lesser than (<) and greater than (>) symbols (also referred to as left or right angle brackets). For instance, a start tag of a container tag or an empty tag element looks like this:

```
<tagname>
```

You always precede an end tag of a container tag element with a forward slash (/) to distinguish it from a start tag:

```
</tagname>
```

To tag a section of text, you contain it within the start and end tags of a tag element. For instance, text contained in a level-one heading tag would look like this, where <H1> is the start tag and </H1> is the end tag:

```
<H1>This is a Level-One Heading</H1>
```

Whenever I refer to "a level-one heading tag," I'm referring to both the start and end tags. When I want to specifically refer to a start tag or an end tag, I'll say "the start tag" or "the end tag." Note, however, that a few tags look like empty tags, but these actually are container tags that have implied end tags.

It is somewhat conventional, although by no means required, to type tag names in ALL CAPS. It helps distinguish HTML tags from the remainder of the text being tagged. As a rule, this book presents tag names in ALL CAPS.

Tag Attributes

Attributes allow you to specify how Web browsers should treat a particular tag. An attribute is included within the actual tag (between the left and right angle brackets), either within a start tag or an empty (stand-alone) tag. End tags can't contain attributes. Most of the tags covered in this tutorial don't use attributes, but you'll use them to include images or hypertext links in a Web page toward the end of this tutorial.

Most attributes are combined with a value to allow you to specify different options for how a Web browser should treat the attribute. Here's the format for including an attribute value in a tag:

`ATTRIBUTE="value"`

For instance, to specify that the middle of an image should be aligned with the line of text it is on, you would include the following attribute value inside the IMG (Image) tag:

`ALIGN="middle"`

Tag attributes are, by convention, usually typed in ALL CAPS, with any values assigned to them typed in lowercase. You don't have to do it this way, but it does make it easier to pick them out. Though in most cases you can get away without placing values between quotation marks, there are enough instances where it won't work that it is a good idea, I think, to stick to adding the quotes.

Nesting HTML Tags

You should always *nest* HTML tags, and never overlap them. For instance, always do this:

`<B><I>Always nest tags inside each other.</I></B>`

Notice that the `<I>...</I>` pair is nested within the `<B>...</B>` pair. Never overlap tags so that the outer one ends before the inner one:

`<B><I>Don't overlap tags, like this.</B></I>`

HTML operates in a hierarchical, top-down manner. A tag element may have other tag elements nested in it or be nested within other tag elements. If you overlap two tags, a browser can't tell what should fall inside of what, and the browser may not be able to display your file at all. Be kind to your browser and those of your potential readers: don't overlap tag elements.

The Scratch Pad Model

The model that this tutorial employs resembles a "scratch pad" approach. Think of your text editor as a scratch pad. As you do the Basic HTML Tutorial, enter the suggested tags and text as though you were jotting them down on a scratch pad; in other words, you don't have to clean the slate each time you move on to a new section. Just move on down the page, leaving everything you have already done in place. Doing so also leaves you with a sample file to which you can return and reference later.

Creating and Saving Your Scratch Pad HTML File

Before you can get started doing the tutorial examples, you need to run Windows Notepad and save your scratch pad HTML file in your working folder (C:\HTML). To do this, just follow these steps:

1. Run Windows Notepad (click on the Start button, and then select Programs, Accessories, Notepad).

TIP Alternatively, you can run Notepad by clicking on the Start button and selecting Run. Just type **notepad** and hit the Enter key. (To rerun Notepad in the same Windows session, just click on Start, select Run, and hit the Enter key.)

2. Save the scratch pad file that you'll use in this morning's tutorial. In Notepad, select File, Save As. Save your file to the C:\HTML folder as **scratch.htm**.

NOTE

When you open a Notepad window in Windows 95, Word Wrap is not turned on. If you type a line of text without hitting Enter, it will just keep right on going without wrapping. To turn on Word Wrap, select Edit, Word Wrap (so that it's checked). Unfortunately, you must reset this option every time you use Notepad if you want Word Wrap on. When you turn Word Wrap on in Notepad in Windows 98, it will stay on for future Notepad sessions (that is, until you turn it back off).

Starting Your Page

Whenever you start a new HTML file, you should begin by including these tags:

- The HTML tag
- The HEAD tag
- The TITLE tag
- The BODY tag

The following sections discuss each of these tags.

TYPOGRAPHY LEGEND

In the tutorials in this book, words and code that you should type are formatted as `bold` and `monospaced` text.

Text that should not be typed by you (that is, text that's shown for the purpose of an example) or text that you've already typed is formatted as `monospaced` text. Any file names or folder names that are referenced are also formatted as `monospaced`.

Italicized text in the input examples does not represent actual typed text. Instead, it indicates what should be typed. *Your Name*, for instance, would indicate that your actual name should be typed.

The HTML Tag

Recall that a tag defines a structural element within an HTML document. The HTML tag defines the topmost element, the HTML document itself, identifying it as an HTML document rather than some other kind of document. The HTML tag is a container tag that has a start and end, and all other text and tags are nested within it.

In your scratch pad file in Notepad, type the start and end HTML tags, putting a single hard return between them, like this:

```
<HTML>
</HTML>
```

NOTE Remember that the HTML start tag (<HTML>) must remain at the very top of your file, and the HTML end tag (</HTML>) must remain at the very bottom of your file. Everything else must fall between these two tags.

The HEAD Tag

The HEAD tag contains information about your HTML file. It also may contain other tags that help to identify your HTML file to the outside world. The HEAD tag is nested within the HTML tag. Type the HEAD tag inside the HTML tag now, as follows:

```
<HTML>
<HEAD>
</HEAD>
</HTML>
```

Usually, the only tag contained within the HEAD tag is the TITLE tag. Other tags also can be contained within the HEAD tag, but of these, only the META, BASE, and LINK tags are useful.

FIND IT ON ▶
THE WEB

NOTE Because of space and time limitations, I won't be covering the META, BASE, or LINK tags. However, at the Web site for this book (**www.callihan.com/create3/**), I've created a page of Web site promotion tips that does cover using the META tag. To find out about the BASE and LINK tags, as well as any other tags not covered here, see my Web Links page (**www.callihan.com/weblinks/**) for links to several full HTML references that are available online.

The TITLE Tag

The TITLE tag is nested inside of the HEAD tag. It identifies your page to the rest of the world. For instance, a search engine like Yahoo! or WebCrawler might display the text included in your TITLE tag as a link to your page. The tag also displays on your browser's title bar, but it doesn't appear as part of the page. Make the title descriptive, but keep it under 50 characters, if possible. Try to use a short title followed by a brief description. Someone else should be able to tell what your page is about simply by looking at the title. Think of it as your welcome mat. Also, many search engines give more weight to words and phrases included in your title, so including a few words or phrases you think others might search for when looking for a page like yours can be a big help in getting visitors to your page. Type the TITLE tag inside the HEAD tag.

NOTE If you want to substitute a title of your choosing for the generic title supplied in the following HTML code, go ahead. Don't, however, bust your noggin right now trying to come up with the perfect title. Sunday morning, when you get around to planning your first Web page, you'll spend more time figuring out what contributes to a good title.

```
<HTML>
<HEAD>
<TITLE>Your Title: Describe Your Title</TITLE>
</HEAD>
</HTML>
```

Officially, the TITLE tag is a required element in each HTML document. While most Web browsers will let you get away with not including a TITLE tag, you should always include one. If you don't include a title, the title of your page appears in some browsers as "Untitled," and in others, the URL for the page appears on the browser's title bar. The same holds true for search engines, which will usually list "Untitled" or the URL of your page if the title is missing, making it much less likely that visitors will come to your page through a search engine.

The BODY Tag

The BODY tag is the complement of the HEAD tag and contains all the tags, or elements, that a browser actually displays as the body of your HTML document. Both the HEAD tag and the BODY tag are nested inside the HTML tag. Note, however, that the BODY tag comes after the HEAD tag; they denote separate parts of the HTML document.

 NOTE The HEAD and BODY tags are the only tags that are nested directly inside the HTML tag. Other than the TITLE tag, or other tags inserted in the HEAD tag above, you should nest all other text and tags inside the BODY tag. Keep both </BODY> and </HTML> end tags at the bottom of your HTML file.

Type the BODY tag after the HEAD tag, but inside the HTML tag, as follows:

```
<HTML>
<HEAD>
<TITLE>Your Title: Describe Your Title</TITLE>
</HEAD>
<BODY>
</BODY>
</HTML>
```

You have started your HTML file. All HTML files begin the same way; only the titles are different. What you have typed so far should look like this:

```
<HTML>
<HEAD>
<TITLE>Your Title: Describe Your Title</TITLE>
</HEAD>
<BODY>
</BODY>
</HTML>
```

Saving a Starting Template

If you want, you can save this as a starting template for creating HTML files. Save it as `start.htm` in C:\HTML, for instance. After you save your file as `start.htm`, save it again as `scratch.htm` in C:\HTML (or whatever working title you want to give it) so you won't accidentally save over your starting template later.

Don't bother hopping over to your browser to check this out yet—it will display nothing but the title in the title bar, as is shown in Figure 2.1.

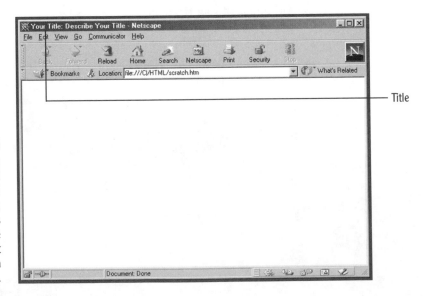

Title

Figure 2.1

When an HTML file with only a TITLE element is loaded into a Web browser, the title is displayed on the title bar, but otherwise you get a blank page.

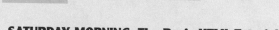

WINDOWS NAVIGATION TIPS

In this book, the words *switch* or *hop* refer to switching between open applications.

You can switch among the open applications in several ways—the best way mainly boils down to your individual preference. Choose the method that works best for you.

✿ **Alt+Tab.** This is my favorite method for hopping between open applications. Just hold down the Alt key and tap the Tab key one or more times to cycle through all currently open applications. This works in all versions of Windows. When the icon for the application you want to hop to is highlighted, just release the Alt key to bring that application to the foreground.

✿ **Alt+Esc.** This is similar to Alt+Tab. It toggles among the open windows, one by one. Hold down the Alt key and tap the Esc key until the window you want comes to the foreground.

✿ **Ctrl+Esc.** This displays the Taskbar at the bottom of the screen—the one that shows buttons for all your open applications—and opens the Start menu. In Windows 3.1, doing this brings up the Task List window, which allows you to select from a list of currently open applications.

As you work through the HTML tutorials today, the figures will show you what each tag looks like in a browser. These figures might not exactly match what you see in the particular browser you're using; therefore, you should use them as cues to hop over to your browser to have a look. Also, you can only debug your HTML file for errors by hopping over to your browser and previewing the HTML file you are actually creating.

NOTE   You've probably noticed that many Web pages have a four-letter file-name extension, *.html, and others have a three-letter extension, *.htm. The second extension came into use because some systems (Windows 3.1 and MS-DOS) only support a three-letter file extension. All Web browsers and Web servers should recognize both file extensions for HTML files.

For this book, I've stuck to using the *.htm file extension, primarily to accommodate readers who are still using Windows 3.1. If you're using a 32-bit version of Windows, such as Windows 95, 98, NT, or 2000, feel free to substitute the *.html file extension, if you wish.

Using Headings to Structure Your Page

You use headings to organize your Web page into hierarchical levels. The top-level heading (denoted by the H1 tag) is the title that will be displayed at the top of your Web page. (Don't confuse this with the title that appears in the browser's title bar, which you just set up using the TITLE tag.) Because the H1 tag functions as the title (or top-level heading) for a Web page, each Web page should have only one H1 tag. (This is the conventional use for this tag. Otherwise, nothing positively forbids including multiple H1 tags in a Web page.)

You use a second-level heading (denoted by the H2 tag) to define a major division in your page, and a third-level heading (using the H3 tag) to define a sublevel division within a major division. Most browsers support up to six heading levels. Within the BODY element that you typed earlier, type six heading-level tags, like this (see Figure 2.2):

```
<BODY>
<H1>This is a top-level heading</H1>
<H2>This is a second-level heading</H2>
<H3>This is a third-level heading</H3>
<H4>This is a fourth-level heading</H4>
<H5>This is a fifth-level heading</H5>
<H6>This is a sixth-level heading</H6>

</BODY>
```

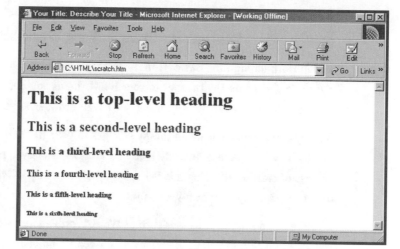

Figure 2.2

Web browsers
display heading
levels in different
font sizes.

As a practical matter, you probably will seldom use more than four heading levels. Displayed in a browser, different level headings appear as different size fonts, from large to small, although each browser decides which fonts to use.

Just because a tag displays similarly or identically in Navigator and Internet Explorer doesn't mean that it will be displayed similarly or identically in other Web browsers, such as NCSA Mosaic, Sun HotJava, and so on. NCSA Mosaic 2.0, for instance, displays H1 through H6 in a normal, non-boldfaced font while using different size fonts than Navigator and Internet Explorer. The only way to be sure how a particular tag is going to make text look in a particular browser is to check it out in that browser.

NOTE Feel free to use the figure illustrations as prompts to save your file in Notepad and hop over to your browser to check out your results. If you're unclear on how to do this, see the sidebars "Windows Navigation Tips" and "Dynamically Updating Your Work." Remember, you don't really know whether you're doing it right until you can actually see it in your Web browser.

DYNAMICALLY UPDATING YOUR WORK

As you work through the Basic HTML Tutorial this morning, you'll want to *dynamically* update the changes to your HTML file as you go, switching back and forth between your text editor and your Web browser to see your results.

Only by being able to make on-the-fly changes to your HTML file can you tell exactly how your page is going to look in a browser while you're still in the process of creating it. Doing this is key to rapidly learning HTML, as well as to quickly creating your own Web pages.

If you're using a word processor such as Word, WordPad, or Windows Write, you won't be able to hop back and forth between it and your browser to dynamically update your work as you go because you can't keep the same file open in both your word processor and your Web browser. That's why I recommend sticking with a text editor such as Windows Notepad—you can have the same file open at the same time in both your text editor and your Web browser.

The following details the steps you should follow to dynamically update your Web page in your browser:

1. Create or open an HTML file in Notepad. Save any changes you make to it. (Select File and Save to save your file; pressing Ctrl+S doesn't work in Notepad.)

2. Leaving your HTML file open in Notepad, run your browser, preferably offline, and open the HTML file you just edited. In Navigator 4.0+ select File, Open Page, Choose File; in Internet Explorer 4.0+ select File, Open, Browse.

3. In the Open dialog box, change to your working folder where you saved your HTML file (C:\HTML). (Click on the Look in drop-down menu, click on the drive letter ([C:]), and then double-click on the HTML folder in the folder view.)

4. Double-click on your HTML file (scratch.htm). In Navigator, make sure the Navigator radio button is selected, and then click on Open. In Internet Explorer, just click on the OK button.

5. Your HTML file (scratch.htm) should now be displayed in your browser, showing the most recent changes you've made to your file.

6. Leaving your HTML file open in your browser, hop back over to Notepad (using the Alt+Tab method described in the sidebar, "Windows Navigation Tips"). In Notepad, make more changes to your HTML file and save those changes.

7. Hop back over to your browser (using Alt+Tab). Click on the Reload button (Navigator) or the Refresh button (Internet Explorer), or press Ctrl + R; to update the display of your page.

8. Repeat steps 6 and 7 frequently to see your work dynamically updated in your browser as you go through this and the other HTML tutorials in this book.

Creating Paragraphs and Line Breaks

The P (Paragraph) and BR (Break) tags let you insert paragraphs and lines of text on your page.

The P (Paragraph) Tag

You can't just type text into an HTML document. Always tag any plain text (text not included in some other element, such as a heading, list, block quote, and so on) that you want to include with the P tag. You shouldn't have any untagged text in an HTML document.

Below the heading tags you typed previously, type the following paragraph, inserting a `<P>` start tag at the start and a `</P>` end tag at the end (see Figure 2.3):

```
<H6>This is a sixth-level heading</H6>
<P>This is paragraph text. This is paragraph text. This is
paragraph text. This is paragraph text. This is paragraph text.
This is paragraph text.</P>
</BODY>
```

The P tag is a container element. In the past, however, it has been common to treat this tag as though it had an implied ending, allowing you to insert the `<P>` start tag at the start of a paragraph while leaving off the `</P>` end tag at the end of a paragraph. The end of a paragraph element is implied by the start of a following block element, such as a heading, a list, another paragraph, and so on. Both HTML 2.0 and HTML 3.2 allowed leaving off the `</P>`. However, HTML 4.0, although it doesn't prohibit this, discourages leaving off the end tag.

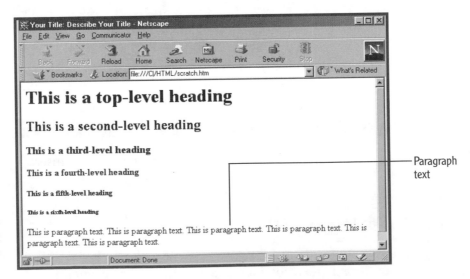

Figure 2.3

All paragraph text is tagged with the P tag.

In most cases, leaving off the `</P>` end tag still works fine, but in a number of situations, due to various browser quirks, leaving off the end tag will have somewhat less than desirable results. Although I encourage you to include the `</P>` end tags, I'll point out as you go through the HTML tutorials the instances in which you should always add the end tag.

Because the latest standard for HTML, HTML 4.0, discourages leaving off the `</P>` end tag, all of the examples in this book include the `</P>` end tags.

A Web browser automatically wraps text in an HTML file to fit inside its window. Therefore, you don't have to insert returns at the ends of your lines to get them to fit inside a browser window. It wouldn't work anyway because Web browsers completely ignore hard returns. Let Notepad wrap your text (turn on Word Wrap), but this is purely for your convenience while working in Notepad. It will have no effect on where the text breaks in your Web browser.

Nesting Paragraphs

Generally, your paragraphs are nested in the BODY tag. You also can nest paragraphs in block quotes (BLOCKQUOTE), glossary definitions (DD), list items (LI), and address blocks (ADDRESS). A paragraph can contain plain text, highlighting (B, I, EM, STRONG, and so on), special characters (like accented characters or the copyright symbol), line breaks (BR), hypertext links (A), and inline images (IMG). You can learn about these codes later in this session.

Don't Use Multiple P Tags to Add Blank Lines

Generally, a P tag that contains no text has no effect. No browsers that I know of let you add blank lines by simply adding P tags. To illustrate this

Figure 2.4

The multiple P tags
inserted between
two paragraphs
should be
completely ignored
by a Web browser,
as shown here.

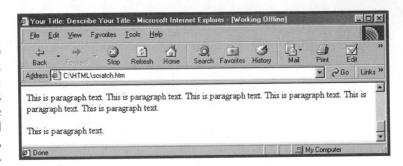

point, following the text paragraph you just typed, add three P tags, followed by another text paragraph (see Figure 2.4):

```
<P>This is paragraph text. This is paragraph text. This is
paragraph text. This is paragraph text. This is paragraph text.
This is paragraph text.</P>
```

```
<P></P>
```

```
<P></P>
```

```
<P></P>
```

```
<P>This is paragraph text.</P>
```

Go ahead and hop over to your Web browser to see what this looks like.
Multiple P tags, with or without their end tags, will probably have no
effect. Most browsers completely ignore them, as shown in Figure 2.4.
Even if a browser does display them, you wouldn't want to write exclusively for it anyway.

The BR (Break) Tag

The BR (Break) tag is an empty, or stand-alone, tag that simply inserts a
line break. Type three text lines separated by BR tags:

```
<P>These lines are separated by BR (Break) tags.<BR>
These lines are separated by BR (Break) tags.<BR>
These lines are separated by BR (Break) tags.</P>
```

As Figure 2.5 shows, only a single line break separates these lines when a
browser displays them. (Paragraphs, you may remember, are separated by
a line break and an extra blank line.)

Figure 2.5

Use the BR (Break) tag to insert a line break at the end of a line.

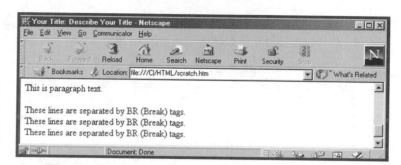

 TIP You can use the BR tag almost anywhere you have text, not just inside of P tags. You can put it inside an H1 or H2 tag to force a heading to show up on two lines, for instance.

Using Multiple BR Tags to Add Blank Lines

You might think you could use multiple BR tags to add blank lines to your page. To see what happens when you try this, type a line of text followed by four BR tags:

```
<P>Four BR (Break) tags follow this line.<BR>
<BR>
<BR>
<BR>
Four BR (Break) tags precede this line.</P>
```

You're not supposed to get away with such a maneuver (according to the official HTML specs, that is). Netscape Navigator, however, has always let you get away with it, and the latest versions of Internet Explorer also let you do it, as shown in Figure 2.6.

Both Navigator and Internet Explorer treat multiple BR tags in a *nonstandard* fashion. To quote from the draft specification for HTML 4.0, "a sequence of contiguous white space characters such as spaces, horizontal tabs, form feeds and line breaks, should be replaced by a single word space."

Figure 2.6

Both Navigator and
Internet Explorer
will display
multiple BR tags,
but in
contravention of
the standards for
HTML.

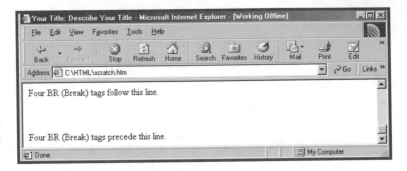

So should you or shouldn't you use BR tags for blank lines? Even though
Netscape Navigator, Internet Explorer, and any number of other Web
browsers let you use multiple BR tags, it still doesn't constitute standard
HTML. The best bet is to avoid nonstandard HTML, even if your
favorite Web browser allows you to get away with using it (even if that
Web browser happens to be Navigator). Besides, you can get the same
result in a perfectly legal way.

TIP

This trick for inserting blank lines into a Web page works for all browsers (even Lynx).
To insert blank lines into your HTML file, enclose regular hard returns inside the PRE
(Preformatted Text) tag:

```
<P>Inserting a PRE tag containing hard returns will add extra
space between paragraphs.</P>
<PRE>


</PRE>
<P>This line should be three lines down.</P>
```

For more information on the PRE tag, see the section, "Using Preformatted Text," later in
this session.

Spacing, Tabs, and Returns:
For Your Eyes Only

In HTML, the tags themselves do all your page's formatting. A browser ignores more than one space inserted into text (two, five, or ten spaces all appear as if they are a single space), as well as all tabs and hard returns (unless they're inside a PRE tag). Any formatting of your HTML file using extra spaces or tabs and returns is *for your eyes only*. So feel free to use all the extra spaces, tabs, and returns you want to make your raw HTML files more readable as you work on them.

TIP   Other than inserting a totally transparent image, the only way to insert multiple horizontal spaces in your HTML file is to use nonbreakable space characters. You insert these into an HTML file as either   or   To simulate a paragraph tab, for example, you would insert   three times at the start of a paragraph:

This will work in virtually all Web browsers, although there are a couple X-Windows Web browsers that won't display nonbreakable spaces at all, displaying them as zero-width characters. For more information on inserting special characters, see "Inserting Non-Keyboard Characters" later in this session.

Adding Comments

You can also add comments to annotate your HTML files. The comment tag is a stand-alone tag that enables you to include messages, for future reference, that will not be displayed in a Web browser in your HTML files. What is a little confusing about this tag, however, is that no "name" is included in the tag. Instead, a comment always begins with a <!-- and ends with a -->.

Any text inserted between these is comment text that a browser completely ignores. Here's an example of the form in which you would enter a comment into an HTML file:

```
<!--Put your comment here-->
```

Now, go ahead and type a comment between two lines of text, like this:

```
<P>This line is followed by a comment.</P>
<!--Comments are not displayed by a browser.-->
<P>This line follows a comment.</P>
```

The above two paragraph lines appear in a Web browser without any additional vertical space between them (other than the space normally added between the two paragraphs). A browser will ignore any text inside the Comment tag.

Highlighting Your Text

Just as in a normal book or report, an HTML document can use text highlighting to clarify the text's meaning. For instance, you can easily bold or italicize text in an HTML file to emphasize particular words or phrases.

Using Italic and Bold Highlighting

HTML has two ways to include italic or bold text on your Web page. The first way involves using "literal" tags: the I (Italic) and B (Bold) tags. The second way is to use "logical" tags: the EM (Emphasis) and STRONG (Strong Emphasis) tags. Most browsers should display the I (Italic) and EM (Emphasis) tags identically, just as they should display the B (Bold) and STRONG (Strong Emphasis) tags identically.

So what's the difference? None, really. The basic philosophy behind HTML is to logically represent the elements of a page rather than literally describe them. The browser can freely interpret the logical elements of an HTML page and display them as it sees fit. Thus, the philosophically

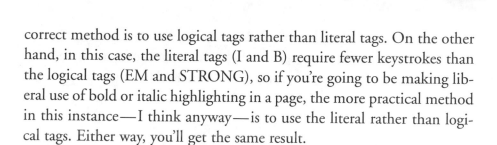

correct method is to use logical tags rather than literal tags. On the other hand, in this case, the literal tags (I and B) require fewer keystrokes than the logical tags (EM and STRONG), so if you're going to be making liberal use of bold or italic highlighting in a page, the more practical method in this instance—I think anyway—is to use the literal rather than logical tags. Either way, you'll get the same result.

As an example of using the I, B, EM, and STRONG tags for text highlighting, type the following lines of text using these tags, as shown here (see Figure 2.7):

```
<P><I>This is italic text.</I></P>
<P><B>This is bold text.</B></P>
<P><EM>This is emphasized text.</EM></P>
<P><STRONG>This is strongly emphasized text.</STRONG></P>
<P><I><B>This is bold italic text.</B></I></P>
```

You can use two other tags—CITE (Citation) and VAR (Variable)—to highlight text, but all Web browsers I know of interpret them exactly like the I (Italic) or EM (Emphasis) tags.

Embedding Monospaced Text

You may want to embed monospaced text within a paragraph to, for example, request keyboard input or to represent screen output. A

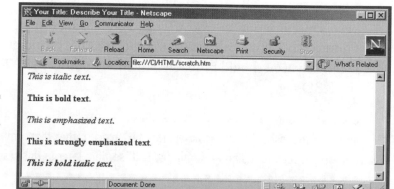

Figure 2.7

You can use literal tags (I and B) or logical tags (EM and STRONG) to italicize or bold text.

monospaced font, also called a fixed-pitch font, is a font in which all the characters occupy the same amount of space on a line. (In a *proportional font,* on the other hand, each character occupies a unique amount of space on a line.) For example, the following line uses a monospaced font:

```
This line uses a monospaced font.
```

The most widely used tag for embedding monospaced text is the TT (Teletype) tag. It appears as a monospaced font in all Web browsers. You can think of it as a general-purpose monospaced text tag that you can use whenever you want to embed monospaced text within a paragraph. Two other tags, the CODE and SAMP tags, produce the same results as the TT tag.

The only other possibly useful tag is the KBD (Keyboard) tag. Unfortunately, how a Web browser displays this tag is rather unpredictable. Navigator displays it the same as the TT tag. Earlier versions of Internet Explorer display it in a boldface monospaced font, although the latest version of Internet Explorer follows Navigator's example. NCSA Mosaic 2.0 displays this tag as an italicized proportional font.

Type the following as an example of using the TT and KBD tags (see Figure 2.8):

```
<P>This is regular text. <TT>This is an example of the TT (Tele-
type or Typewriter Text) tag.</TT> This is regular text.
<KBD>This is an example of the KBD (Keyboard) tag.</KBD></P>
```

The KBD tag might be useful because it would allow you to distinguish between screen output (the TT tag) and keyboard input (the KBD tag). However, because both Navigator and Internet Explorer treat these tags identically, you should probably just stick to using the TT tag and ignore the KBD tag.

NOTE   To insert monospaced text as a separate text block rather than embedding it inside a paragraph, see the "Using Preformatted Text" section, later in this session.

Figure 2.8

The tendency among current Web browsers is to display text marked with the TT and KBD tags identically.

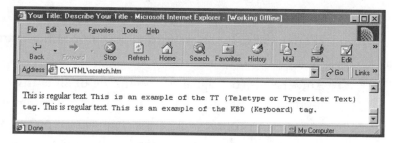

Inserting Non-Keyboard Characters

You may need to enter a special code for a character into your HTML file under two circumstances: if you want to insert a reserved character that is used to parse (interpret and display) an HTML file, and if you want to enter a special, or extended, character that isn't part of the regular keyboard character set.

You insert both of these characters into an HTML file in the form of a numerical entity code or a named entity code. Numerical entity codes are inserted in the following form, where *number* is a three-digit decimal number from 000 to 255:

&#*number*;

Named entity codes are inserted in the following form, where *name* is the name of a character as listed in the HTML specs:

&*name*;

Reserved Characters

HTML uses the <, >, &, and " characters to parse, or interpret, an HTML document for display. Except for angle brackets, you rarely need to automatically replace these characters with their entity codes:

✿ Angle brackets (< and >) should always be replaced by their corresponding entity codes if you want to display them "as is" in an HTML file.

- Double quotes (") only need to be replaced if they're part of an HTML tag that you want to appear as is rather than as interpreted by a browser.

- Ampersands (&) signal the beginning of an entity code but only need to be replaced if they're part of an HTML entity code that you want to appear as is rather than as interpreted by a browser. You never need to replace stand-alone ampersands.

◆◆◆◆◆◆◆◆◆◆◆◆◆◆◆◆◆◆◆◆◆◆◆◆◆◆◆◆◆◆◆◆◆◆◆◆◆◆

If you're using a word processor to create HTML files, be sure to turn off the "smart quotes" feature. When creating HTML files, you always want to use regular "keyboard" quotes. In other words, each quotation mark should be straight up and down, not curled to the left or right.

◆◆◆◆◆◆◆◆◆◆◆◆◆◆◆◆◆◆◆◆◆◆◆◆◆◆◆◆◆◆◆◆◆◆◆◆◆◆

You can use character entities exclusively to insert any of these characters into an HTML file when you want an HTML tag to appear on your Web page as is rather than as interpreted by the browser. To have a browser show "<EM>" onscreen instead of interpreting it as a formatting code, you need to enter it like this:

```
&lt;EM&gt;
```

All Web browsers recognize the named entity codes for these characters, so you don't have to use the numerical entity codes here. For an easy reference, Table 2.1 shows the named entity codes for inserting HTML reserved characters.

Special Characters

Suppose you want to post a page devoted to an article you've written, and you want to protect it by showing your copyright. Because the copyright symbol (©) isn't available on the keyboard, you can't just type it into your

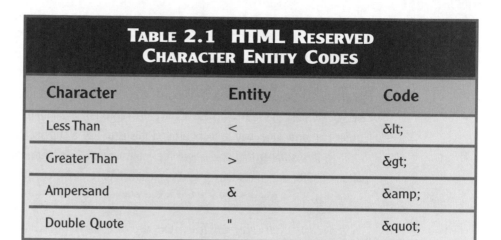

Character	Entity	Code
Less Than	<	&lt;
Greater Than	>	&gt;
Ampersand	&	&amp;
Double Quote	"	&quot;

HTML document as you would a normal keyboard character. Instead, you must use a special code that tells the browser to insert the character where you want it.

In HTML, such characters can be entered two ways: as numerical entity codes or named entity codes. You can insert the copyright symbol, for example, by using its numerical entity code (©) or its named entity code (©).

HTML uses the ISO 8859-1 character set, which is an 8-bit character set that provides 256 positions (000 through 255). Of these, however, 000 through 032 and 127 correspond to control characters, and 128 through 159 are designated as undisplayable. Thus, only the last 96 codes (160 through 255) represent all the special characters that, according to the ISO 8859-1 standard, should be legally used on a Web page. These include many special symbols (cent, copyright, degree, and so on), plus many accented characters (like a capital A with an acute accent) that are commonly used in many foreign languages.

Numerical character entities use the actual decimal numeration of the character in the ISO 8859-1 character set. As noted previously, you could insert a copyright symbol into a Web page by using its numerical character entity like this:

`&#169;`

Named entity codes have been designated to correspond to many of these special characters. Again, to insert a copyright symbol using its named character entity, you would type:

`&copy;`

Whether a Web browser will display a named character entity is another matter. Other than the uppercase and lowercase accented characters (A-grave, a-acute, and so on) that many foreign languages require, only the copyright and registration signs have anything close to universal support. Certain Web browsers can interpret and display almost all of these named entities, but other than those just mentioned, Netscape Navigator won't. Feel free to use the named entity codes for the copyright or registration symbol and for any of the accented characters, but otherwise stick to the numerical character entities.

CAUTION Although the ISO 8859-1 character set is used to designate special characters to insert in a Web page, it is not the universal native character set for all computer operating systems. It is the native character set for both UNIX and Windows, but not for the Macintosh or MS-DOS. The native character set of the Macintosh, however, doesn't contain all of the characters that are included in the ISO 8859-1 character set, including fourteen of the standard special characters (160 through 255). Internet Explorer 4.0+ for the Macintosh substitutes the ISO 8859-1 character set (which it calls the Western (Latin 1) character set) for the Macintosh's native character set to display Web pages, so it will display the missing characters. In other Macintosh browsers, however, if you try to use any of these missing characters, you'll see a different character than the one that you intend. The solution is to avoid using these characters on a Web page. In Appendix B, "Special Characters," all of the non-Macintosh characters are clearly identified.

Table 2.2 shows some of the most commonly used special characters, their numerical and named entity codes, and support by browsers (universal support for named entities cannot be guaranteed).

TABLE 2.2 SPECIAL CHARACTERS			
Character	**Number**	**Name**	**Name Support**
Trademark	&#153;	&trade;	Not Navigator (all versions)
Cent	&#162;	&cent;	4.0+ browsers only*
Copyright	&#169;	&copy;	All browsers
Registered	&#174;	&reg;	All browsers
Multiply	&#215;	&times;	4.0+ browsers only*
Divide	&#247;	&divide;	4.0+ browsers only*
* Netscape Navigator 4.0+ or Microsoft Internet Explorer 4.0+			

Table 2.2 is just a partial list of special characters you can insert into an HTML file. For a full listing of all the special characters you can use, see Appendix B, "Special Characters."

CAUTION   Named entity codes such as © or ® are case-sensitive. You should type them exactly as they are listed. À and à, for instance, are entity names for two separate accented characters: an uppercase *A* with a grave accent and a lowercase *a* with a grave accent, respectively.

Go ahead and enter the following example of using the numerical entity code for the copyright symbol and the named entity code for the registered symbol (see Figure 2.9):

```
<H2>&#169; Copyright 1997.</H2>
<H2>Crumbies&reg;</H2>
```

Using Block Quotes

The BLOCKQUOTE (Block Quote) tag double-indents a block of text from both margins. You usually use it to display quotations, as the name of the tag implies. But you aren't limited to using it on quotations; you can use it to double-indent any block of text.

Figure 2.9

You can insert special characters such as the copyright and registered symbols using numerical or named entity codes.

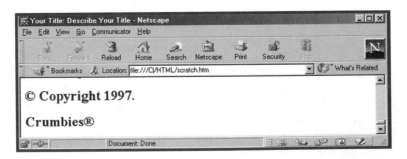

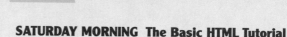

Type a paragraph of text, followed by a paragraph of text inside a BLOCKQUOTE tag (see Figure 2.10):

```
<P>In <EM>Notes from the Underground</EM>, Dostoevsky plumbs
the depths of human psychology, revealing the complexity and
contradictions underlying even the most normal and decent of
human beings:</P>
<BLOCKQUOTE>
<P>Every man has some reminiscenses which he would not tell to
everyone, but only to his friends. He has others which he would
not reveal even to his friends, but only to himself, and that in
secret. But finally there are still others which a man is even
afraid to tell himself, and every decent man has a considerable
number of such things in his mind.</P>
</BLOCKQUOTE>
```

According to the specification for the tag, you aren't supposed to put raw text inside a block quote—text inserted in a block quote is supposed to be nested inside a paragraph, heading, list, definition list, preformatted text, or another block quote. Browsers don't care, however, whether you insert block quote text inside of a P tag. Using the P tag to nest text inside a BLOCKQUOTE tag does, however, enable you to include multiple paragraphs within a block quote, for instance.

The BLOCKQUOTE tag is fairly commonly used as a formatting device to indent text in from the margins of a Web page. You should be aware,

Figure 2.10

The BLOCKQUOTE tag is used to double-indent text from the margins.

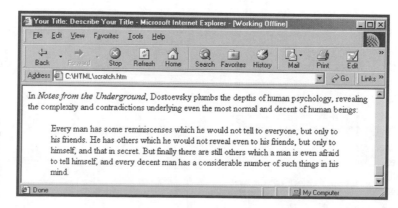

however, that though this works fine for recent browsers, some earlier browsers display block quote text in a font other than a normal proportional font. Internet Explorer 2.0, the default browser for Windows 95, displays block quote text in a bolded italic font, for instance. NCSA Mosaic 2.0 displays block quote text in a bolded font. So, you might want to think twice before using it simply as a formatting device to indent text. If you use BLOCKQUOTE to display an indented quotation, however, then it is no big deal that an occasional browser might italicize or bold it.

Using BR (Break) Tags in a Block Quote

You can use BR (Break) tags in a block quote to display stanzas of poetry, the verses of a song, or other indented text for which you don't want the lines to wrap. Type a paragraph of text, followed by a paragraph of text using BR tags inserted inside a BLOCKQUOTE tag (see Figure 2.11).

```
<P>In <EM>Porgy and Bess</EM>, in the song "Summertime," George
Gershwin evokes the hazy, lazy days of a Southern summer:</P>
<BLOCKQUOTE>
<P>Summertime and the living is easy,<BR>
Fish are jumping and the cotton is high.<BR>
Oh your Daddy's rich and your Ma is good looking,<BR>
So hush little baby, don't you cry.</P>
</BLOCKQUOTE>
```

Figure 2.11

By combining BR tags with the BLOCKQUOTE tag, you can create indented stanzas for a poem or song.

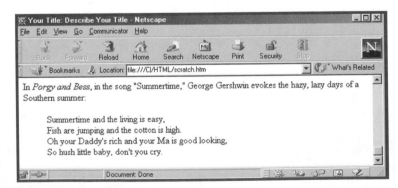

Using Preformatted Text

You use the PRE (Preformatted Text) tag to display text in a monospaced fixed-pitch font. As its name implies, you use the PRE tag to display text as is, including all spaces and hard returns. The primary use for this tag is to display text in a tabular or columnar format in which you want to make sure that columns are properly aligned.

TIP

Always use spaces, not tabs, to align columns when using the PRE tag because different browsers can display tabs in PRE tagged text differently.

Actually, the PRE tag is the original "tables" tag for HTML. Unlike the TABLE tag (part of HTML 3.2 but not HTML 2.0), all Web browsers support it, which is a real advantage. It can be particularly handy for displaying worksheets or reports. Another common usage is for displaying program code or output.

CAUTION

When typing tabular or columnar text to be tagged with a PRE tag, make sure that you have a monospaced fixed-pitch font such as Courier turned on in your text editor or word processor. Notepad automatically displays all text in a monospaced font. Word processors, however, by default normally use a proportional font. Many HTML editors will automatically display PRE tagged text in a monospaced font, but some won't.

For an example of using the PRE tag, type a table using rows and columns (see Figure 2.12):

```
<PRE>
          Sales Figures for First Quarter of 1996
   ----------------------------------------------------------

             January   February      March       Totals
   Anderson  $ 10,200  $   20,015  $   14,685  $   44,900
   Baker       30,500      25,885      50,225     106,610
   Peterson    15,900      20,115      18,890      54,905
   Wilson      40,100      35,000      29,000     104,100

             --------   ---------   ---------   ---------
   Totals    $ 96,700  $ 101,015   $ 112,800   $ 310,515
</PRE>
```

To double-indent preformatted text in both Netscape Navigator and NCSA Mosaic, put it inside a BLOCKQUOTE tag. Enclose the PRE tag text you just typed inside a BLOCKQUOTE tag, as follows:

```
<PRE>

<BLOCKQUOTE>
          Sales Figures for First Quarter of 1996
   ----------------------------------------------------------

             January   February      March       Totals
   Anderson  $ 10,200  $   20,015  $   14,685  $   44,900
   Baker       30,500      25,885      50,225     106,610
   Peterson    15,900      20,115      18,890      54,905
   Wilson      40,100      35,000      29,000     104,100

             --------   ---------   ---------   ---------
   Totals    $ 96,700  $ 101,015   $ 112,800   $ 310,515
</BLOCKQUOTE>

</PRE>
```

Figure 2.12

The PRE tag displays text blocks in a monospaced font, preserving all spaces and line breaks in columnar and tabular text.

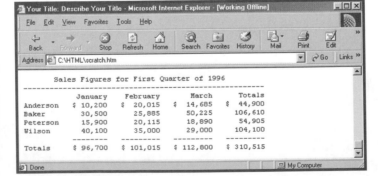

This won't work in Internet Explorer 2.0, which will still display the table flush left. Also, you might think that you could reverse the nesting order here, placing the PRE tags inside the BLOCKQUOTE tags, but a bug in Internet Explorer 4.0 will still cause it to be displayed flush to the left margin. This has been fixed in versions 4.01 and later of Internet Explorer, but plenty of people are still using version 4.0, so you'd better just stick to putting the BLOCKQUOTE tags inside the PRE tags.

Take a Break?

This seems like a good place to take a break. Get up and stretch those arms and legs. Pour another cup of coffee. Or take the dog for a walk. I'll see you back in five or ten minutes for the remainder of this session.

Creating Lists

Only headings and paragraph text elements are used more commonly than lists. Many Web pages are nothing but lists of hypertext links. You, like anyone else surfing the Web, have been on that merry-go-round a few times—going from one page of lists to another page of lists to another. If you're going to create Web pages, you need to know how to make lists! There are two types of lists: ordered and unordered. An ordered list is simply a numbered list, and an unordered list is a bulleted list.

TIP You don't have to physically type the numbers for the items in an ordered list or insert bullet characters for an unordered list. A Web browser will automatically number list items in an ordered list and insert bullet characters in an unordered list.

The OL (Ordered List) Tag

The OL (Ordered List) tag defines a sequentially numbered list of items. Therefore, the OL tag must surround the entire list. The LI (List Item) tag is nested inside the OL tag and defines each individual item within the list.

Create an ordered list to see how these tags work together (see Figure 2.13):

```
<P>When visiting Florence, one should be sure to visit:</P>
<OL>
<LI>The Church of Santa Maria Novella
<LI>The Medici Chapels
<LI>The Church of San Lorenzo
<LI>The Baptistry of St. John
</OL>
```

NOTE The LI (List Item) tag is actually a container tag with an implied ending. Leaving off the end tag is customary in this instance and approved by the latest HTML standards.

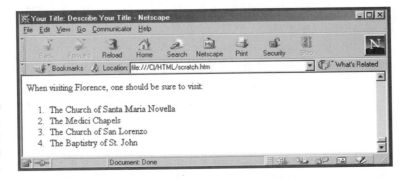

Figure 2.13

The OL (Ordered List) tag is used to create a numbered list.

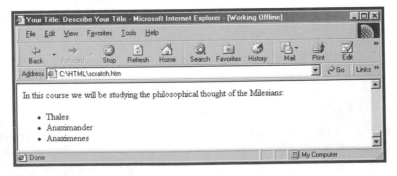

Figure 2.14

The UL (Unordered List) tag is used to create a bulleted list.

The UL (Unordered List) Tag

The UL (Unordered List) tag defines a bulleted list of items. Once again, the LI (List Item) tag is nested inside the UL tag and defines each item within the list. Create a bulleted list (see Figure 2.14):

```
<P>In this course we will be studying the philosophical thought
of the Milesians:</P>
<UL>
<LI>Thales
<LI>Anaximander
<LI>Anaximenes
</UL>
```

Nesting Lists

You can nest a list inside another list. The browser automatically indents nested list levels. You can nest the same or different kinds of lists.

The following list examples use spaces to indent the different nested levels of the list. The only purpose of this is to make the code more readable during editing, as a Web browser will completely ignore any additional spaces you insert. Feel free to insert spaces or tabs to approximate the layout shown here. Create a nested bulleted list:

```
<UL>
<LI>Some Pre-Socratic Philosophers
   <UL>
   <LI>The Milesians
     <UL>
     <LI>Thales
     <LI>Anaximander
     <LI>Anaximenes
     </UL>
```

```
<LI>The Eleatics
   <UL>
   <LI>Parmenides
   <LI>Anaxagoras
   </UL>
   </UL>
</UL>
```

You should be aware that how the different levels of an unordered list are displayed might vary somewhat from browser to browser, as shown in Figures 2.15 and 2.16.

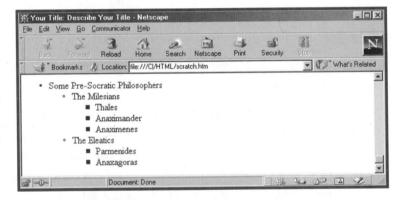

Figure 2.15

Netscape Navigator displays a multilevel bulleted list like this.

Figure 2.16

Internet Explorer displays a multilevel bulleted list like this.

Mixing Lists

You can nest an ordered list within an unordered list (see Figure 2.17):

```
<UL>
<LI>King-Side Openings
   <OL>
   <LI>Ruy Lopez
   <LI>King Bishop's Opening
   <LI>King's Gambit
   </OL>
<LI>Queen-Side Openings
   <OL>
   <LI>Queen's Gambit Declined
   <LI>Queen's Gambit Accepted
   <LI>English Opening
   </OL>
</UL>
```

Two other list tags, the DIR and MENU tags, can also be used, but they display in the vast majority of browsers exactly the same as the UL tag, so there isn't much reason to use them. The HTML 4.0 specification also strongly recommends that the UL tag be used instead.

Figure 2.17

You can nest a numbered (ordered) list inside a bulleted (unordered) list and vice versa.

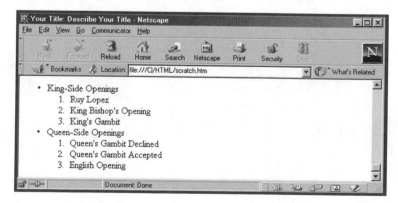

Creating Definition Lists

The DL (Definition List) tag allows you to create glossaries, or lists of terms and definitions. A glossary actually consists of three tag elements that all work together: the DL tag to define the list, the DT (Definition Term) tag to define the terms, and the DD (Definition Description) tag to define the definitions. Set up a short glossary now (see Figure 2.18):

```
<DL>
<DT>Appeal
<DD>A proceeding by which the decision of a lower court may be
appealed to a higher court.
<DT>Arrest
<DD>The legal apprehension and restraint of someone charged with
a crime so that they might be brought before a court to stand
trial.
<DT>Bail
<DD>A security offered to a court in exchange for a person's
release and as assurance of their appearance in court when
required.
</DL>
```

As you've probably noticed, the end tags for the DT and DD tags are implied, the same as for LI end tags in a regular list. The only difference is that a glossary, or definition list, has a two-part item (both a term and a description) rather than a one-part item. As long as you keep this in mind, you should have no trouble creating glossaries.

Figure 2.18

A definition list (or glossary) is created using three tags: the DL (Definition List), DT (Definition Term), and DD (Definition Description) tags.

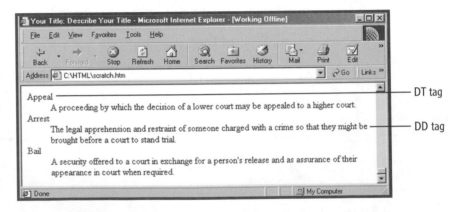

By itself, a glossary list is a bit bland. You can dress it up by adding emphasis or tagging the definition terms with a heading tag. Here is an example of adding bold italic emphasis to a definition term:

```
<DT><I><B>Appeal</B></I>
```

Here is an example of tagging a definition term using an H3 heading tag:

```
<DT><H3>Appeal</H3>
```

Creating Hypertext Links

If you've surfed the Web at all, you should be quite familiar with hypertext links. You've probably used hypertext links not only to jump to and view another Web page or jump to a specific place in either the same or another Web page, but also to read a Gopher file, display an image, download a program, send an e-mail message, play an audio or video clip, run a script, access a database, telnet to a server, and so on. You can use hypertext links to jump to anything that has an address on the Internet (not just on the Web), as long as you don't need a password. Of course, what happens after you make the jump depends on where you go.

In a sense, the Web is a kind of giant "What's behind door #3?" game, which perhaps helps explain much of its basic appeal. It's all quite easy and transparent: just click and go. However, explaining how to make this happen on your Web page isn't nearly as easy or transparent. This section will make the A (Anchor) tag as clear as possible. The three basic kinds of hypertext links are as follows:

- **Links to other HTML documents or data objects.** These are by far the most commonly used links on the Web. They allow you to jump from one Web page to another, as well as to anything else that has an address on the Internet (not just the Web), such as Gopher files, FTP archives, images, and so on.

- **Links to other places in the same HTML document.** These links allow you to jump from one place in a Web page to another point on the same Web page. Many Web pages have directories or "tables of contents" at the beginning of the page, allowing you to decide which part of the page you would like to view and then click on the link to jump to that section of the page or document.

⚙ **Links to places in other HTML documents.** These links are quite similar to links to places in the same document, except you can jump to certain sections on other pages. If you've clicked on a hypertext link and then jumped to some point halfway down another Web page, you've used this type of link.

You use the A tag to anchor one or both ends of a hypertext link. If you're linking to another Web page or data object, you only need one anchor. If you're linking to another location in the same or another Web page, you need to use two anchors, one functioning as your launchpad, so to speak, and the other as your landing spot. The second anchor is often called a "target anchor."

Anatomy of the A (Anchor) Tag

Think of a hypertext link as being composed of the following three elements:

⚙ The start and end tags

⚙ The link target

⚙ The link text

Figure 2.19 illustrates the three parts of a hypertext link.

Figure 2.19

A hypertext link has three parts: the start and end tags, the link target, and the link text.

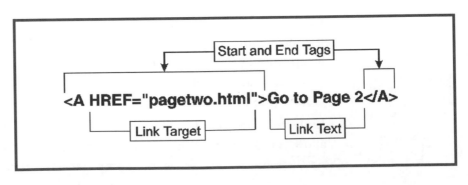

In Figure 2.19, the HREF (Hypertext Reference) attribute specifies the URL, or address, of the object of the link, which here is simply another Web page. Note that the full address (URL) is not given, just the file name. This means that the object of the link, most commonly another Web page, is located in the same folder as the Web page from which the link is being made. If you wanted to make a link with a Web page somewhere else on the Web, you'd have to include the full URL (`http://www.somewhere.com/somepage.html`, or something like that), rather than just the file name (somepage.html). For more information on using the A tag's HREF attribute, see the following section, "Linking to a File or Data Object."

When using the A tag, you must include either an HREF attribute or a NAME attribute. The NAME attribute identifies the anchor as a target anchor. For more information on using the A tag's NAME attribute, see "Linking to a Place in the Same HTML File" and "Linking to a Place in Another HTML File" later in this section.

Linking to a File or Data Object

You can form an HTML link to anything on the Web that has an address. To create a hypertext link that jumps to a file that is somewhere on the Web (as opposed to a folder included in your own Web site), you include the whole URL of the file to which you want to jump. Type the following example to create a real hypertext link that links to the World Wide Web Consortium's home page (see Figure 2.20):

```
<P>You can find out more about the WWW at the home page of the
<A HREF="http://www.w3.org/">W3 Consortium</A>.</P>
```

Figure 2.20

The underlining flags a hypertext link to the home page of the W3 Consortium.

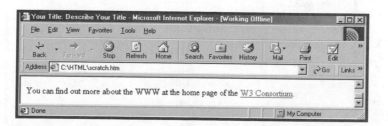

NOTE Notice that the A tag falls inside a P tag. Since the A tag is an inline element, it should always be nested inside of a block element, such as the P tag, instead of being nested directly inside of the BODY tag.

When you click on the hypertext link shown in Figure 2.20, a hypertext "jump" takes you to the target address, displaying the page shown in Figure 2.21. Feel free to hop over to your browser to check this out. You'll have to go online to check out the link, however.

Linking to Data Objects

A data object is any file located on the Internet. It might be an image file, a sound file, a video file, or just a text file. You're not limited to linking only to files located on Web servers (HTTP servers). You can link to files on an FTP server or a Gopher server, for instance.

Your browser should be able to directly display any text file or GIF or JPEG graphic on a Web, FTP, or Gopher server. Other kinds of files, such as sound, animation, or video files, may require that a compatible viewer or player be installed.

Figure 2.21

The home page of the W3C appears when you click on the link shown in Figure 2.20.

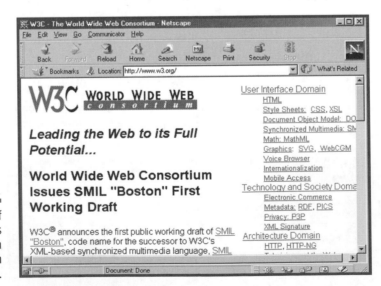

Linking to a Place in the Same HTML File

Linking to another place in the same HTML file requires two anchors, an HREF anchor and a NAME anchor (or target anchor). An HREF anchor that links to a NAME anchor has a special form:

```
<A HREF="#anchorname">anchortext</A>
```

In an HREF anchor, the # sign indicates that the following is the name of a target anchor—the # sign combined with the following anchor name is called a "fragment identifier."

Anytime you create a hypertext link using a fragment identifier to link to another location in your Web page, you need to also insert the corresponding target anchor. Target anchors are inserted in the following format:

```
<A NAME="anchorname"></A>
```

The main thing is that the anchor name must match exactly in both anchor tags. Notice, however, that only the anchor name, and not the # sign, is included in the target anchor. The anchor name must also be unique—you can't use the same anchor name twice in a Web page.

Some of the more common uses for linking HREF and NAME anchors on the same page are to create a directory or table of contents that links to the major headings of a page, make cross references between different

```
<A HREF="#two">Section Two</A><BR>

<A HREF="#three">Section Three</A></P>

<H3><A NAME="one">Section One</A></H3>

<P>This is the text following the first subheading. This is the
text following the first subheading. This is the text following
the first subheading. This is the text following the first sub-
heading. This is the text following the first subheading. This
is the text following the first subheading.</P>

<H3><A NAME="two">Section Two</A></H3>

<P>This is the text following the second subheading. This is the
text following the second subheading. This is the text following
the second subheading. This is the text following the second
subheading. This is the text following the second subheading.
This is the text following the second subheading.</P>

<H3><A NAME="three">Section Three</A></H3>

<P>This is the text following the third subheading. This is the
text following the third subheading. This is the text following
the third subheading. This is the text following the third sub-
heading. This is the text following the third subheading. This
is the text following the third subheading.</P>
```

Because only the first subheading and subsection is shown in Figure 2.22, you should save your file and hop over to your browser to check out how this whole example looks. Click on the table of contents links to jump to the different subsections. (Click on the Back button to return to the table of contents.)

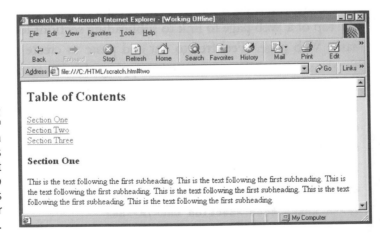

Figure 2.22

You can create a table of contents using hypertext links that will jump to subheadings within your document.

Linking to a Place in Another HTML File

Just as you can make a hypertext link with a place in the same HTML file, you can make a link with a place in another HTML file. Both work the same way, except in the second instance the NAME anchor (your landing spot) is placed in an entirely different HTML file from the one where the link is being made. The form for an HREF anchor that links to a place in another HTML file is:

```
<A HREF="address#anchorname">anchortext</A>
```

This actually combines the forms for linking to another page and linking to a place on a page. In the above example, *address* refers to the URL of the HTML file that the link will jump to (this can be a full URL or just an HTML file name if it is located in the same folder, for instance); *anchorname* refers to the anchor name assigned in the target anchor; and *anchortext* refers to the text that is displayed as the hypertext link. Move back down to the bottom of your HTML file and enter the following example, just above the </BODY> end tag, to create a hypertext link that jumps to a place in another HTML file (see Figure 2.23):

```
<P>Go to <A HREF="links.htm#parttwo">Part Two</A> of the <A
HREF="links.htm">How to Use Links</A> web page.</P>
</BODY>
```

Figure 2.23

The first link jumps to a place in the How to Use Links Web page, and the second link jumps to the Web page itself.

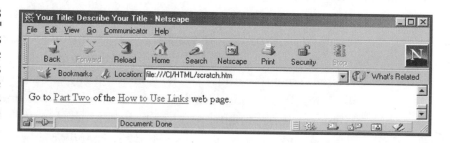

The preceding HTML includes links both to Part Two of the How to Use Links Web page and to the whole How to Use Links Web page. The only difference between linking to a location in a Web page and simply linking directly to that Web page is that you add the target name (also called a fragment identifier), here #parttwo, to the HREF string value.

I've included links.htm with the example files that you installed in C:\HTML. To check out how this link works, just click on the Part Two link (click on the Back button to return). If you view the page source in your browser, or open it directly in Notepad, you can see the target anchor that the link jumps to:

```
<H2><A NAME="parttwo"></A>Part Two</H2>
```

Creating Link Lists

So far, the discussion has focused on creating lists and creating links but hasn't explained creating link lists. A *link list* is a list of hypertext links, usually bulleted but sometimes numbered. Because link lists are so ubiquitous, everybody should know how to create them. To create a link list, all you need to do is combine an unordered list and some hypertext links.

Creating a Simple Link List

A simple link list includes only the hypertext link and the link text, without any following descriptive text. You can include whatever you want as the link text, but it should be informative and descriptive of the page you're linking to because you're not adding any descriptive text outside of the links. It is a good idea to use the title or the level-one heading of the Web page you're linking to as the link text, which usually will fill the bill, although occasionally you may need to expand or abbreviate it. Go ahead and set up a simple list of actual yo-yo links using the titles of the linked Web pages as the link text (see Figure 2.24):

```
<H2>Yo Yo Links</H2>
<UL>
```

```
<LI><A
HREF="http://pages.nyu.edu/~tqm3413/yoyo/index.htm">Tomer's Page
of Exotic Yo-Yo</A>
<LI><A HREF="http://www.socool.com/socool/yo-yo.html">Just Say
YO!!!</A>
<LI><A HREF="http://www.pd.net/yoyo/">American Yo-Yo
Association</A>
<LI><A HREF="http://www.socool.com/socool/yo_hist.html">The
History of the Yo-Yo</A>
</UL>
```

NOTE When you enter Web addresses (URLs), you should always type them exactly as they appear. UNIX commands are case-sensitive, and most Web servers still run UNIX.

Creating a Link List with Descriptions

A simple list of links can prove somewhat empty. It would be nice to add more information so visitors would have a clearer idea of what awaits at the other end of the link. One option is to edit the link text to include more information than the title affords. However, it is best to try to keep the actual link text as concise as possible so that a visitor can scan it at a glance. The solution is to add explanatory text following the hypertext link. In the list of links you just typed, add some explanatory text for each link (see Figure 2.25):

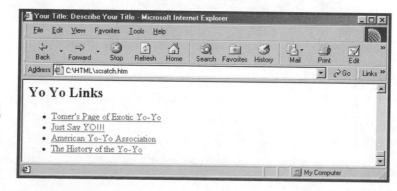

Figure 2.24

In a simple link list, the link text and the link items are the same.

```
<H2>Yo Yo Links</H2>
<UL>
<LI><A
HREF="http://pages.nyu.edu/~tqm3413/yoyo/index.htm">Tomer's Page
of Exotic Yo-Yo</A> Dedicated to the "little-known, original,
unusual, difficult, or otherwise interesting tricks."
<LI><A HREF="http://www.socool.com/socool/yo-yo.html">Just Say
YO!!!</A> Features the Web's first Yo-Yo animation.
<LI><A HREF="http://www.pd.net/yoyo/">American Yo-Yo
Association</A> Read past issues of the AYYA Newsletter.
<LI><A HREF="http://www.socool.com/socool/yo_hist.html">The History of the
Yo-Yo</A> All you want to know about Yo-Yo history.
</UL>
```

Other Ways to Create Link Lists

The preceding examples illustrate the most simple and direct ways to create link lists. A variation you might want to try is using a definition list in which the hypertext links are inserted in the DT tags, with the descriptions inserted in the DD tags. You could also tag the definition terms with a heading tag to display the links more prominently. Using a definition list for a list of links can be particularly handy if you want to provide more than just a sentence or two of explanatory or descriptive text. Later, in the Intermediate HTML Tutorial and the Tables Tutorial, I'll show you two other ways to create indented link lists using colorful 3-D bullet icons.

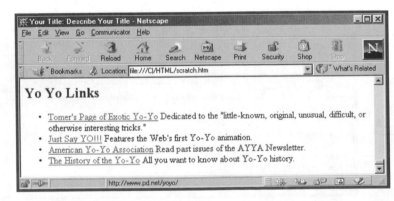

Figure 2.25

Sometimes a short list of links with explanations is better than a long one without.

Using Inline Images

The IMG (Image) tag allows you to display inline images on your Web page. The term *inline* here means that an image is inserted at a particular location in a line within a Web page.

The most commonly used formats for inline images are GIF and JPEG. All current graphical Web browsers display GIF and JPEG files as inline images. These two graphic formats tend to serve different purposes. GIF images are limited to 256 colors but can have a color set to transparent. They can also be interlaced, allowing the image to be progressively displayed while its file is still being downloaded to the browser. GIF images can also be animated. JPEG images can select from a palette of up to 16.7 million colors but can't be transparent or animated. JPEG images also can't be interlaced, although a recent variant of the JPEG format, the progressive JPEG, is displayed progressively as it is downloaded—It Is supported only by more recent Web browsers, however.

A rule of thumb is to use JPEG images when you want to include a photographic image, or a graphic using a gradient fill effect, where reducing the number of colors to 256 or fewer will negatively affect image quality (for example, by producing a banding effect). When you want to include a non-photographic image, in most cases you should stick to using GIFs because they're much less likely to require more than 256 colors to display effectively.

A relatively new image format that is rapidly gaining support on the Web is the PNG graphic format. Like GIF images, PNG images can have a color set to transparent and be progressively displayed while still being downloaded. Additionally, the PNG format supports up to 48-bit true color images (the JPEG format supports up to 24-bit true color images). PNG, at first glance, offers the best of both GIF and JPEG. Both the latest versions of Navigator and Internet Explorer support PNG graphics. Paint Shop Pro, available on the CD-ROM, can open, edit, and save PNG images. The only holdup is that a lot of older browsers are still in use. The best advice, unless you want to create a Web site aimed only at the latest browsers, is to stick with GIF and JPEG images.

The IMG tag is an empty, or stand-alone, element. Its form is:

```
<IMG SRC="imagefile">
```

The SRC (Source) attribute is a required attribute that identifies the full or partial address (URL) or the name of the file to display. Now, insert an inline graphic into your HTML file (see Figure 2.26):

```
<P>The inline graphic, SAMPLE.GIF, is displayed here:</P>
<P><IMG SRC="sample.gif"></P>
```

Notice that the IMG tag is nested in a P tag. That's because the IMG tag inserts an *inline* image—so if you want an image to be displayed on its own line, you need to nest it in a P or other block element tag.

TIP

If the graphic file you want to display as an inline image resides in the same folder as its HTML file, in the SRC attribute, you only need to refer to the name of the graphic file ("sample.gif," for instance), rather than its whole address. For example, any of the sample graphic files you've copied from the CD-ROM to C:\HTML can be included in any HTML file you save in that same folder just by including its file name in the IMG tag.

Figure 2.26

All graphical Web browsers can display inline graphic images.

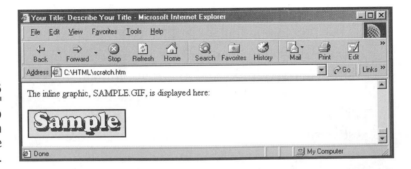

You *can* link to a graphics file anywhere on the Web and display it on your Web page by using the IMG tag. For instance, you might do something like this:

```
<IMG SRC="http://www.somewhere.com/someimage.gif">
```

Doing so, however, is universally frowned upon on the Web. Not only might you be violating somebody's copyright, you most certainly would be generating traffic on that person's server simply so you can display a particular inline image on your Web page. Also, that person can tell you are doing it and trace it back to you. It may not be against the law, but a complaint to whoever is running your server could get you kicked off your server. Bottom line: it's not the way to make friends on the Web. In other words, only directly link to an image on another's server if you have permission.

It's perfectly okay to link to others' Web pages, though. That's how you make friends on the Web. Just don't claim their Web stuff as your own. And if they give you permission to use any of their graphics, you can download them to your server and include them on your own Web page. But don't just go around downloading and using other people's graphics. Plenty of repositories of public domain graphics exist on the Web. See Appendix A, "Web Resources," for references to where you can find public domain graphics on the Web.

Using the ALT Attribute

The ALT attribute can be included in the IMG tag to help identify an image. In the newer browsers, for instance, if you pass the cursor over an image, the contents of any included ALT attribute will be displayed. Also, because surfing the Web can often be like wading through hip-deep molasses, a lot of people do it with the display of images turned off to help speed things up. And a lot of people still use text-based browsers, such as Lynx, which don't display images at all. Using the ALT attribute will clue these surfers in on the content or purpose of an image. Enter the following to create an example of an inline image with an ALT attribute:

```
<P><IMG SRC="sample.gif" ALT="A sample graphic"></P>
```

In the latest versions of Netscape Navigator and Internet Explorer, the ALT attribute value appears as a pop-up caption box when the cursor is passed over the image. When viewed in Lynx, the message "A sample graphic" is displayed, rather than just "[Image]." In a graphical Web browser with image-loading turned off, the message "A sample graphic" would appear alongside the image icon, as shown in Figure 2.27.

If your graphic has informational import, you should always include an ALT attribute (`ALT="Georgy-Porgy's Home Page"` or `ALT="Diagram of the X-27P Circuit Board"`, for example). This is especially important where an image is being used by itself to perform a function, such as displaying the title of a Web page in a banner graphic (where no corresponding H1 element is included), or functioning as a navigational icon or image link where no text is included on the Web page to describe the link. Including an ALT attribute will allow somebody using a text-only browser or a graphical Web browser with graphics turned off to see what is going on. It can also help a visually impaired user who's using a Braille or speech browser to know what's what on your page.

TIP

If an image is decorative and serves no informational purpose, insert an ALT attribute with a blank attribute value: `ALT=""`. That way, you won't clutter up a Web page in a text-only browser with `[Image]` references. Also, if you're using images as icon bullets, include this ALT attribute to cue users of text-only browsers that the image is a bullet: `ALT="*"`.

Figure 2.27

SAMPLE.GIF is pictured here, first without the ALT attribute and then with the ALT attribute, as shown in Navigator with the display of images turned off.

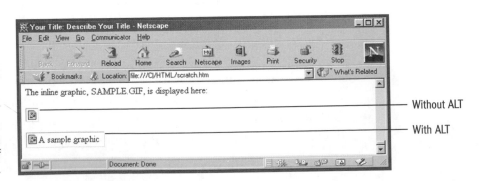

Without ALT

With ALT

Using the ALIGN Attribute in Inline Images

The ALIGN attribute allows you to position an inline image relative to the line of text that it is on. All current graphical Web browsers should recognize these values: "top," "middle," and "bottom."

Insert an inline image using the "top" ALIGN value:

```
<P>The image on this line <IMG ALIGN="top" SRC="top.gif"> is
top-aligned.</P>
```

Insert an inline image using the "middle" ALIGN value:

```
<P>The image on this line <IMG ALIGN="middle" SRC="middle.gif">
is middle-aligned.</P>
```

Insert an inline image using the "bottom" ALIGN value:

```
<P>The image on this line <IMG ALIGN="bottom" SRC="bottom.gif">
is bottom-aligned.</P>
```

Figure 2.28 shows these examples as they appear in a Web browser.

Figure 2.28

Inline images can be aligned relative to the baseline of the line they are on.

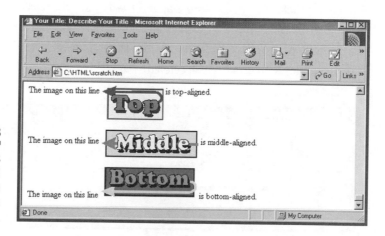

Using Horizontal Rules

The HR (Horizontal Rule) tag is an empty (or stand-alone) element that allows you to add horizontal rules to your Web pages. Set up a text paragraph followed by an HR tag:

```
<P>A horizontal rule is displayed below this line.</P>

<HR>
```

Figure 2.29 shows a horizontal rule displayed in Netscape Navigator.

In the Intermediate HTML Tutorial, scheduled for Saturday afternoon, I'll be showing you more things you can do with horizontal rules, including setting their width, alignment, and shading settings. I'll also be showing you how to use a graphical rule, which is just an inline image, as a colorful replacement for a horizontal rule.

Signing Your Work

You generally use the ADDRESS tag to define an address block (or signature block) for your Web page. This is usually used to identify you as the author or owner of a Web page and provide a visitor to your site with a means of contacting you. A horizontal rule usually separates your address block from the rest of your page. Using the following example as

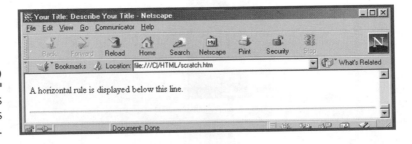

Figure 2.29

Navigator displays a horizontal rule as a shaded line.

a guide, add an address block at the bottom of your page, substituting your name and company or organization:

```
<HR>
<ADDRESS>
Johnny Doe<BR>
Fantastic Creations, Inc.<BR>
</ADDRESS>
</BODY>
```

The ADDRESS tag is a block element, so there is no need to nest a P tag inside of it. The BR (Break) tags are used to single-space the address block.

All current Web browsers should display text inserted in an ADDRESS element in italics, but a few earlier browsers do not. To ensure that your address block will be in italics in all Web browsers, you should bracket it with an I (Italic) tag, as shown here.

```
<HR>
<ADDRESS>
<I>
Johnny Doe<BR>
Fantastic Creations, Inc.<BR>
</I>
</ADDRESS>
```

Adding a Mailto Link to Your Address

The above example only identifies you as the author or owner of your Web page; it doesn't provide any way for a visitor to your page to contact you. A large part of the fun of creating a Web page is getting great feedback from visitors.

If you're putting up a business page, you could include an 800 number, fax number, and even your company's mailing address. If you're creating a non-business page, however, you probably don't want to include this type of personal information on your page.

You could just type in your e-mail address so visitors could e-mail you, but this isn't very interactive. HTML has a better solution: a mailto link. Go ahead and add the following mailto link to your address block (feel free to substitute your e-mail address):

```
<HR>
<ADDRESS>
<I>
Johnny Doe<BR>
Fantastic Creations, Inc.<BR>
E-Mail: <A HREF="mailto:jd@fantastic-creations.com">jd@fantastic-
creations.com</A><BR>
</I>
</ADDRESS>
```

A mailto link is actually just a hypertext link that links to your e-mail address. In a browser that supports mailto links, clicking on the link will cause an e-mail composition window already addressed to you to pop up, in which your visitor can easily compose and send an e-mail message to you. See Figure 2.30 for an example of a mailto pop-up window in Internet Explorer.

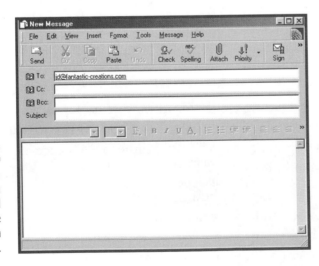

Figure 2.30

When you click on a mailto link, you can send an e-mail message to the address included in the link.

PREVENTING SPAM

Unfortunately, someone always comes along to spoil the party—in this case, the spammer. As a defensive measure against getting spammed, some people avoid posting either their name or e-mail address on their Web pages, providing only a guestbook link to allow visitors to give them feedback. AOL users apparently have to be particularly careful about revealing their screen names or other personal information (in chat rooms or message boards, for instance), which can help a spammer gain access to their information in AOL's member directory. AOL provides a guestbook you can easily add to your Web pages. Using a guestbook instead of your name and e-mail address can also be a good way to help shield any children using your e-mail account from receiving pornographic, violent, or other undesirable spam messages.

On the other hand, I have my name and e-mail address on dozens of Web pages and only get what I consider to be a moderate amount of spam, mostly originating from providing my e-mail address in online forms, I suspect (which I've stopped doing). Of course, I'm not on AOL, either.

I'd hate to see everybody with a Web page end up concealing his or her identity and e-mail address just to counter spam—such a cure would be worse than the disease, I believe. Openness is a large part of what makes the Web such a great place. Thankfully, most people don't want to hide behind masks and pseudonyms—they want to be seen, read, and known. I know I do!

One alternative is to get a free Web-based e-mail address (commonly referred to as a *Web mail* address) through Hotmail, Yahoo!, Netcenter, or some other Web mail provider. Post that e-mail address on your Web pages. You could also use it in any chat rooms that you frequent or type it in any online forms you have to fill out. Then, if that address starts to get overly spammed, just get another one! If you're concerned about having to continually update your pages with new e-mail addresses, use a link to a contact page instead—that way, you'll only have to update it in one place. You can give real visitors (not spammers) your permanent (unpublished) e-mail address when you reply to them, so they can add it to their address books. If you're concerned about hackers, crackers, and spoofers being able to harvest your e-mail address directly from your e-mail messages, just add "HATES SPAM," or something similar, to your e-mail address (*yourname*HATES SPAM@*yourdomain*.com, for instance), instructing the recipient to remove "HATES SPAM" when he or she replies.

Not all browsers support mailto links. If you're using Internet Explorer, you need to have either Internet Mail (with I.E. 3.x) or Outlook Express (with I.E. 4.0+) installed. (If you're using Microsoft Exchange or Outlook as your e-mail program, you won't be able to use mailto links.) Even if your browser supports mailto links, your e-mail program has to be configured properly to send e-mail. Therefore, no matter which way you cut it, you are going to have viewers who can't use a mailto link.

Does that mean you should avoid mailto links? Absolutely not! The solution is to make sure that your full e-mail address is used as the link text for your mailto link. This means you need to enter your e-mail address twice for a mailto link, as shown in the following example. That way, if someone can't use your mailto link, he or she can always click and drag to copy your e-mail address or just write it down and then send you a message using his or her regular e-mail client.

Adding Your URL to Your Address

If your home page is different from the page you are currently creating, you might want to add a hypertext link to it. Your home page might serve as an index or directory to the rest of your Web pages. By including the URL of your home page in the address block of all of your other Web pages, you can give visitors to your page an easy way to get back to your home page. Because you're probably creating your first Web page in this tutorial, you won't actually have a home page yet that you can link to. In the following example, just enter the dummy hypertext link as an example of adding your URL to your address block (see Figure 2.31).

```
<HR>

<ADDRESS>

<I>

Johnny Doe<BR>

Fantastic Creations, Inc.<BR>

E-Mail: <A HREF="mailto:jd@fantastic-creations.com">jd@fantastic-
creations. com</A><BR>

URL: <A HREF="http://www.fantastic-creations.com">http://www.
fantastic-creations.com</A><BR>

</I>

</ADDRESS>
```

Saving Your Work

Save the HTML file you just created. You can use it later as a reference. When you first saved it, you named it `scratch.htm`. If more than one person is going to be doing this tutorial and you want to make sure that this file doesn't get overwritten, you might want to give it a new name (`jm-scratch.htm`, for instance, if your name is John Miller or Jill Moore).

Figure 2.31

An address block might contain your name, company name, street address, phone numbers, as well as a mailto link to your e-mail address and a hypertext link to your home page.

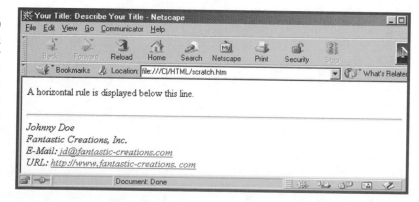

Wrapping Up

You should now have a working knowledge of basic HTML. Don't worry if you don't remember or fully understand everything that you've done in this tutorial; the best way to learn is simply by doing. You've also saved your scratch pad file, either as `scratch.htm` or with another name you've given it, so you can come back and use it as a reference later. Feel free to load it into your text editor and view it in your Web browser to re-familiarize yourself with how a particular tag works.

The Basic HTML Tutorial has covered everything you need to know to be able to plan and create your first Web page. If doing the Basic HTML Tutorial has taken you most or all of the day, or you just feel you have reached the point of information overload for today, feel free to call it a day (or a night). The Intermediate HTML Tutorial and the Tables Tutorial are both optional and not required for you to plan and create your first Web page tomorrow. I'll see you tomorrow for the Sunday Morning session, "Planning Your First Web Page."

If, however, you have time and energy left after doing the Basic HTML Tutorial and are ready for more, get up and stretch those muscles, have some lunch, check your e-mail. I'll see you back in a half hour or so for the Intermediate HTML Tutorial.

The Intermediate HTML Tutorial

- Superscripts, subscripts, underlining, and strikethrough
- Horizontally aligning paragraphs, headings, and divisions
- Wrapping text around images
- Fancy 3-D icon link lists
- Font sizes, colors, and faces
- Background colors and images

This tutorial is optional. The Basic HTML Tutorial covered everything you need to know for tomorrow, and if you haven't yet completed the Saturday Morning session, you should finish it before attempting to do this afternoon's tutorial. After doing both tutorials, you'll have that much more to put into practice when you plan and create your first Web page.

The Intermediate HTML Tutorial covers

- Some HTML 2.0 features not covered in the Basic HTML Tutorial, including creating banner graphics and image links
- Most of HTML 3.2, including horizontally aligning document elements, wrapping text around images, creating indented icon link lists, and making font size, color, and face changes
- Some of the new HTML 4.0 features, including marking insertions and deletions, and an example of applying styles to a span of text

This tutorial does not cover the more advanced features of HTML such as forms, scripts or applets, embedded objects, style sheets, or frames. Tables, although not covered in this tutorial, are covered in a separate bonus tutorial that you can do this evening if you have the time and energy. In Appendix A, "Web Resources," you'll find links to where you can find out about using these more advanced HTML features. Another good reference is Prima Tech's *Learn HTML In a Weekend (Revised Edition)*, also authored by me, which includes software tutorials for creating

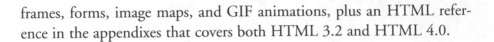

frames, forms, image maps, and GIF animations, plus an HTML reference in the appendixes that covers both HTML 3.2 and HTML 4.0.

NOTE　You should have already installed the example graphic files for this tutorial at the start of the Basic HTML Tutorial. If you haven't installed these files, please return to "Installing the Example Files" in the Saturday Morning session before doing this tutorial.

Getting Started

All of the example files used in this tutorial were installed with the tutorial example files that you installed for the Basic HTML Tutorial. You don't need to install anything extra to do this tutorial.

While you could use just about any graphical Web browser to do the Basic HTML Tutorial, for this tutorial you'll need to use at least an HTML 3.2-compliant Web browser. At minimum, you should use Netscape Navigator 2.0 or greater or Microsoft Internet Explorer 3.0 or greater. You can also use Opera 3.6—an evaluation version is included on the CD-ROM. To preview the HTML 4.0 sections of this tutorial, you'll need an HTML 4.0-compliant browser, such as Netscape Navigator 4.x or Microsoft Internet Explorer 4.x/5.x. I've tested this tutorial with the release versions of Navigator 4.7 and Internet Explorer 5.0.

As with the Basic HTML Tutorial, I recommend that you use Windows Notepad to do this tutorial. If you're using Windows 95, just remember to turn on Word Wrap (select Edit, Word Wrap).

Loading Your Starting Template

Load the starting template (start.htm) that you saved this morning. You should be able to find it in C:\HTML, unless you've saved it somewhere else. It should look like the following listing (if you didn't save the template, just retype it now):

```
<HTML>
<HEAD>
<TITLE>Your Title: Describe Your Title</TITLE>
</HEAD>
<BODY>
</BODY>
</HTML>
```

NOTE

● ●

If you substituted a TITLE element of your own for "Your Title: Describe Your Title," don't worry if your version of **start.htm** differs in this regard. Otherwise, your **start.htm** should look like my example.

● ●

Save your scratch pad file that you'll be using in this afternoon's tutorial. In Notepad, select File, Save As. Change the folder where you are going to save your file to C:\HTML, then save your file as scratch2.htm.

Working with Text

This section covers some things that you can do when working with text, including using additional HTML 3.2 text highlighting tags, some new HTML 4.0 text highlighting tags, as well as right-aligning and center-aligning paragraphs, headings, and other document sections.

HTML 3.2 Text Highlighting Tags

HTML 3.2 recognizes a number of character rendering tags, including the SUP (Superscript), SUB (Subscript), U (Underline), and STRIKE (Strikethrough) tags.

The SUP and SUB tags are highly useful tags that can be used wherever you need superscripts or subscripts. The STRIKE tag renders text as strikethrough, which can be handy if you're using the Web in workgroup document preparation processes. Most current Web browsers support these tags. The U tag was originally a proposed HTML 3.0 tag and has

Figure 3.1

In HTML 3.2, you can add superscripting, subscripting, underlining, and strikethrough to text.

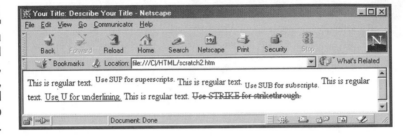

been supported in most recent browsers. It was not supported, however, in Netscape Navigator 2.0, which is still used by lots of surfers, so you may want to avoid using it. To check out how these tags look in your browser, enter the following (see Figure 3.1 to see what this looks like in a browser):

```
<P>This is regular text. <SUP>Use SUP for superscripts.</SUP>
This is regular text. <SUB>Use SUB for subscripts.</SUB> This is
regular text. <U>Use U for underlining.</U> This is regular
text. <STRIKE>Use STRIKE for strikethrough.</STRIKE></P>
```

TIP

Many earlier browsers, as well as text-based browsers such as Lynx, won't display superscripts or subscripts. To account for those browsers, enclose superscripts or subscripts within parentheses to set them apart from preceding or following text. For instance, to include a superscripted trademark symbol, you might type:

`Xerox<SUP>(TM)</SUP>`

That way, it appears in Lynx as "Xerox(TM)" rather than as "XeroxTM." The tradeoff here, of course, is that in a browser that does support superscripting, you're stuck with the parentheses—but, oh well, who ever said it was a perfect world?

HTML 4.0 Text Highlighting Tags

A number of new text highlighting tags have been incorporated in HTML 4.0. These include the DEL (Delete), INS (Insert), S (Strikethrough),

Q (Quote), and SPAN tags. So far, the DEL and INS tags are only supported by the 4.x and 5.x versions of Internet Explorer. The 4.x version of Navigator does not support either of these tags. Neither browser yet supports the Q tag, but both support the S tag. The SPAN tag is supported by versions of both Navigator and Internet Explorer greater than 4.0.

The DEL (Delete), INS (Insert), and S (Strikethrough) Tags

The DEL (Delete) and INS (Insert) tags allow you to mark deletions and insertions in an HTML file. Enter the following for an example of using these tags (see Figure 3.2):

```
<P><DEL>This text is marked for deletion.</DEL> This is regular
text. <INS>This text is marked for insertion.</INS></P>
```

The S (Strikethrough) tag works exactly the same as the STRIKE or DEL tags. Because it isn't supported in versions of Netscape Navigator earlier than 4.0, you should just use the STRIKE tag instead.

The Q (Quote) Tag

The Q (Quote) tag could potentially be quite useful. Its purpose is to insert language-specific quotation marks, such as curly quotes for English, for instance. The LANG attribute is used to specify the language (LANG="en-us", for instance). It is even supposed to substitute single

Figure 3.2

In HTML 4.0, you can mark deletions and insertions, but so far this only works in Internet Explorer 4.x/5.x.

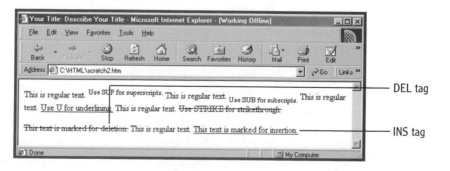

quotes for a nested quotation. Unfortunately, however, no browser, not even Internet Explorer 5.x, supports this tag.

The SPAN Tag

The SPAN tag is a kind of general-purpose text highlighting element. As its name implies, it can be used to "span" a string of text. By itself, the SPAN tag does absolutely nothing. For it to come to life, you need to create a style for it.

For an example of using the SPAN tag, first insert the following:

```
<P>This is regular text. This is <SPAN>SPANNED TEXT</SPAN>. This
is regular text.</P>
```

Next, enter the following example, nested inside the HEAD tag, to create a style for the SPAN tag:

```
<TITLE>Your Title: Describe Your Title</TITLE>
<STYLE type="text/css">
<!--
SPAN {font-family: sans-serif; font-style: italic; font-size:
125%; color: #FF8000}
-->
</STYLE>
</HEAD>
```

 NOTE   Notice the comment tags (`<!--` and `-->`) that are nested inside the STYLE tag in the previous example—these are included to mask the contents of the STYLE tag from earlier browsers that aren't savvy to style sheets. The comment tags also keep search engine robots from indexing and displaying the contents of your STYLE tag rather than the first sentences or paragraph of your page. Browsers that understand style sheets, however, will ignore the comment tags.

Figure 3.3 shows how the spanned text now appears in a browser that supports style sheets, after a style has been created for the SPAN tag.

Figure 3.3

In HTML 4.0, you can use the SPAN tag to apply a style to a "span" of text.

This is just a small sample of what can be done with style sheets. Later, if you want to find out more about using style sheets, here are some links that you can investigate:

- Creating Your First Style Sheet by Eric Meyer at **webreview.com/wr/pub/97/10/10/style/**

- Cascading Style Sheets by W3C at **www.w3.org/Style/CSS/**

- WebDeveloper.com's Guide to Cascading Style Sheets at **www.webdeveloper.com/html/html_css_1.html**

- Cascading Style Sheets by Web Design Group at **www.htmlhelp.com/reference/css/**

- Web Review's CSS Browser Compatibility Charts at **webreview.com/wr/pub/97/10/10/style/index.html**

Aligning Paragraphs, Headings, and Divisions

You can use the ALIGN attribute to horizontally align paragraphs and headings. You can center-align or right-align paragraphs, headings, and document divisions (left alignment is the default). Additionally, you can use the CENTER tag to center-align any of these elements, plus many other document elements. The following sections look at each of these individually.

Aligning Headings and Paragraphs

You can use the ALIGN attribute to center-align or right-align headings and paragraphs by using an attribute value of either "center" or "right" ("left" is the default). For instance, to center-align a level-two heading, you would tag your heading like this:

```
<H2 ALIGN="center">Your Heading Here</H2>
```

You would right-align a level-two heading like this:

```
<H2 ALIGN="right">Your Heading Here</H2>
```

You would center-align or right-align paragraph text in exactly the same way. For instance, to center-align a text paragraph, you would tag your paragraph like this:

```
<P ALIGN="center">Your paragraph text here.</P>
```

You would right-align a text paragraph like this:

```
<P ALIGN="right">Your paragraph text here.</P>
```

To see what this looks like in your browser, enter the following, save your file, and hop over to your browser to check it out (see Figure 3.4):

```
<H3 ALIGN="right">This is a Right-Aligned Level-Three Heading</H3>
<P ALIGN="right">This is a right-aligned text paragraph. This is a
right-aligned text paragraph. This is a right-aligned text para-
graph. This is a right-aligned text paragraph.</P>
<H3 ALIGN="center">This is a Center-Aligned Level-Three Heading</H3>
<P ALIGN="center">This is a center-aligned text paragraph. This is
a center-aligned text paragraph. This is a center-aligned text
paragraph. This is a center-aligned text paragraph.</P>
```

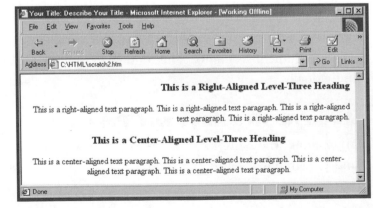

Figure 3.4

You can right- or center-align headings and paragraphs.

Aligning Document Divisions

The DIV tag defines a division within a document. Within it you can nest and align headings, paragraphs, unordered and ordered lists, definition lists, preformatted text, address blocks, tables, and even images.

The DIV tag is an HTML 3.2 element that was previously an HTML 3.0 proposed tag. It allows you to block tag a whole section (a division) of a document as center- or right-aligned.

Enter the following for an example of using the DIV tag to apply center alignment to a document division that includes a level-two heading, a paragraph, and a bullet list:

```
<DIV ALIGN="center">
<H2>Level-Two Heading</H2>
<P>This paragraph, and the level-two heading above it, is
centered using the DIV tag's ALIGN attribute.</P>
<UL>
<LI>First list item.
<LI>Second list item.
</UL>
</DIV>
```

Style sheets, which are part of HTML 4.0, make this tag even more useful, allowing users to apply different formatting or display characteristics to different sections of a document, such as a table of contents, an index, or a glossary. For some links to where you can find out more about using style sheets, see my Web Links site at **www.callihan.com/weblinks/**.

FIND IT ON ▶
THE WEB

Figure 3.5

You can center- or right-align a document division—here including a heading, paragraph text, and a bullet list—using the DIV tag.

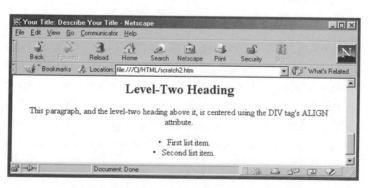

NOTE

A shareware software program, CoffeeCup StyleSheet Maker++, that can help automate creating HTML style sheets for your Web pages is included on the CD-ROM. For links to more style sheet utilities, see my Web Tools site at **www.callihan.com/webtools/**.

Using the CENTER Tag

The CENTER tag is a Netscape extension that has been included in HTML 3.2, where it now represents a shortcut for `<DIV ALIGN="center">`. Anything that can be nested inside a DIV element can also be nested in a CENTER element. All fairly recent browsers should support the CENTER tag.

For an example of using the CENTER element to center-align text and other document elements, copy and paste the text you just entered as an example of using the DIV tag, then edit it, replacing `<DIV ALIGN= "center">` and `</DIV>` with `<CENTER>` and `</CENTER>`, so it looks like this:

```
<CENTER>
<H2>Level-Two Heading</H2>
<P>This paragraph, and the level-two heading above it, is
centered-aligned using the CENTER tag.</P>
<UL>
<LI>First list item.
<LI>Second list item.
</UL>
</CENTER>
```

The end result in your browser should look exactly the same as using the DIV tag with center alignment set, as shown previously in Figure 3.5.

CAUTION

Don't forget to close the two previous examples. If you forget the end tags (`</DIV>` or `</CENTER>`), all of the following examples will also be centered.

Working with Images

The Basic HTML Tutorial covered adding inline images to your Web page, as well as top-aligning, middle-aligning, and bottom-aligning an inline image relative to a line of text. It also covered using the ALT attribute with inline images to make life easier for users of text-only browsers or graphical browsers with the graphics turned off. This section of the Intermediate HTML Tutorial covers several additional things you can do with inline images: using a banner graphic, right-aligning or center-aligning graphics, wrapping text around a graphic, and creating image links.

Adding a Banner Graphic

A banner graphic is an inline image that runs along the top of your Web page. It might include your company name or logo, or a piece of art to add some graphic appeal and pizzazz to your page. You don't have to create a banner graphic right now—the following example uses a sample banner graphic that is included with the example files.

To add a banner graphic to your Web page, go to the top of your Web page and add the following (see Figure 3.6):

```
<BODY>
<P ALIGN="center"><IMG SRC="banner.gif" WIDTH="595" HEIGHT="134"
ALT="My Banner Graphic"></P>
<H1 ALIGN="center">The Intermediate HTML Tutorial</H1>
```

Even if your banner graphic stretches across your entire browser window, it is a good idea to place it on a center-aligned paragraph. That way, it will always be centered, regardless of the screen resolution and the size of the browser window. I also included a centered level-one heading, because it is fairly common for a banner graphic to be followed by the main heading for the page.

You'll also notice that an ALT attribute is included in the IMG tag. It is a good idea to include ALT attributes in your images, which will assist a

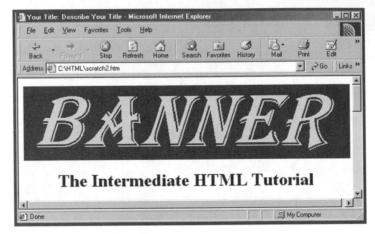

Figure 3.6

A banner graphic
runs across the top
of a Web page.

visually impaired visitor using a Braille browser to know what is what. See "Using the ALT Attribute" in the Basic HTML Tutorial for more information on using this attribute.

Also, in this example, the SRC attribute uses a relative URL, the file name of the banner graphic file. As long as an image is in the same folder as the Web page in which you want to display it, you only need to use the file name as the SRC attribute value. (For more information on absolute versus relative URLs, see "Using Relative URLs" later in this tutorial.)

You can specify the height and width in pixels of an inline image using the HEIGHT and WIDTH attributes. Normally, a Web browser has to download an image before it can allocate space for it on a Web page. This means that if you have a relatively large graphic, everything else has to wait until the image downloads. A banner graphic, usually the largest graphic on your page, can be especially guilty of this. If you include HEIGHT and WIDTH attributes, a browser can allocate space for your image and then display the remainder of the page without waiting for the banner graphic to download completely.

If you're substituting your own banner graphic here, you'll need to change the HEIGHT and WIDTH attribute values in the previous example to match the actual size of your image. It is a good idea to try to keep the

width of your image to less than 600 pixels—otherwise your banner image may exceed the maximum width of a browser window running in 640 × 480 resolution.

The advice is often given on the Web that you should set the HEIGHT and WIDTH attributes for *all* images you want to include in a Web page. I, quite frankly, don't bother doing this for small graphics such as icon bullets, but I do set them in any other images I include. I also don't bother to include these attributes in the other sample images that are used in this tutorial because the scratch pad file you are creating will only be viewed by you locally.

◆ ◆

You may be tempted to use the HEIGHT and WIDTH attributes to resize your image as it appears in a browser window. This is strongly discouraged. If you want to alter the size of your image as it appears in a browser window, you should resize it in your image editor (and then include the actual dimensions of your image in the HEIGHT and WIDTH attributes). Decreasing the size of your image in the browser is a waste of bandwidth; increasing the size of your image in your browser won't improve the resolution of the image (it'll be the same image, just blown up bigger) and will make any image flaws (such as the "jaggies") all the more noticeable.

You can also set a percentage value for the WIDTH attribute (WIDTH="75%", for instance), which will cause the width of the image to be resized relative to the width of the browser window. This should probably be avoided, except in the case of a graphic rule (see "Using Graphic Rules" later in this tutorial).

◆ ◆

Using Interlaced and Transparent GIF Graphics

An interlaced GIF will load progressively over several passes, generating a kind of "venetian blind" effect. This allows the reader to see what the whole image is going to look like before it has been completely downloaded.

A transparent GIF is a GIF graphic that has one of its colors set to transparent, allowing any background color or background image to show through the graphic. This can be handy if you want your graphic to look as if it's floating on top of the background.

Banner graphics are often set to be both interlaced and transparent. For information on how to create interlaced and transparent GIF images, see the Sunday Evening bonus session, "The Graphics Tutorial."

Aligning Images

The default horizontal alignment of an image is flush with the left margin. Contrary to what you might think, you can't use the ALIGN attribute in the IMG tag to center-align or right-align an image. Rather, you need to nest the IMG tag in a paragraph (or other block element) in which center alignment or right alignment has been set.

Return to the bottom of your file, just before the </BODY> and </HTML> end tags, and enter the following to right-align an image using paragraph alignment (see Figure 3.7):

```
<P ALIGN="right"><IMG SRC="right.gif"></P>
```

To center-align an image using paragraph alignment, enter the following (see Figure 3.8):

```
<P ALIGN="center"><IMG SRC="center.gif"></P>
```

You also can use the DIV or the CENTER tag to horizontally align an image. The CENTER tag is the more widely supported, but the DIV tag allows you to right-align an image as well. Because some browsers may

Figure 3.7

You can right-align an image in an HTML 3.2-compliant Web browser by placing it inside a right-aligned paragraph.

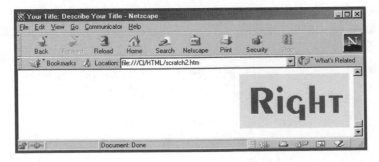

Figure 3.8

You can center-align an image in an HTML 3.2-compliant Web browser by placing it inside a center-aligned paragraph.

not recognize the CENTER tag as a block element and the DIV tag is only supported in the latest browsers, my recommendation is that you stick to nesting images that you want to be horizontally aligned in a center-aligned or a right-aligned paragraph.

Wrapping Text around Images

In the Basic HTML Tutorial, you learned how to align an image relative to a line of text using the ALIGN attribute values of "top," "bottom," and "middle." In addition to these attribute values, you can set two other ALIGN attribute values: "left" and "right." You might think that the purpose of these attributes is to align an image at either the left or right margin, but that's not so. Rather, these attributes are used to wrap text around the right side or left side of an image.

Wrapping Text around a Left-Aligned Image

Enter the following as an example of wrapping text around a left-aligned image:

```
<P><IMG ALIGN="left" SRC="left.gif">If you set left-alignment in
an inline image, the text will wrap around the right side of the
graphic. If you set left-alignment in an inline image, the text
will wrap around the right side of the graphic. If you set left-
alignment in an inline image, the text will wrap around the
right side of the graphic.<BR CLEAR="left"></P>
```

 NOTE You're probably wondering what the `<BR CLEAR="left">` code is doing at the end of the paragraph. You'll notice similar BR tags using the CLEAR attribute in some of the following examples. Their purpose is to *stop* the text from wrapping—otherwise, the following image is liable to wrap as well. Later, in "Using the BR Tag's CLEAR Attribute," I'll tell you more about using this attribute.

Wrapping Text around a Right-Aligned Image

Enter the following as an example of wrapping text around a right-aligned image (see Figure 3.9):

```
<P><IMG ALIGN="right" SRC="right.gif">If you set right-alignment
in an inline image, the text will wrap around the left side of
the graphic. If you set right-alignment in an inline image, the
text will wrap around the left side of the graphic. If you set
right-alignment in an inline image, the text will wrap around
the left side of the graphic.<BR CLEAR="right"></P>
```

You aren't limited to just wrapping text around an image. All other elements, including headings, lists, and other images, will wrap around an image with either left alignment or right alignment set.

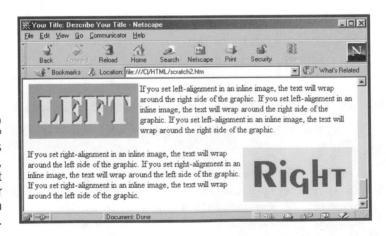

Figure 3.9

Using the IMG tag's ALIGN attribute, you can wrap text around the left or right side of an image.

Adding Spacing between an Image and Wrapping Text

When you hopped over to take a look at the last couple of examples in your browser, you may have noticed that text wrapping around an image, especially around a left-aligned image, is not separated from the image by much space. To add spacing between wrapping text and a left- or right-aligned image, you can insert an HSPACE (Horizontal Space) attribute in the IMG tag. Edit the example you created for wrapping text around a left-aligned image and add the following to insert 10 pixels on either side of the image (see Figure 3.10):

```
<P><IMG ALIGN="left" SRC="left.gif" HSPACE="10">If you set left-
alignment in an inline image, the text will wrap around the
right side of the graphic. If you set left-alignment in an
inline image, the text will wrap around the right side of the
graphic. If you set left-alignment in an inline image, the text
will wrap around the right side of the graphic.<BR
CLEAR="left"></P>
```

Flowing Text between Images

You not only can wrap text around the right or left side of an image, you can also flow text between two images. For example, enter the following (see Figure 3.11):

```
<P><IMG ALIGN="left" SRC="left.gif"><IMG ALIGN="right"
SRC="right.gif">Text will flow between a left-aligned and a
right-aligned image. Text will flow between a left-aligned and a
right-aligned image.<BR CLEAR="all"></P>
```

Flowing an Image between Two Other Images

You can even flow a non-aligned image between a left-aligned image and a right-aligned one. To make this even slicker, stick the whole thing in a center-aligned paragraph, so the flowing, non-aligned image is centered

Figure 3.10

Using the IMG tag's HSPACE attribute, which adds space to the left and right of an image, you can add space between an image and wrapping text.

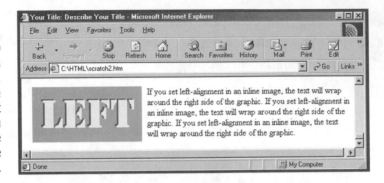

Figure 3.11

You can flow text between a left-aligned and a right-aligned image in an HTML 3.2-compliant Web browser.

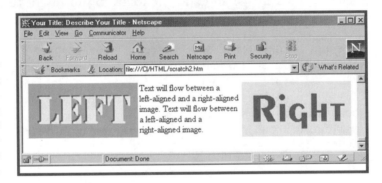

between the two aligned images. This is a bit of a parlor trick, but both Navigator and Internet Explorer handle it fine. I've seen a couple of other supposedly HTML 3.2-compliant browsers flub it though, usually not aligning the middle image quite even with the other images. For an example of how to do this, enter the following (see Figure 3.12):

```
<P><IMG ALIGN="left" SRC="one.gif"><IMG ALIGN="right"
SRC="three.gif"></P><P ALIGN="center"><IMG SRC="two.gif"><BR
CLEAR="all"></P>
```

Notice in the above example that two P tags are used—the left-aligned image and the right-aligned image are nested in the first paragraph, and the image that flows between the other two images is nested in the second paragraph.

Figure 3.12

You can also flow an image between a left-aligned and a right-aligned image.

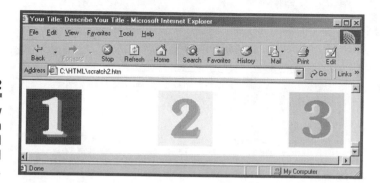

Using the BR Tag's CLEAR Attribute

The BR tag's CLEAR attribute, as its name indicates, is used to cause whatever follows to *clear* a left-aligned image, a right-aligned image, or both. In the previous examples, for instance, it was used to ensure that each following example cleared the previous one. If the BR tag's CLEAR attribute is set to "left," it causes whatever follows to clear and move down below a left-aligned image. A "right" attribute value causes whatever follows to clear a right-aligned image. An "all" attribute value causes whatever follows to clear either a left-aligned or a right-aligned image, or both.

Clearing a Left-Aligned Image

To see how this works with a left-aligned graphic, insert the following into the example you just created for wrapping text around a left-aligned image (you can copy and paste it if you want):

```
<P><IMG ALIGN="left" SRC="left.gif">If you set left-alignment in
an inline image, the text will wrap around the right side of the
graphic.
```

```
<BR CLEAR="left">
```

```
If you set left-alignment in an inline image, the text will wrap
around the right side of the graphic. If you set left-alignment
in an inline image, the text will wrap around the right side of
the graphic.</P>
```

Figure 3.13

A BR tag with
CLEAR="left" set
will cause following
text to break past a
left-aligned image.

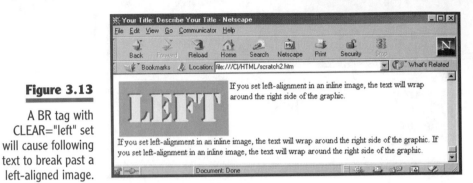

As Figure 3.13 shows, the CLEAR="left" attribute has the effect of moving all following text past a left-aligned graphic to a position where the left margin is clear.

Clearing a Right-Aligned Image

To see how this works with a right-aligned graphic, insert the following as indicated into the example you created for wrapping text around a right-aligned image (you can copy and paste it if you want):

```
<P><IMG ALIGN="right" SRC="right.gif">If you set right-alignment
in an inline image, the text will wrap around the left side of
the graphic.
<BR CLEAR="right">
If you set right-alignment in an inline image, the text will
wrap around the left side of the graphic. If you set right-
alignment in an inline image, the text will wrap around the left
side of the graphic.</P>
```

As you can see in Figure 3.14, the CLEAR="right" attribute has the effect of moving all following text past a right-aligned graphic to a position where the right margin is clear.

Clearing Both Left-Aligned and Right-Aligned Images

Finally, to see how this works when flowing text between both a left-aligned and a right-aligned graphic, insert the following into the example

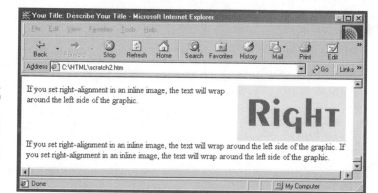

Figure 3.14

Figure 3.14

A BR tag with CLEAR="right" set will cause following text to break past a right-aligned image.

you created for flowing text between a left-aligned and a right-aligned image (you can copy and paste it if you want):

```
<P><IMG ALIGN="left" SRC="left.gif"><IMG ALIGN="right"
SRC="right.gif">Text will flow between a left-aligned and a
right-aligned image.
<BR CLEAR="all">
Text will flow between a left-aligned and a right-aligned
image.</P>
```

As Figure 3.15 shows, the CLEAR="all" attribute has the effect of moving all following text past a left-aligned or a right-aligned graphic to a position where both margins are clear.

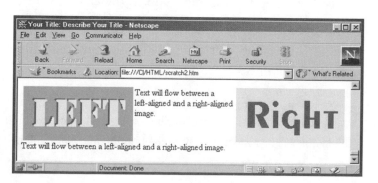

Figure 3.15

A BR tag with CLEAR="all" set will cause following text to break past both a left-aligned image and a right-aligned image.

Working with Image Links

In the Basic HTML Tutorial, you learned how to place inline images on your page, and you also learned how to create hypertext links. What you haven't learned yet is how to create an inline image that functions as a hypertext link, where clicking on the image will activate the link. Hey, if you want to brag about knowing HTML, you've got to know how to create image links!

Including an Image in a Link

To activate an image as a hypertext link, all you have to do is nest it inside an A tag, like this:

```
<P><A HREF="link.htm">
<IMG SRC="link.gif">This is the text.</A></P>
```

TIP You'll be using this text in later examples. If you copy the example you just created to the Clipboard now (highlight it with the cursor and press Ctrl+C), you won't have to retype it later.

In the previous example, the Web page that is linked to, link.htm, is included with the tutorial example files you installed to C:HTML. To test it, just click on the image in your browser (click on the Back button to return).

Figure 3.16 shows that when an image is placed inside a hypertext link, the image itself becomes a hot link.

TIP If you include an ALIGN="right" attribute value in the IMG tag in the previous example, the image will be displayed flush to the right margin while still being part of the link.

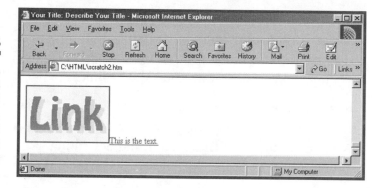

Figure 3.16

The image, displayed with a blue border, and the link text, underlined with a blue line, are both part of the same hypertext link.

Using an Image Link by Itself

In the previous example, the link included both the image and the text, meaning that clicking on either one would activate the link. You can also specify the image as the link but not the text. To do this in the example, you would move the </A> end tag so only the image is enclosed within the A start and end tags, like this (see Figure 3.17):

```
<P><A HREF="link.htm">
<IMG SRC="link.gif"></A>This is the text.</P>
```

Creating Navigational Icons

A navigational icon is often used when a picture by itself is enough to convey the action that will occur when the user activates the link. For instance, a left-hand arrow at the top or bottom of a page indicates

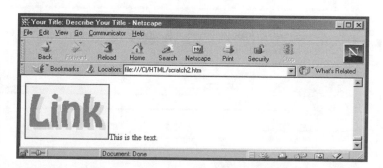

Figure 3.17

When you place the image inside the hypertext link, the image will function as the link.

returning to the previous page, a right-hand arrow indicates going to the next page, and a house indicates returning to the home page. You create a navigational icon by nesting only an image inside the A tag, without any accompanying text inside or outside the link.

To accommodate text-only browsers or graphical browsers with graphics turned off, you should always include ALT text in a navigational icon's IMG tag, indicating that it's a link and describing what it links to. Here's an example of including ALT text in an image link:

```
<P><A HREF="prev.htm">
<IMG SRC="back.gif" ALT="Go to Previous Page"></A></P>
```

Figure 3.18 shows the navigational icon as it appears in a Web browser with the display of graphics turned on. Figure 3.19 shows this same image with the display of graphics turned off.

You can check this in your browser. The following steps show you how to turn off the display of graphics in both Netscape Navigator 4.0+ and Internet Explorer 4.0+.

Figure 3.18

Navigational icons are usually displayed by themselves, without any accompanying text included in the link.

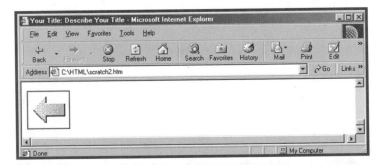

Figure 3.19

Including ALT text in the IMG tag for a navigational icon will clue in users who have turned off the display of graphics or use a text-only browser.

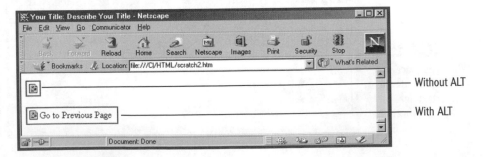

In Netscape Navigator 4.0 or greater:

1. Select Edit, Preferences, and select Advanced in the Categories menu.

2. Uncheck the "Automatically load images" check box. Click on OK.

3. Exit and then rerun Navigator, and then reload your HTML file.

In Internet Explorer 4.0 or greater:

1. In IE 4.0 only, select View, Options. In IE 4.1 or greater, select View, Internet Options. In IE 5.x, select Tools, Internet Options.

2. Select the Advanced tab. Under Multimedia, click on the "Show pictures" check box so that it is unchecked. Click on OK.

3. Click on the Refresh button (or press Ctrl+R).

CAUTION

Don't forget to turn display of images back on! (Otherwise, the example graphics for the following examples won't display in your browser.) Repeat the previous steps to turn display of images back on, rechecking the "Automatically load images" check box in Navigator and the "Show pictures" check box in Internet Explorer. Just press Ctrl+R (or click on the Refresh or Reload button) to reactivate display of images in your browser. (You don't need to exit and rerun Navigator to turn display of images back on—just to turn it off.)

Controlling the Border around an Image Link

The default width of the border around an image link is 2 pixels in Netscape Navigator. The IMG tag's BORDER attribute allows you to specify a custom width for the border. For instance, to increase the width of the border around the image link to 10 pixels, you would do the following:

```
<P><A HREF="link.htm">
<IMG SRC="link.gif" BORDER="10">This is the text.</A></P>
```

NOTE If you earlier copied the example text preceding Figure 3.16 to the Clipboard, you can paste it for each of the following examples and edit as shown. If not, then just type the following example, copy it, and paste it for the following examples, editing as shown.

As shown in Figure 3.20, when you increase the border width to 10 pixels, you really increase it.

Turning Off the Image Link Border

Navigational icons often have their borders turned off. You may want to turn off the border of an image link in other situations. Edit the previous example to turn off the image link border (see Figure 3.21):

```
<P><A HREF="link.htm">
<IMG SRC="link.gif" BORDER="0">This is the text.</A></P>
```

TIP Navigational icons are often displayed with their borders turned off, especially if the image used is self-explanatory (such as a house image for a link that jumps back to the home page, for instance).

Figure 3.20

Using the BORDER attribute in the IMG tag, you can increase the width of the border around an image link.

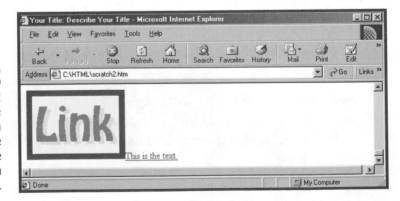

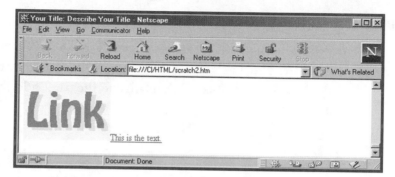

Figure 3.21

Sometimes you want an image without a border to be a link.

Positioning Link Text Relative to an Image Link

All the examples so far have lined up the text at the bottom and to the right of the image link. It might be nice to align the link text with the middle of the image. Just insert an `ALIGN="middle"` attribute value inside the IMG tag, like this:

```
<P><A HREF="link.htm">
<IMG SRC="link.gif" ALIGN="middle">This is the text.</A></P>
```

See Figure 3.22 for how this should look in a Web browser.

To align the link text with the top of the image link, just insert `ALIGN="top"` as the attribute value (bottom alignment is the default). (You can position only a single line of text relative to an image using `ALIGN="top"`—any additional lines will wrap below the image.)

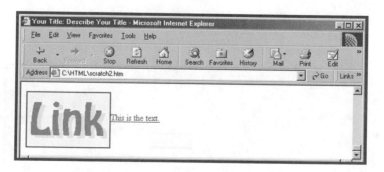

Figure 3.22

You can middle-align an image link relative to the link text.

Horizontally Aligning an Image Link

You can also align an image link relative to the Web page by using an ALIGN attribute in the P tag that contains the link. For example, to center the link text and image link relative to the page, add the following (see Figure 3.23):

```
<P ALIGN="center"><A HREF="link.htm">
<IMG SRC="link.gif" ALIGN="middle">This is the text.</A></P>
```

Using a right-aligned paragraph in the HTML code for Figure 3.23 rather than a center-aligned one would cause the link text and image link to be right-aligned. Left alignment, on the other hand, is the default.

Displaying the Link Text under the Image Link

You can also center the link text under the image link by inserting a BR tag in front of the link text, as shown here (see Figure 3.24):

```
<P ALIGN="center"><A HREF="link.htm">
<IMG SRC="link.gif" ALIGN="middle"><BR>This is the text.</A></P>
```

Reversing the Position of the Image Link and Link Text

You can reverse the relative position of an image link and its associated link text by placing the image link after the link text. To check this out, enter the following example (see Figure 3.25):

```
<P ALIGN="center"><A HREF="link.htm">This is the text.
<IMG SRC="link.gif"></A></P>
```

Figure 3.23

You can center an image link and link text by placing them in a center-aligned paragraph.

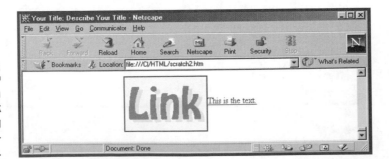

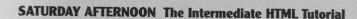

Figure 3.24

By inserting a BR tag, you can position link text beneath an image link.

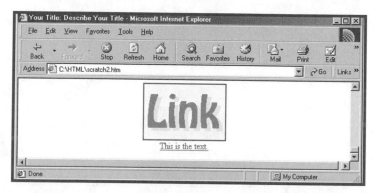

Figure 3.25

You can also put the link text to the left of the image link.

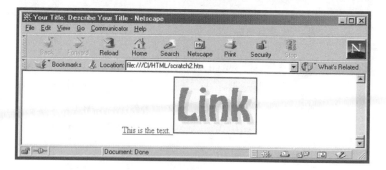

Displaying the Link Text above the Image Link

You can also display link text above the image link if you put the link text ahead of the image. Then all you need to do is put a BR tag at the end of the link text, as shown here (see Figure 3.26):

```
<P ALIGN="center"><A HREF="link.htm">This is the text.<BR>
<IMG SRC="link.gif"></A></P>
```

CAUTION

◆ ◆

If you don't add the `</P>` end tag at the end of a center-aligned or right-aligned paragraph, a bug in Internet Explorer 3.02 will cause it to also apply the horizontal alignment (center alignment or right alignment) to any following list. The next code example is an ordered list (OL), so if you've been leaving off the `</P>` end tag, be sure to add it at the end of the previous code example.

◆ ◆

Figure 3.26

You can center link
text directly above
an image link.

Working with Lists

The Basic HTML Tutorial covered creating ordered (numbered) lists and
unordered (bulleted) lists. It also covered nesting lists within each other
and mixing and matching lists. This section of the Intermediate HTML
Tutorial covers additional ways you can control the display of ordered and
unordered lists.

Specifying the Number Type

You can use the TYPE attribute to specify the number type for an ordered
(OL) list. The values that you can use with the TYPE attribute are "A,"
"a," "I," "i," and "1," for specifying uppercase letters, lowercase letters,
uppercase Roman numerals, lowercase Roman numerals, or Arabic numbers, respectively. Enter the following for an example of specifying uppercase Roman numerals for an ordered list (see Figure 3.27):

```
<OL TYPE="I">
<LI>This is item one.
<LI>This is item two.
<LI>This is item three.
<LI>This is item four.
</OL>
```

Figure 3.27

The TYPE="I"
attribute causes an
ordered list to be
displayed with
uppercase Roman
numerals.

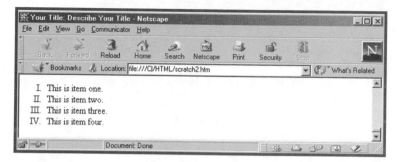

Creating a Multilevel Outline

You might expect Web browsers to vary the number types of nested ordered (numbered) lists automatically. After all, they usually vary the bullet types of nested unordered (bulleted) lists, as you saw in the Basic HTML Tutorial this morning. But no current Web browser automatically varies the number type in nested ordered lists.

To vary the number types of nested ordered lists, you need to use the TYPE attribute of the OL tag. As mentioned in the previous section, you use the values "A," "a," "I," "i," and "1" for specifying uppercase letters, lowercase letters, uppercase Roman numerals, lowercase Roman numerals, or Arabic numbers, respectively. This allows you to create a multilevel outline.

CAUTION You should realize, however, that this can look awful in a Web browser that doesn't support the TYPE attribute for ordered lists, so if you use this feature, you might want to label your page as "HTML 3.2 or greater only."

TIP For this and the following example, tab or space to create the indents—this is for your eyes only and will have no effect when displayed in a browser. Your browser will automatically indent nested ordered lists. Also, be careful that you "nest" instead of "overlap" the different nested outline levels.

Enter the following as an example of creating a multilevel outline using TYPE attributes:

```
<OL TYPE="I">
<LI>Level-one outline level.
  <OL TYPE="A">
  <LI>Level-two outline level.
    <OL TYPE="1">
    <LI>Level-three outline level.
      <OL TYPE="a">
      <LI>Level-four outline level.
      <LI>Level-four outline level.
      </OL>
    <LI>Level-three outline level.
    </OL>
  <LI>Level-two outline level.
  </OL>
<LI>Level-one outline level.
</OL>
```

Figure 3.28 shows how this appears in an HTML 3.2-compliant Web browser. Remember—the indenting you see in the figure (or in your browser) comes from nesting the OL tags; it has nothing to do with any spaces or tabs you may have added here.

You can dress up your outline by bolding or italicizing different levels. You can also apply any of the heading-level tags to have your different outline levels appear in fonts of varying sizes. Later in this tutorial, you'll

Figure 3.28

By using the TYPE attribute to assign different number types, you can create a multilevel outline.

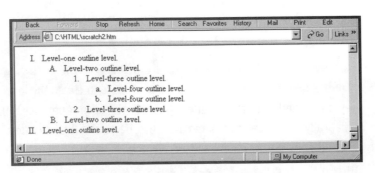

learn how to use the FONT tag to specify font sizes and colors, which you can also use to further emphasize your outline levels. When you use any of these tags to vary the size or color of an outline level, always nest the OL start and end tags inside the tags you want to use to visually differentiate your outline levels.

Including Paragraphs in a Multilevel Outline

You can insert paragraphs inside a multilevel outline by inserting a paragraph following a list item. The paragraph will automatically line up vertically with the text of the preceding list item. For instance, insert the following (see Figure 3.29):

```
<OL TYPE="I">
<LI>Level-one outline level.
<P>Paragraph text following a list item will automatically be
indented flush with the list item text.</P>
  <OL TYPE="A">
  <LI>Level-two outline level.
  <P>Paragraph text following a list item will automatically be
indented flush with the list item text.</P>
      <OL TYPE="1">
      <LI>Level-three outline level.
      <P>Paragraph text following a list item will automatically
be indented flush with the list item text.</P>
        <OL TYPE="a">
        <LI>Level-four outline level.
        <LI>Level-four outline level.
        </OL>
      <LI>Level-three outline level.
      </OL>
  <LI>Level-two outline level.
  </OL>
<LI>Level-one outline level.
</OL>
```

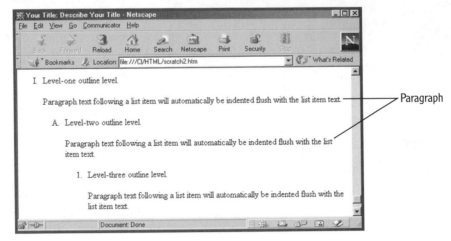

Paragraph

Figure 3.29

Paragraphs
included in a
multilevel outline
automatically
line up vertically
with the preceding
list item.

◆ ◆

CAUTION This is another case where you want to be sure to add the `</P>` end tag if you want a
paragraph to be displayed properly. That's because Navigator and Internet Explorer
won't add extra space between the paragraph and the following list items without it.

◆ ◆

Starting and Restarting Numbering in an Ordered List

You can use the START attribute in an OL start tag to start the numbering sequence at a particular number. You can use the VALUE attribute in
an LI tag to restart the numbering sequence at a particular number. For
an example of first starting the numbering sequence at 3, then restarting
it at 8, enter the following (see Figure 3.30):

```
<OL START="3">
<LI>This should be numbered as 3
<LI>This should be numbered as 4.
<LI VALUE="8">This should be numbered as 8.
<LI>This should be numbered as 9.
</OL>
```

Figure 3.30

You can use the OL tag's START attribute and the LI tag's VALUE attribute to start or restart the numbering of an ordered list.

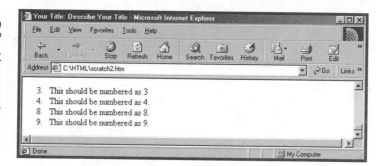

The numbering sequence will be started or restarted using the current TYPE attribute value. For instance, if TYPE="A" is used in the OL tag, then START="3" in an OL tag or VALUE="3" in an LI tag would start or restart the numbering at "C."

Specifying Bullet Types in Unordered Lists

You can also use the TYPE attribute with unordered (bulleted) lists to specify the type of bullet to display. The values that you can use with the UL tag's TYPE attribute are "disc," "circle," and "square." (In all browsers that I know of, the default sequence for nested bullet lists is a disc for the first level, a circle for the second level, and a square for the third level.) Enter the following for an example of specifying a bullet-type sequence other than the default for a bullet list three levels deep (see Figure 3.31):

```
<UL TYPE="square">
<LI>First-level bullet.
<LI>First-level bullet.
  <UL TYPE="disc">
  <LI>Second-level bullet.
  <LI>Second-level bullet.
    <UL TYPE="circle">
    <LI>Third-level bullet.
    <LI>Third-level bullet.
    </UL>
  </UL>
</UL>
```

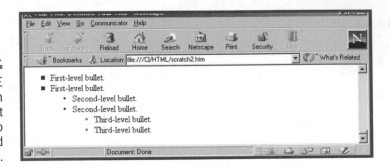

Figure 3.31

Using the TYPE attribute, you can assign nondefault bullet types to nested unordered lists (UL).

TIP Just as you can include automatically indented paragraphs in an outline, you can do the same in a nested bulleted list. Just insert paragraphs following a list item but inside the list, and they will automatically line up to match the list item's indentation. (Don't forget to add the `</P>` end tags at the end of the paragraphs.)

Take a Break?

Ready for a breather? Coming up next, I'm going to be showing you how to create those fancy 3-D icon bullet link lists I've been telling you about, so you might want to take the chance now to get up and get some of the kinks out. Do some deep breathing. Unglue your eyes from the screen and stare at the horizon. Grab a snack or a soda. I'll see you back in five to ten minutes.

Creating Icon Link Lists

An *icon link list* is a list of hypertext links that uses colorful 3-D graphical icon bullets (inline images) rather than plain, black-and-white bullets like those you get when you create an unordered list by using the UL tag. This is a good way to add some pizzazz to your Web page.

For creating the icon link list, you'll be using the same links and link descriptions you used to create a regular link list in the Basic HTML

Tutorial. You can copy and paste these from `scratch.htm`, or you can just retype them, as shown here:

```
<A HREF="http://pages.nyu.edu/~tqm3413/yoyo/index.htm">Tomer's
Page of Exotic Yo-Yo</A> Dedicated to the "little-known,
original, unusual, difficult, or otherwise interesting tricks."
<A HREF="http://www.socool.com/socool/yo-yo.html">Just Say
YO!!!</A> Features the Web's first YoYo animation.
<A HREF="http://www.pd.net/yoyo/">American Yo-Yo Association</A>
Read past issues of the AYYA Newsletter.
<A HREF="http://www.socool.com/socool/yo_hist.html">The History
of the Yo-Yo</A> All you want to know about Yo-Yo history.
```

This method for creating an icon link list uses left-aligned bullet icons and BR tags. To add the bullet icons, insert the following codes (see Figure 3.32):

```
<P><IMG SRC="redball.gif" ALIGN="left" HSPACE="5" VSPACE="4">
<A HREF="http://pages.nyu.edu/~tqm3413/yoyo/index.htm">Tomer's Page of
Exotic Yo-Yo</A> Dedicated to the "little-known, original, unusual,
difficult, or otherwise interesting tricks."<BR CLEAR="left">
<IMG SRC="redball.gif" ALIGN="left" HSPACE="5" VSPACE="4">
<A HREF="http://www.socool.com/socool/yo-yo.html">Just Say YO!!!</A>
Features the Web's first YoYo animation. <BR CLEAR="left">
<IMG SRC="redball.gif" ALIGN="left" HSPACE="5" VSPACE="4">
<A HREF="http://www.pd.net/yoyo/">American Yo-Yo Association</A> Read
past issues of the AYYA Newsletter.<BR CLEAR="left">
<IMG SRC="redball.gif" ALIGN="left" HSPACE="5" VSPACE="4">
<A HREF="http://www.socool.com/socool/yo_hist.html">The History of
the Yo-Yo</A> All you want to know about Yo-Yo history.<BR
CLEAR="left"></P>
```

Figure 3.32

An indented icon bullet list can be created by using left-aligned bullet images and BR tags with the CLEAR attribute.

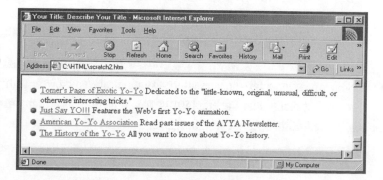

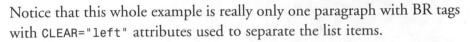

Notice that this whole example is really only one paragraph with BR tags with CLEAR="left" attributes used to separate the list items.

Only the first item in the list has enough description text to wrap and be indented in a browser. Feel free to add more description text to the previous example, so that the other list items will also wrap and be indented.

A limitation of this particular method is that it only allows two lines of text in a list item—a third line won't be indented but will be flush to the left margin. Further increasing the VSPACE attribute value (which is what creates the indent effect) will move the bullet icon too far down relative to the text where it is inserted. For that reason, you need to be careful not to add more text than can be contained on two lines. Be sure to test this for the lowest common denominator, running your browser in a screen resolution of 640×480 pixels, or with the width of your browser window reset to 640 pixels or fewer.

Another limitation of this method is that you don't have very much control over how a browser will align your icon bullet relative to the following text. The Windows versions of both Netscape Navigator and Microsoft Internet Explorer display this almost identically, but the Macintosh versions of both of these browsers will display the bullet icon at least a pixel lower than the Windows versions.

To increase or decrease the amount of horizontal space that is displayed between the icon bullet and the following link and description text, just increase or decrease the HSPACE attribute values.

If a browser doesn't support left-aligning the bullet icons, any wrapping text will be displayed flush to the left margin, so you don't have to worry about this overly messing up older browsers.

TIP Someone using a text-only browser or a graphical Web browser with graphics turned off might not realize that the graphics are icon bullets. To clue them in, you might want to edit the IMG tags for the icon bullets, adding **ALT="*"**, so they look like this:

```
<IMG SRC="redball.gif" ALIGN="top" HSPACE=5 VSPACE=5 ALT="*">
```

If you're wondering where to get more graphic icons to spice up your Web page, you can find a collection of them and other Web art on the CD-ROM. You can also find a collection of Web art images, including many icon bullet images, available for download from this book's Web site at **www.callihan.com/create3/**.

In the Saturday Evening bonus session, "The Tables Tutorial," I'll be showing you how to create icon link lists that allow for an unlimited number of indented lines.

Working with Rules

You learned how to use the HR (Horizontal Rule) tag in the Basic HTML Tutorial. In the following section, I'll show you how to create custom horizontal rules by changing the height, width, alignment, and shading of a horizontal rule. I'll also show you how to use inline images as graphic rules, which lets you include fancy and colorful horizontal rules in your Web pages.

Creating Custom Horizontal Rules

The default horizontal rule looks rather bland. True, it does have some shading to give it a bit of a 3-D look—although it is entirely washed out in Internet Explorer if you've set your browser's background to white. So this section covers some things you can do to dress up your horizontal rules, including changing their height, width, and alignment.

The attributes used here in the HR tag were all originally Netscape Navigator extensions. HTML 3.2 includes them, so they now qualify as "official HTML." Most current Web browsers support these attributes.

Changing the Height of a Horizontal Rule

To change the height of a horizontal rule, set the SIZE attribute value in the HR tag. The value you set is the rule's height, or thickness, in pixels. Enter the following for an example of creating a horizontal rule that has

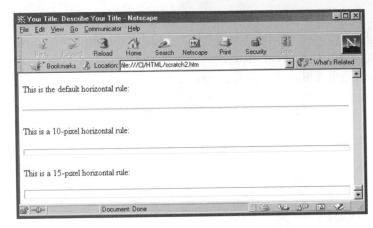

Figure 3.33

You can vary the
thickness of a
horizontal rule.

a thickness of 10 pixels and another one that has a thickness of 15 pixels, along with a regular rule so you can see the difference (see Figure 3.33):

```
<P>This is the default horizontal rule:</P>
<HR>
<P>This is a 10-pixel horizontal rule:</P>
<HR SIZE="10">
<P>This is a 15-pixel horizontal rule:</P>
<HR SIZE="15">
```

Using Unshaded Horizontal Rules

The default setting for a horizontal rule is "shaded." To set an unshaded horizontal rule, just add the NOSHADE attribute to the HR tag, as shown here:

```
<P>This 15-pixel horizontal rule is unshaded:</P>
<HR SIZE="15" NOSHADE>
```

The following figures, Figure 3.34 and Figure 3.35, show how this looks in the Windows versions of Netscape Navigator and Internet Explorer, which take somewhat different approaches to displaying unshaded horizontal rules.

As you can see, the Windows version of Navigator displays an unshaded rule filled in gray with rounded-off corners, and the Windows version of

Figure 3.34

The Windows version of Internet Explorer displays an unshaded horizontal rule shaded in gray and with square corners.

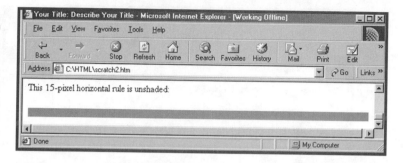

Figure 3.35

The Windows version of Navigator displays an unshaded horizontal rule shaded in gray with rounded-off corners.

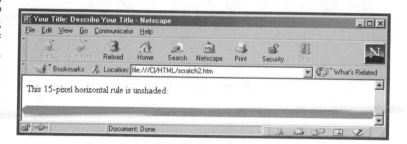

Internet Explorer displays it also filled in gray but with square corners. The Macintosh versions of these browsers, however, differ from their Windows versions in how they display this example—both display it filled in black with square corners, as does NCSA Mosaic 2.0 for Windows. So the only uniformity you can expect from an unshaded rule is that it'll be filled, in gray or black.

Changing the Width of a Horizontal Rule

You also can change the width of a horizontal rule, either by setting the width in actual pixels or by specifying a percentage of the total width of the browser window. By default, horizontal rules are centered in the browser window. Enter the following for an example of creating a 15-pixel horizontal rule with a width that is 75 percent of a browser's window (see Figure 3.36):

```
<P>This 15-pixel horizontal rule has a width of 75 percent:</P>
<HR WIDTH="75%" SIZE="15" NOSHADE>
```

Figure 3.36

A horizontal rule
with a percentage
width is
automatically
centered.

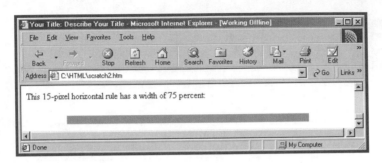

CAUTION

You might be tempted to stack horizontal rules of different widths to generate an effect similar to this:

Be advised that in a Web browser that doesn't support setting the WIDTH attribute for the HR tag, your effect will turn out to look something like this:

This is a good example of a situation in which both Navigator and Internet Explorer support doing something, but you probably still shouldn't do it. The general rule is not to do tricks specific to only a few browsers if they're going to mess up other browsers. One way around this is to provide alternative pages, or at least label your page as "HTML 3.2 Only." Both Netscape and Microsoft have button images you can use to link your site directly to theirs, so your visitors can download the latest versions of their browsers.

Setting the Alignment of a Horizontal Rule

You can use the ALIGN attribute in the HR tag to left-align or right-align a horizontal rule (center alignment is the default). Both Netscape Navigator and Internet Explorer support left- or right-aligning a horizontal rule. Enter

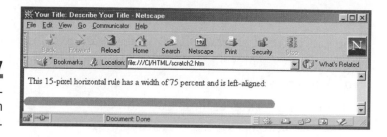

Figure 3.37

You can either left-align or right-align a horizontal rule.

the following for an example of doing this (see Figure 3.37):

```
<P>This 15-pixel horizontal rule has a width of 75 percent and
is left-aligned:</P>
<HR ALIGN="left" WIDTH="75%" SIZE="15" NOSHADE>
```

Using Graphic Rules

Horizontal rules probably work best as simple separators. Their main advantage is that they consume very few bytes. If you want a rule that is more colorful, however, you'll need to use a graphic rule. A graphic rule is actually just an inline image shaped in the form of a rule. The main disadvantage is that a graphic rule consumes considerably more bytes than a horizontal rule (although you can use the same graphic rule several times without taking up any additional bytes).

Enter the following as an example of inserting a graphic rule on your Web page (see Figure 3.38):

```
<P>This is a graphic rule:</P>
<P><IMG SRC="rain_lin.gif"></P>
```

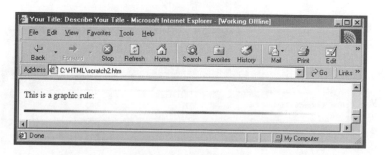

Figure 3.38

Instead of a plain ordinary horizontal rule, you can use a fancy graphic rule.

Centering a Graphic Rule

You can center a graphic rule as you would any inline image simply by placing it in a center-aligned paragraph. Edit the example you just created to center it, like this (see Figure 3.39):

```
<P>This is a centered graphic rule:</P>
<P ALIGN="center"><IMG SRC="rain_lin.gif"></P>
```

Setting the Width and Height of a Graphic Rule

Just as with any other inline image, you can set the height and width of a graphic rule. Earlier, I recommended that you use the actual height and width dimensions of your image when setting the HEIGHT and WIDTH attributes for an inline image. Every rule has an exception, however. The benefits of being able to adjust the height and width of a graphic rule, on the fly, in your browser simply outweigh the small disadvantages that might accrue. Because graphic rules usually don't have diagonal or curved edges and lines, you don't have to worry about the "jaggies," for instance. Even if you decrease the size of a graphic rule, the bandwidth wastage is usually very small—in most cases, however, you'll probably be increasing, rather than decreasing, the dimensions of your graphic rules.

I also advised you previously against using width percentages to resize inline images. Once again, graphic rules are an exception to the rule. That's because being able to dynamically resize the width of a graphic rule relative to the width of a browser window is, I think anyway, a pretty neat effect, and the disadvantages are negligible.

Figure 3.39

You can center a graphic rule by placing it in a center-aligned paragraph.

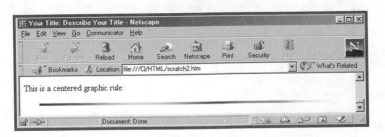

So, feel free to experiment with resetting the height and width of any graphic rules you want to use—in fact, varying the width and height of the same graphic rule is one way to add some visual variety to your Web page without costing you any additional bytes. Just don't do it with your other inline images (resize them in your image editor, not your browser).

The following is an example of a graphic rule, nested in a center-aligned paragraph, with a height set at 15 pixels and a width set at 95 percent of the browser window (see Figure 3.40):

```
<P>This is a centered graphic rule with its height and width set
at 15 pixels and 95 percent:</P>
<P ALIGN="center"><IMG SRC="rain_lin.gif" HEIGHT="15"
WIDTH="95%"></P>
```

TIP

The capability to set the width and height of an inline image allows a neat trick for creating a graphic rule. It also lets you create graphic rules that are much smaller, byte-wise, than a normal graphic rule. To do this, in your graphics editor, create a small graphic (10 x 10 pixels) using the color of your choice as the background and save it to C:\HTML as a GIF or JPEG file. Next, insert the graphic into your Web page as an inline image and then set the height and width attributes to 10 pixels and 75 percent, for instance:

```
<P ALIGN="center"><IMG SRC="yourfile.gif" HEIGHT="10" WIDTH="75%">
```

If your graphic is red, then a red graphic rule 10 pixels high and extending across 75 percent of the browser window will be displayed, even though the actual size of the graphic is only 10 x 10 pixels. You can also experiment in your image editor with using fills other than solid color fills, such as pattern or gradient fills, for instance, to achieve more varied effects.

Figure 3.40

The benefits of being able to dynamically resize a graphic rule in a browser are considerable, and the disadvantages are negligible.

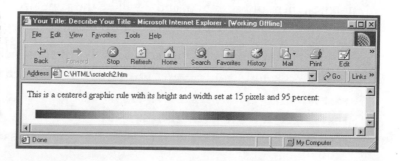

Working with Fonts

The FONT tag allows you to change font sizes, colors, and faces. In the following sections, I'll show you how to apply the FONT tag's SIZE, COLOR, and FACE attributes.

Changing Font Sizes

The FONT tag allows you to specify the size of a section of text. The FONT tag uses the SIZE attribute to change the size of a font. You can set font sizes using absolute or relative size values.

Setting Absolute Font Sizes

Seven absolute (or fixed) font sizes, numbered from 1 to 7, can be applied using the FONT tag's SIZE attribute. The default font size corresponds to a size of 3. Sizes 1 and 2 set font sizes that are two sizes and one size smaller than the default font size, and sizes 4, 5, and 6 set font sizes that are progressively larger than the default font size. Generally, when it comes to the larger font sizes, 4 is the same size as an H3 tag, 5 the same size as an H2 tag, 6 the same size as an H1 tag, and 7 one size larger than an H1 tag. (The clinker here, however, is the Macintosh version of Internet Explorer 4.x. It allows users to bump up the Mac's relatively diminutive default font size by clicking a Larger button, but does so simply by bumping all of the font sizes up one notch, with the exception of the largest font size [7], which stays the same. As a result, if the Larger button has been clicked once, then font sizes 6 and 7 will be the same size; if the Larger button has been clicked twice to bump up the font size two notches, then font sizes 5, 6, and 7 will be the same size. No other browser on the Mac, however, does these kinds of font shenanigans.)

To see what these different font sizes look like in your Web browser, enter the following and then hop over to your browser (see Figure 3.41):

```
<P><FONT SIZE="1">Font Size 1.</FONT><BR>
<FONT SIZE="2">Font Size 2.</FONT><BR>
<FONT SIZE="3">Font Size 3 (the default).</FONT><BR>
```

```
<FONT SIZE="4">Font Size 4.</FONT><BR>
<FONT SIZE="5">Font Size 5.</FONT><BR>
<FONT SIZE="6">Font Size 6.</FONT><BR>
<FONT SIZE="7">Font Size 7.</FONT></P>
```

TIP You can also nest font tags inside each other, so you could do something like this to switch back to the default font size in the middle of a larger set font size:

```
<FONT SIZE="4">This is Font Size 4. <FONT SIZE="3">This is the default size font.</FONT> This is Font Size 4 again.</FONT>.
```

Setting Relative Font Sizes

You also can set relative font sizes. Relative font-size changes are indicated by either a plus (+) or minus (-) sign preceding the font size number. For instance, FONT SIZE="+1" indicates a font size that is one size larger than the base font. Because the default base font is the same as a Size 3 absolute font, a Size +1 relative font would be the same as a Size 4 absolute font (3 + 1 = 4). For instance, enter the following for an example of using relative font-size changes to indicate the seven possible font sizes (see Figure 3.42):

```
<P><FONT SIZE="-2">Font Size -2.</FONT><BR>
<FONT SIZE="-1">Font Size -1.</FONT><BR>
Default Font Size.<BR>
<FONT SIZE="+1">Font Size +1.</FONT><BR>
<FONT SIZE="+2">Font Size +2.</FONT><BR>
<FONT SIZE="+3">Font Size +3.</FONT><BR>
<FONT SIZE="+4">Font Size +4.</FONT></P>
```

You'll notice that a relative -2 is the same as an absolute 1, -1 is the same as 2, +1 is the same as 4, and so on. The default font size, which requires no font-size change, is the same as 3.

Now, you may be asking, "If relative fonts are just another way to specify the same fonts as absolute fonts, why bother?" The next section, "Setting the Base Font," provides the answer to that question.

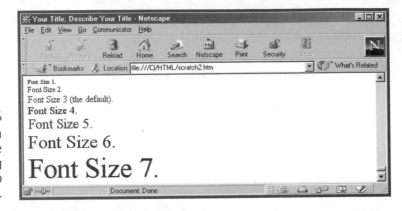

Figure 3.41

You can set seven different absolute font sizes, ranging from very small to fairly large.

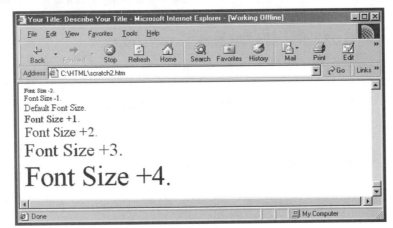

Figure 3.42

You can set seven different relative font sizes.

Setting the Base Font

The BASEFONT tag allows you to change the size of the *base font*—the default font used in text. You can set it to any of the absolute font sizes, 1 through 7 (3 is the default). It's a stand-alone (or empty) tag. You set the base font size the same way you set an absolute font size. For instance, to increase the base font size one notch for text following the BASEFONT tag, you would set the base font to an absolute font size of 4, like this:

```
<BASEFONT SIZE="4">
```

When you change the base font size using the BASEFONT tag, all following relative font sizes will change relative to the new base font. For

instance, if you change the base font size to 4 as above, then a relative font size of +1 would be the same as an absolute font size of 5 (4 + 1 = 5).

You can insert the BASEFONT tag at any point within a Web page to set the base font to any of the absolute font sizes. It stays in effect until another BASEFONT tag changes the base font to another size. It not only affects relative font sizes, but also any SMALL and BIG font changes (described next in the session), as well as the size of all paragraph text, character rendering (italic, bold, and so on), list elements, definition lists, block quotes, predefined text, and address blocks that follow it. Headings and text set with absolute font-size tags are not affected, however. Text inside of tables is also not affected.

CAUTION You may be tempted to use the BASEFONT tag to set a relative font size—`<BASEFONT SIZE="+1">`, for instance. This actually works fine in Navigator, which increases the default base font size one notch (resetting the default base font size from an absolute size of 3 to a size of 4). Internet Explorer, however, will resize the base font relative to a starting size of 1, meaning that the new base font size will actually shrink a notch (to a size of 2, rather than jumping up to a size of 4). Don't set relative font-size changes in the BASE-FONT tag, in other words. If you want to bump up the base font size a notch, *always* do it using an absolute font-size change—`<BASEFONT SIZE="4">`, for instance.

Using the BIG and SMALL Tags

The BIG and SMALL tags are Netscape extensions that were later incorporated into HTML 3.2. They are container tags that specify a font size that is one size smaller or one size bigger than the current base font size. These tags can be a quick and easy way to bump up or down the size of nested text. To get even larger or smaller font sizes, you can nest BIG and SMALL tags (`<BIG><BIG>...</BIG></BIG>`, for instance). To try using these tags, enter this example (see Figure 3.43):

```
<P><SMALL>This is a smaller font.</SMALL> This is a regular
font. <BIG>This is a bigger font.</BIG> <BIG><BIG>This is an
even bigger font.</BIG></P>
```

Figure 3.43

You can use the
BIG and SMALL
tags to increase or
decrease font sizes.

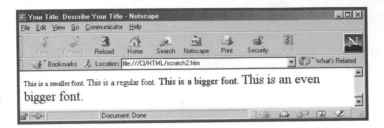

FONT-SIZE TAGS IN HTML 4.0

If you check out the specification for HTML 4.0, you may notice that a number
of tags used to change the font sizes, colors, or faces—the FONT, BASEFONT,
BIG, and SMALL tags—have been "deprecated." This just means that a more
recent standard is available to achieve the same result—cascading style
sheets, in this case. It doesn't mean that you shouldn't use these tags—that
would be the case only if they had been "obsoleted." Current and future
browsers are required to continue supporting all deprecated tags but may
drop support for obsoleted tags. Their long history (they started out as
Netscape extensions before being officially incorporated into HTML 3.2)
ensures that they will be supported by both current and future browsers. On
the other hand, Cascading Style Sheets, level 1 (CSS1)—the initial standard
for style sheets—has yet to be fully supported even by the most recent
browsers. Older graphical browsers, still being used by loads of surfers, don't
support them at all.

Another reason to use these tags is that they are easier and more straightfor-
ward than are style sheets for a novice HTML user to learn and apply. Even
HTML experts can find applying styles a bit sticky, considering that there is
little uniformity in how even the most recent browsers implement styles.

So many pages have already been created using the FONT, BASEFONT, BIG,
and SMALL tags that it is not likely that these tags will ever be obsoleted in
future versions of HTML (the BIG and SMALL tags are only slightly more likely
to be obsoleted than the FONT and BASEFONT tags, I think).

Changing Font Colors

The FONT tag uses the COLOR attribute to change the color of a font. To specify a font color, you can either use one of 16 color names that match the Windows 16-color palette, or you can use RGB hex codes—which is more difficult but gives you access to a lot more colors.

Setting Font Colors Using the 16 Color Names

The 16 Windows color names are black, white, aqua, blue, fuchsia, gray, green, lime, maroon, navy, olive, purple, red, silver, teal, and yellow. Enter the following for an example of specifying font colors using color names (this example omits black and white):

```
<P><FONT SIZE=7>
<FONT COLOR="aqua">Aqua </FONT><FONT COLOR="blue">Blue </FONT>
<FONT COLOR="fuchsia">Fuchsia </FONT><FONT COLOR="gray">Gray </FONT>
<FONT COLOR="green">Green </FONT><FONT COLOR="lime">Lime </FONT>
<FONT COLOR="maroon">Maroon </FONT><FONT COLOR="navy">Navy </FONT>
<FONT COLOR="olive">Olive </FONT><FONT COLOR="purple">Purple </FONT>
<FONT COLOR="red">Red </FONT><FONT COLOR="silver">Silver </FONT>
<FONT COLOR="teal">Teal </FONT><FONT COLOR="yellow">Yellow </FONT>
</FONT></P>
```

The illustration in Figure 3.44, shown here in monochrome, gives only a rough idea of what this looks like in a browser. Be sure to hop over to your browser to see what the colors really look like.

Setting Font Colors Using RGB Hex Codes

Setting the font color using RGB hex codes involves specifying values from 0 to 255 (00 to FF, in hexadecimal) for the red, green, and blue components of a color, providing you with a grand total of no less than 16.7 million colors from which to choose.

If you're wondering why the RGB codes are set as hexadecimal, rather than decimal, values, the reason is that you can count in hexadecimal

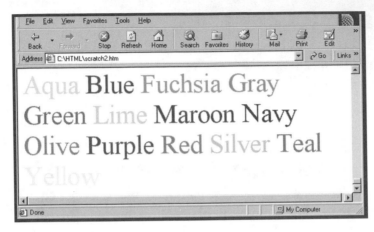

Figure 3.44

You can use 16 color names, including black and white (not shown here), to set font colors.

from 0 to 255 using only two-digit numbers. The hexadecimal equivalent to 159, for instance, is 9F.

You set the RGB hex code for a color in the FONT tag in this general form, where *rr* is the hex value for red, *gg* the hex value for green, and *bb* the hex value for blue:

```
<FONT COLOR="#rrggbb">This is the text to be colored.</FONT>
```

For instance, a red color here could be specified as #FF0000, a lime green color as #00FF00, and a blue color as #0000FF. (FF is the highest hexadecimal number, equaling 255, whereas 00 is the lowest, equaling 0.) Enter the following example of assigning font colors using RGB hex codes (the example also sets the font size so it will be more visible in your browser; see Figure 3.45):

```
<P><FONT SIZE="7">
<FONT COLOR="#FF6633">"Orange" (FF6633) </FONT>
<FONT COLOR="#CC9900">"Gold" (CC9900) </FONT>
<FONT COLOR="#6600FF">"Violet" (6600FF) </FONT>
<FONT COLOR="#FF9999">"Salmon" (FF9999) </FONT>
<FONT COLOR="#CC0000">"Brick Red" (CC0000) </FONT>
<FONT COLOR="#3399FF">"Sky Blue" (3399FF) </FONT>
</FONT></P>
```

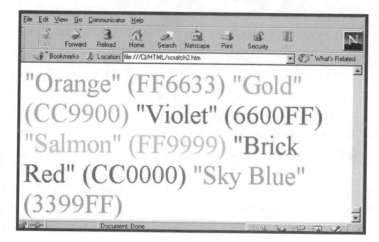

Figure 3.45

Here are just some of the many colors you can set using RGB hex codes.

Browsers on systems that can display only 256 colors use *dithering* to display colors that aren't included in the browser or system palette that is used for those systems. Sometimes this is fine, other times decidedly not. The only colors that definitely won't be dithered on 256-color systems are those included in the 216-color browser-safe palette (often referred to as the "Netscape palette," because that's where this started, but other browsers now also use the same palette). Other colors, if they aren't also included in a particular system's 256-color palette, will be dithered on 256-color systems.

◀◀◀◀◀◀◀◀◀◀◀◀◀◀◀◀◀◀◀◀◀◀◀◀◀◀◀◀◀◀◀◀◀◀

Dithering is a technique for simulating colors that are not present in a system's color palette. Colors not present are simulated by intermingling pixels of two or more palette colors, tricking the human eye, which perceives a single color. The resulting color may look very similar to the intended color, but it may also look quite different, appearing mottled or grainy, and in a color quite different from the intended one, depending on how well colors present in the palette are able to simulate the color that isn't.

◀◀◀◀◀◀◀◀◀◀◀◀◀◀◀◀◀◀◀◀◀◀◀◀◀◀◀◀◀◀◀◀◀◀

TIP

If you stick to hexadecimal codes 00, 33, 66, 99, CC, and FF when inserting RGB hex codes, you'll be selecting colors from the browser-safe palette, helping to ensure that your page will display fine on 256-color systems. You'll also reduce the number of colors from which you must select to 216. The background, text, and link colors set in the example are all combinations of these codes. This will have the added benefit of making sure that your colors will display as anticipated on a 256-color system.

Showing you how to count in hexadecimal or explaining how an RGB color scheme works is beyond the scope of this book. Quite frankly, unless you already know hex and RGB color theory, the only practical way is to use some kind of color chart, wheel, or cube that allows you to select the color you want and get the corresponding hex code.

A number of places on the Web have color cubes or charts that show you all of the browser-safe colors and their RGB hex codes. Here are two of the best:

FIND IT ON ▶
THE WEB

- ❖ Victor Engel's No Dither Netscape Color Palette at **the-light.com/netcol.html**

- ❖ Doug Jacobson's RGB Color Chart at **www.phoenix.net/~jacobson/rgb.html**

I've also included a file, colors.html, with the example files in the HTML Tutorials folder. Just open it in your browser to see a table including all of the browser-safe colors and their corresponding RGB hex codes.

Many HTML editors also have color pickers, which allow you to choose the color you want and then insert the RGB hex code into your Web page for you. Generally, however, they won't identify the browser-safe colors.

Changing Font Faces

The FACE attribute for the FONT tag was originally a Microsoft extension. It wasn't included in HTML 3.2 but was later incorporated into HTML 4.0. It allows you to specify a font, or list of fonts, in which you

would like to have text displayed. A browser that supports this attribute will check to see if any of the fonts specified are present on a local computer and then display the text in that font if it is available. If not, it will display the text in the default font.

One of the tricks to using this attribute is to specify a list of fonts that will snag as many computers as possible. You should realize that just because a font is available on your system doesn't mean that it will be available on someone else's system. If most systems aren't liable to have a particular font, there really isn't much point in specifying it. For that reason, I don't think trying to specify one particular font is the way to go, and you certainly shouldn't base the design of your Web page on having any one particular font available. Even if you stick with fonts that are included with Windows, you should realize that those fonts may not be available on a Macintosh or a UNIX system.

A good way to use this attribute is to specify a list of fonts that fit into the same category, such as serif, sans serif, or monospaced fonts. For instance, to maximize the chances that the following example will be displayed in a sans serif font, enter the following (see Figure 3.46):

```
<P><FONT SIZE="6" COLOR="blue" FACE="Verdana, Arial,
Helvetica">This text will be in either Verdana, Arial, or
Helvetica, depending on which fonts are installed on a local
system.</FONT></P>
```

You're not limited to listing only font faces that are available on your own system—Helvetica, a Postscript font face, is included in the previous example because it is more likely to be present on a Macintosh system, which is less likely to have Verdana or Arial available. Enter the following for an example of specifying a pair of monospaced fonts (Courier New and Courier) that should ensure that one or the other will display on both Windows and Macintosh systems (see Figure 3.47):

```
<P><B><FONT SIZE="6" COLOR="blue" FACE="Courier New,
Courier">This text will be in a bold Courier New or Courier
font face, depending on which fonts are installed on a local
system.</FONT></B></P>
```

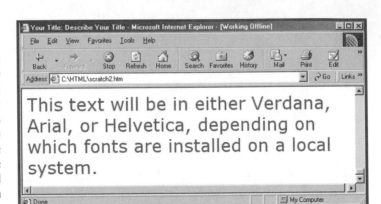

Figure 3.46

You can specify a list of font faces in the FONT tag's FACE attribute to increase the chance that at least one (here Verdana) will be available on a local system.

In the previous example, the FONT tag is also nested inside of a B (Bold) tag to render the monospaced font as a bolded font.

 TIP   On Windows systems, Adobe Type Manager must be installed for Postscript fonts to be finely rendered—otherwise, a lower-quality bitmap representation will be displayed. For that reason, when including a list of font faces in the FONT tag, you should always precede any Postscript fonts (Helvetica, Times, Palatino, and Courier, for instance) by one or more True Type fonts (Arial, Times New Roman, Verdana, and Courier New, for instance).

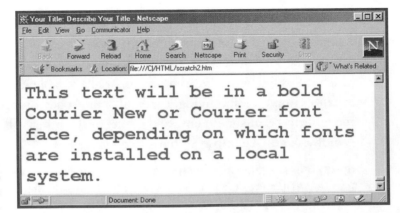

Figure 3.47

To display a monospaced font, both Courier New (shown here) and Courier can be specified to increase the chances that both Windows and Macintosh systems will display a monospaced font.

Using Background Colors and Images

Using a background color or image is a great way to dress up the appearance of your Web page. In the following sections, I'll be showing you how to set a background color (as well as matching text and link colors) and how to use a background image with your Web page.

Using a Background Color

Using the right background color is a simple and easy way to make your Web page look really great. (Or really horrible, depending on the color you choose!) In this section, I'll show you how to set a background color and matching text and link colors.

You can set the colors for the background, text, and links by using these attributes of the BODY tag: BGCOLOR sets the background color, TEXT the text (or foreground) color, LINK the color of hypertext links, VLINK the color of visited links, and ALINK the color of activated links (where you hold down the mouse button on a link but haven't released it). As with the FONT tag's COLOR attribute, you can set these attributes using any of the 16 color names (black, white, aqua, blue, fuchsia, gray, green, lime, maroon, navy, olive, purple, red, silver, teal, and yellow) or by using RGB hexadecimal codes.

The general form for entering these attributes as color names is shown here, where *colorname* is one of the 16 color names given:

```
<BODY BGCOLOR="colorname" TEXT="colorname" LINK="colorname"
VLINK="colorname" ALINK="colorname"
```

The general form for entering these attributes as RGB hexadecimal codes is shown here, where *rrggbb* is three hexadecimal numbers forming the RGB code for setting the red, green, and blue components of an RGB color:

```
<BODY BGCOLOR="#rrggbb" TEXT="#rrggbb" LINK="#rrggbb"
VLINK="#rrggbb" ALINK="#rrggbb"
```

The following example sets the colors for the background, the text (or foreground), and the three varieties of links—regular, visited, and activated.

TIP

When setting a light text color against a darker background color, it is a good idea to bump up the base font size one notch (insert **<BASEFONT SIZE="4">** at the top of your page, just below the **<BODY>** tag) to help make the text font more legible.

Go to the top of your HTML file and add the following to the BODY tag as an example of setting these attributes (bump up the base font size a notch as well while you're at it):

```
<BODY BGCOLOR="#6699CC" TEXT="#FFFFCC" LINK="#00FF33"
VLINK="#99CC00" ALINK="#FF0000">
<BASEFONT SIZE="4">
```

This sets the background color to slate blue, text to light yellow, links to bright green, visited links to a darker green, and activated links to bright red. The base font size is also bumped up one notch.

Because the illustrations in this book are not printed in color, Figure 3.48 can only show you the contrast and tone of the colors you set in the example. To see what it really looks like, hop over to your Web browser.

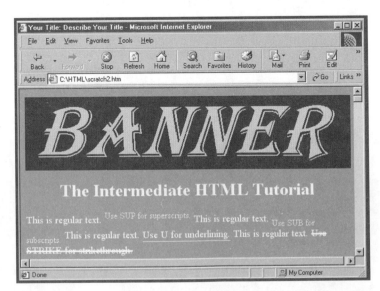

Figure 3.48

You can set a background color, as well as matching text and link colors.

CAUTION

♦ ♦

If you decide to set colors (and nothing says you have to), you should try to avoid color combinations that make your text font less readable. Some color combinations can render a Web page entirely unusable.

♦ ♦

Using a Background Image

The BACKGROUND attribute of the BODY tag allows you to specify a background image. Background images are usually quite small (usually not larger than 100 x 100 pixels)—a Web browser will *tile* the image so that it fills the whole background of the browser window (similar to how tiles are laid on a bathroom wall or floor). Background images are usually created so they can be seamlessly tiled, meaning that you can't easily distinguish the seams between the tiled images; the tiled images appear to be a continuous pattern or texture.

TIP

■ ■

You can create your own seamless background image instead of using one of many ready-made background images available on the Web. Paint Shop Pro 5, included on the CD-ROM, has a nifty feature that allows you to select any area within an image and then convert it into a seamless background image. Just select an area in an image with the Selection tool, and then select Selections and Convert to Seamless Pattern.

■ ■

A background image can be a GIF, JPEG, or PNG file. The general format for entering this attribute is shown as follows, with *filename* referring to a graphic file located in the same folder as the Web page and with *URL* referring to the address (relative or absolute) of a graphic file located in a different folder than the Web page:

```
<BODY BACKGROUND="filename or URL">
```

A key consideration when using background images is to avoid busy or high-contrast images. If you're going to use a dark background image, you should set the color of your text and links to a lighter color. The

following example inserts a background image that is close in color and tone to the background color you added previously, so you won't have to change the other colors (see Figure 3.49):

```
<BODY BACKGROUND="back_pool.jpg" BGCOLOR="#6699CC" TEXT="#FFFFCC"
LINK="#00FF33" VLINK="#99CC00" ALINK="#FF0000">
<BASEFONT SIZE="4">
```

TIP

To allow for surfers who've turned off display of images, it is a good idea to always set a background color that is similar in color and tone to the background image you've set. That way, any text and link colors that you've set will still display legibly against the background color if the background image has been turned off.

Save the HTML file you just created. You can use it later as a reference. When you first saved it, you named it scratch2.htm. If more than one person will be doing this tutorial and you want to make sure that this file doesn't get overwritten, you might want to give it a new name; you could use your initials in the file name (jm-scratch2.htm, if your name is John Moore or June Miller, for instance).

Figure 3.49

One of the more effective ways to add visual appeal to your Web page is to use a background image.

Using Relative URLs (Optional)

This is an optional section—you don't need to read it to plan and create your first Web page tomorrow. If you're running short on time, feel free to skip it for now. (Don't skip it forever, however—knowing how to use relative URLs is one of the keys to being able to create more complex and sophisticated Web sites.)

In the tutorials and work sessions for this book, I'm having you save your HTML files and image files all in the same folder. This is primarily for convenience sake, so you can get your feet wet first before diving into the deep end of the pool. By saving your files all in the same folder, you only have to include the file name as the URL for a hypertext link or an inline image.

However, if you get into creating more complicated Web sites, organized into separate projects, for instance, each with its own main page and subpages, then you'll definitely start to outgrow simply saving all your files in the same folder. You'll then want to organize your separate Web page projects in their own separate folders. You may also want to create a separate folder just to hold your images (this way, different Web page projects can share many of the same images, as well).

You've already seen examples of *absolute URLs*—the URL for this book's Web site (`http://www.callihan.com/create3/index.htm`), for instance, is an absolute URL (also called a "full URL"). An absolute URL expresses the location of the object of a URL in absolute terms, listing the server type (`http://`), the domain name (`www.callihan.com/`), the folder path (`create3/`), and the object of the link (`index.htm`).

However, when a file is included within the folder structure of your own Web site, there is no need to include everything that would be included in an absolute URL. By using a *relative URL*, which states the position of the link object in relation to the current folder (the folder where the linking HTML file is saved), you only need to include information in your link that is not common to both. For instance, whenever I've had you create a link or inline image that only specifies the file name, you've been using a relative

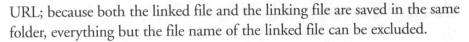

URL; because both the linked file and the linking file are saved in the same folder, everything but the file name of the linked file can be excluded.

Another reason to use relative URLs rather than absolute URLs when linking to files that are internal to your own Web site is that you can create and test your site entirely on your local computer, and then transfer your site up onto a server without having to change any of the links. This is because absolute links on your local computer and absolute links on your server will be different (because they are on different machines), but relative links (because they are relative to the current folder) will be the same.

Figure 3.50 shows a hypothetical Web site organized into folders and subfolders. In the following explanations, I'll be referring quite often to the different folders illustrated in this figure, so be sure to refer back to it frequently to refresh your mental picture of what's going on.

NOTE   In the following explanations I'll be describing the relationships between folders in terms of familial relationships.

The phrase *child folder* refers to a folder that is inside (a child of) the linking file's folder. In Figure 3.50, for instance, the images, products, and support folders are all child folders of the My Pages folder.

The phrase *parent folder* refers to the folder in which a linking file's folder is located. In Figure 3.50, for instance, the My Pages folder is the parent folder of the images, products, and support folders.

The phrase *grandparent folder* refers to the parent folder of a parent folder. In Figure 3.50, for instance, the My Pages folder is the grandparent folder of the technical and sales folders. The phrase *grandchild folder*, on the other hand, refers to the opposite relation—in the illustration, the technical folder is a grandchild folder of the My Pages folder.

The phrase *sibling folder* refers to child folders located in the same parent folder. Other relationships can be set up here, such as between two cousins, between an aunt or uncle and a niece or nephew, and so on.

While reading the following sections, please feel free to refer back to Figure 3.50 frequently for a visual representation of these relationships.

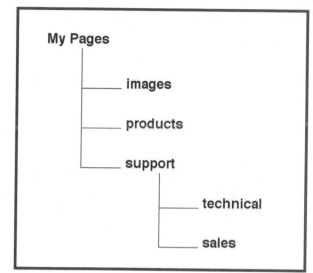

Figure 3.50

The My Pages folder contains the images, products, and support folders, and the support folder contains the technical and sales folders.

Linking to a File in a Child Folder

Now, suppose you want to link from your home page (My Pages > index.html) to an inline image stored in the images folder (My Pages > images > headline.gif). In that case, the IMG tag would only need to include the following:

```
<IMG SRC="images/headline.gif">
```

Linking to an HTML file in a subfolder works exactly the same way. Suppose you want to link from your home page (My Pages > index.html) to a product catalog you've saved in the products folder (My Pages > products > catalog.html). In that case, the hypertext link would need to look like this:

```
<A HREF="products/catalog.html">
```

That's pretty simple. If you want to link to a file that is in a child folder (or subfolder) of the linking file's folder, you only need to include the name of the child folder, a forward slash, and the file name of the file you're linking to. A common mistake is to insert a forward slash in front of the child folder (in UNIX, forward slashes come after, not before,

folder names). Another common mistake is to use backward slashes (\) instead of forward slashes.

Linking to a File in a Grandchild Folder

But what if you want to link to a file that's located in a subfolder of a subfolder (a grandchild folder, in other words) of the linking file's folder? Suppose that you want to link from your home page (My Pages > index.html) to a page of support phone numbers you've saved in the technical folder that is in the support folder (My Pages > support> technical > numbers.html). In that case, the hypertext link would need to look like this:

```
<A HREF="support/technical/numbers.html">
```

Linking to a File in a Parent Folder

Linking back up, from a child folder to a parent folder, gets a little trickier. For instance, assume that you want to create a link in your catalog page (My Pages > products > catalog.html) to your home page (My Pages > index.html). In that case, the hypertext link would need to look like this:

```
<A HREF="../index.html">
```

Notice the two dots and the forward slash (../). In UNIX, this refers to a parent folder of the current folder. So this URL tells the browser to step up one level (to the parent folder of the linking file's folder), and then to open `index.html`.

Linking to a File in a Grandparent Folder

What if you want to link back up to a file stored in a parent of the parent of the linking file's folder? For instance, suppose you want to create a link in your page of support numbers (My Pages > support > technical > numbers.html) that links back to your home page (My Pages > index.html). In that case, the link would need to look like this:

```
<A HREF="../../index.html">
```

In other words, for each level you want to step back up, you just insert two dots and a forward slash (../).

Linking to a File in a Sibling Folder

What about linking between files located in separate child folders of the same parent folder? Assume, for instance, that you want to add a link to your product catalog page (My Pages > products > catalog.html) that links to an FAQ (*Frequently Asked Questions*) page, faq.html, that you've saved in the support folder (My pages > support > faq.html). That requires stepping up one level (to the parent folder) and then stepping back down one level (to the sibling folder). To do this, the link would need to look like this:

```
<A HREF="../support/faq.html">
```

Linking to a File in a Child Folder of a Sibling Folder

What if you want to link to a file located in a child folder of a sibling folder (that is, to a nephew or niece folder)? Assume, for instance, that you want to create a link in your product catalog page (My Pages > products > catalog.html) to a page of technical support numbers, numbers.html, that you've saved in the technical folder (My Pages > support > technical > numbers.html). In that case, the link would need to look like this:

```
<A HREF="../support/technical/numbers.html">
```

Now, assume that you want to make a link in the other direction, from numbers.html (in My Pages > support > technical) to catalog.html (in My Pages > products). That link would need to look like this:

```
<A HREF="../../products/catalog.html">
```

Here you're actually stepping back up two levels (../../) on the tree, and then walking down another branch (the products folder).

TIP When creating subfolders in a multi-folder Web site, you should avoid using any upper-case letters in your folder or file names. This is because file and folder names on UNIX servers are case-sensitive. If you make a habit of always using lowercase letters in file and folder names that are part of your Web site, you'll run into a lot fewer problems if you later transfer your Web site up onto a UNIX server. You must also eliminate any spaces in your Web site's file and folder names (you can substitute underscores (_) in their place, if you wish).

Wrapping Up

If you've made it this far, you're doing well. As I mentioned at the start of this session, you didn't need to complete this tutorial to plan and create your first Web page tomorrow. So, if you've been able to complete all or part of this tutorial, congrats!

If you are not completely exhausted and want to learn even *more* HTML, you can do the Tables Tutorial that I've scheduled as a bonus session for tonight. If your eyes are ready to fall out of their sockets, however, feel free to come back and do the Tables Tutorial at a later date. As with the Intermediate HTML Tutorial, you don't need to do it to be able to plan and create your first Web page tomorrow.

But don't burn the midnight oil! You're going to need a good night's sleep, because I've got lots more scheduled for you tomorrow when you'll be planning and creating your first Web page.

SATURDAY EVENING

The Tables Tutorial

(BONUS SESSION)

- ✿ Defining columns and rows
- ✿ Controlling borders and spacing
- ✿ Spanning columns and rows
- ✿ Using background colors and images
- ✿ Creating icon link lists using tables

One of the weaknesses of HTML 2.0 was its inability to display information or data in a tabular format, except by including it as raw text (spaces included) inside a PRE (Preformatted Text) element—a solution that, although highly practical, was rather bland, at best. Originally a proposed HTML 3.0 feature, tables have since been included in HTML 3.2. A few additional tags specifically designed for working with tables have also been included in HTML 4.0.

Just because tables were not included in the Intermediate HTML Tutorial, don't think they're an "advanced" HTML feature. Although you'll need to invest some time in learning how tables work and what they can do for you, they're nothing the average user can't master in a relatively short period of time.

This tutorial should take less time to complete than the Basic and Intermediate HTML Tutorials. You should be able to complete it in one to two hours. If you run short on time, feel free to leave any unfinished portion of the tutorial until another day.

NOTE If you've not yet completed the Intermediate HTML Tutorial scheduled for Saturday afternoon, you should finish it before attempting to do the Tables Tutorial.

This tutorial uses two example graphics files that have already been used in previous tutorials. No other example files are required. If the example graphics files have worked properly in the Basic and Intermediate HTML Tutorials, then you're all ready to use them in this tutorial.

If you haven't installed the example files, return to "Installing the Example Files" at the start of the Saturday Morning session and do so now before trying to do this tutorial.

In doing this tutorial, you'll be creating two tables. In the first, you'll learn all the standard HTML 3.2 table tags, along with a couple of the new HTML 4.0 table tags. I'll even show you how to apply some styles to your table. With each new example, you'll just modify the same table you're creating—no need to create a separate table for each example. In the second table, you'll learn how to create a 3-D icon bullet list using tables so that you have no limit on the number of indented lines following the bullet.

Feel free to save your file after each example and hop over to your Web browser to see what it looks like.

TIP   With the example files you copied from the CD-ROM, you'll find a file, **tutor3.htm**, that shows all the examples covered in this tutorial as separate tables. Don't bother to copy and paste each example as a separate table. Instead, make all changes in a single file and use **tutor3.htm** for future reference on how to implement each feature.

Getting Started

All of the example files used in this tutorial were installed with the tutorial example files that you installed for the Basic HTML Tutorial. You don't need to install anything extra to do this tutorial.

For this tutorial you'll need to use at least an HTML 3.2-compliant Web browser. At minimum, you should use Netscape Navigator 2.0 or greater or Microsoft Internet Explorer 3.0 or greater. You can also use the Opera or NeoPlanet browsers, which are included on the CD-ROM. To preview the HTML 4.0 sections of this tutorial, you'll need to use Internet Explorer 4.0+ because no current version of Navigator supports the HTML 4.0 table tags yet. I've tested this tutorial with the release versions of Navigator 4.7 and Internet Explorer 5.0.

I recommend that you use Windows Notepad to do this tutorial. If you're using Windows 95, just remember to turn on Word Wrap when you run Notepad—just select Edit, Word Wrap. (The Windows 98 version of Notepad will leave Word Wrap turned on until you turn it off.)

Loading Your Starting Template

Load the starting template (start.htm) that you saved in the Basic HTML Tutorial. You should be able to find it in C:\HTML, unless you've saved it somewhere else. It should look like the following listing (if you didn't save the template, just retype it now):

```
<HTML>
<HEAD>
<TITLE>Your Title: Describe Your Title</TITLE>
</HEAD>
<BODY>
</BODY>
</HTML>
```

NOTE If you substituted a TITLE element of your own for "Your Title: Describe Your Title," don't worry if your version of **start.htm** differs in this regard. Otherwise, your **start.htm** should look like my example.

Saving Your Scratch Pad File

Save your scratch pad file that you'll be using in this evening's tutorial. In Notepad, select File, Save As. Change the folder where you are going to save your file to C:\HTML, then save your file as scratch3.htm.

Starting Your Table

The TABLE tag needs to bracket your table. All other tags or text to be included in your table should be nested inside the TABLE tag. Enter the following HTML nested in the BODY tag:

```
<BODY>
<P>
<TABLE>
</TABLE>
</P>
</BODY>
```

NOTE   Because the TABLE tag is not a block element but rather an inline element (like the IMG tag, for instance), you should always nest the TABLE tag inside a block element (such as the P tag, for instance).

Defining Columns and Rows

You can use the TR (Table Row) and TD (Table Data) tags to create a grid of rows and columns. Here's an example (see Figure 4.1 for an example of what this will look like in your Web browser):

```
<TABLE>
<TR><TD>1A</TD><TD>1B</TD><TD>1C</TD><TD>1D</TD></TR>
<TR><TD>2A</TD><TD>2B</TD><TD>2C</TD><TD>2D</TD></TR>
</TABLE>
```

Notice that a <TR> start tag and a </TR> end tag bracket each row.

Figure 4.1

A table can consist of columns and rows.

Adding and Controlling Borders

A table hardly looks like a table without a border. Including a BORDER attribute inside the TABLE tag does the trick. Here's an example (see Figure 4.2):

```
<TABLE BORDER="1">
<TR><TD>1A</TD><TD>1B</TD><TD>1C</TD><TD>1D</TD></TR>
```

HTML 3.2 also recognizes the BORDER attribute by itself, whereas HTML 4.0 recognizes the BORDER="border" attribute value. Both of these should have exactly the same result as BORDER="1".

Increasing the value of the BORDER attribute has a result you might not expect. It increases the thickness of the outer border of the table, displaying it in 3-D relief; however, it doesn't affect the appearance of the interior lines of the table. Increase the BORDER value to 6 pixels (see Figure 4.3):

```
<TABLE BORDER="6">
<TR><TD>1A</TD><TD>1B</TD><TD>1C</TD><TD>1D</TD></TR>
```

Figure 4.2

You can add borders to a table.

Figure 4.3

Table borders go
3-D when you
boost their
thickness.

Setting Spacing and Padding

Your table looks a bit cramped, don't you think? The CELLSPACING
attribute adds space between cells, whereas the CELLPADDING attribute
adds space within each cell. Add 6 pixels of spacing and padding, like this
(see Figure 4.4):

```
<TABLE BORDER="6" CELLSPACING="6" CELLPADDING="6">
<TR><TD>1A</TD><TD>1B</TD><TD>1C</TD><TD>1D</TD></TR>
```

Adding Column Headings

What's a table without column headings, right? The TH (Table Heading)
tag works just like the TD tag, except it defines a particular cell as a heading cell rather than as an ordinary data cell. To create a row of four column headings at the top of your table, use the TR tag to define a row;
then, instead of using TD tags, insert TH tags to define the cells, like this
(see Figure 4.5):

Figure 4.4

You can add space
between cells and
padding within
cells.

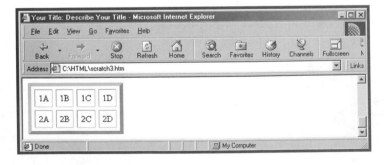

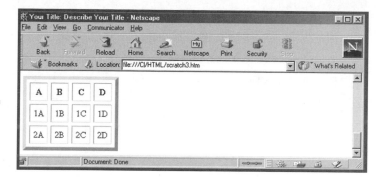

Figure 4.5

Table headings are automatically bolded and centered.

```
<TABLE BORDER="6" CELLSPACING="6" CELLPADDING="6">
<TR><TH>A</TH><TH>B</TH><TH>C</TH><TH>D</TH></TR>
<TR><TD>1A</TD><TD>1B</TD><TD>1C</TD><TD>1D</TD></TR>
```

You'll notice when you view this in your browser that column headings are automatically displayed bolded and centered.

Adding a Caption

The CAPTION tag allows you to specify a caption for your table (see Figure 4.6):

```
<TABLE BORDER="6" CELLSPACING="6" CELLPADDING="6">
<CAPTION>I. Table Example</CAPTION>
```

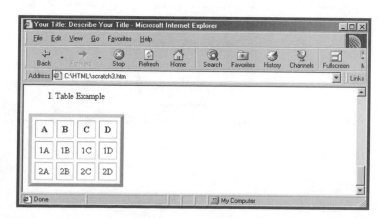

Figure 4.6

You can add a caption to a table.

You can display the caption below the table by setting an `ALIGN="bottom"` attribute value in the CAPTION tag. The HTML 4.0 specifications state that you should also be able to use `ALIGN="left"` or `ALIGN="right"` to display the caption either to the left or right of the table; however, no browser currently supports this. Internet Explorer 4.x/5.x will left-align or right-align the caption above the table, but Navigator 4.x completely ignores these attribute values.

Centering a Table

To center the table, just insert an `ALIGN="center"` attribute value in the TABLE tag (see Figure 4.7):

```
<TABLE ALIGN="center" BORDER="6" CELLSPACING="6" CELLPADDING="6">
<CAPTION>I. Table Example</CAPTION>
```

Alternatively, you can get exactly the same result by nesting your table inside a CENTER tag, a center-aligned paragraph, or a center-aligned DIV tag. To indent your table rather than center it, just nest it inside a BLOCKQUOTE tag.

Figure 4.7

You can center a table by inserting the `ALIGN="center"` attribute value in the TABLE tag.

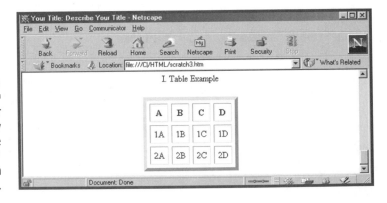

TIP Tables are not block elements but rather inline elements that function on a Web page in a similar fashion to how inline images created with the IMG tag function. Just as with inline images, you can flow text around a table by inserting an **ALIGN="left"** or **ALIGN="right"** attribute value in the TABLE tag. **ALIGN="left"** will flow text around the right side of a table, whereas **ALIGN="right"** will flow text around the left side of a table. Not only can you flow text around a table, but you can flow any other element as well, including even another table. Don't get sidetracked trying to actually do this right now, but if you want to check out how it works, an example of two tables flowing around each other is included in **tutor3.htm**. Just pull it up into your browser to check it out (see Figure 4.8); to check out the codes, just open it in Notepad. Unlike with inline images, however, you cannot flow text or other elements between two tables.

Navigator recognizes the HSPACE and VSPACE attributes in the TABLE tag, but Internet Explorer doesn't. One trick you can use that will achieve about the same result is to nest one table, with borders turned on, inside of another table, a single-cell table with borders turned off. In the second table, with the borders turned off, just insert a CELL-PADDING attribute in the TABLE tag to set an invisible space around the first (nested) table. To wrap text or other elements around your nested table, be sure the ALIGN attribute (left or right) is inserted in the TABLE tag of the outside table (not the inside, or nested, table).

Figure 4.8

You can display two tables side by side by using the ALIGN="left" and ALIGN="right" attribute values.

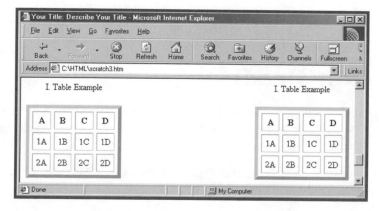

Setting Table Width and Height

You can include WIDTH and HEIGHT attributes to specify the size of your table. You can use either absolute values (number of pixels) or relative values (percentages). Specify a width of 75 percent, like this (see Figure 4.9):

```
<TABLE ALIGN="center" BORDER="6" CELLSPACING="6" CELLPADDING="6"
WIDTH="75%">
<CAPTION>I. Table Example</CAPTION>
```

You can also set the HEIGHT attribute in the TABLE tag, although it's generally less useful than setting the WIDTH attribute. You can use this technique to increase the row heights in a table by setting an absolute value (number of pixels) for the height of the table that is greater than the normal height.

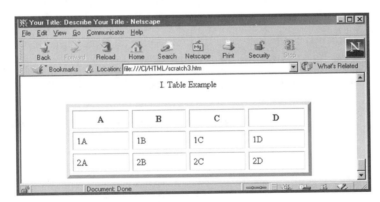

Figure 4.9

You can set the width of a table to a percentage (here, 75 percent) of a browser window.

Adding Row Headings

Now you can add some row headings. To create a row heading, just add a TH cell (instead of a TD cell) at the start of a table row, like this (see Figure 4.10):

```
<TABLE ALIGN="center" BORDER="6" CELLSPACING="6" CELLPADDING="6"
WIDTH="75%">
```

```
<CAPTION>I. Table Example</CAPTION>
<TR><TH></TH><TH>A</TH><TH>B</TH><TH>C</TH><TH>D</TH></TR>
<TR><TH>Row
1:</TH><TD>1A</TD><TD>1B</TD><TD>1C</TD><TD>1D</TD></TR>
<TR><TH>Row
2:</TH><TD>2A</TD><TD>2B</TD><TD>2C</TD><TD>2D</TD></TR>
</TABLE>
```

You'll notice when you view this in your browser that row headings are formatted just like column headings—centered and bolded.

Horizontally Aligning Cell Contents

Right now, the text in the data cells is left-aligned. Use the ALIGN attribute to right-align the two rows of data cells, like this (see Figure 4.11):

```
<CAPTION>I. Table Example</CAPTION>
<TR><TH></TH><TH>A</TH><TH>B</TH><TH>C</TH><TH>D</TH></TR>
<TR ALIGN="right"><TH>Row
1:</TH><TD>1A</TD><TD>1B</TD><TD>1C</TD><TD>1D</TD></TR>
<TR ALIGN="right"><TH>Row
2:</TH><TD>2A</TD><TD>2B</TD><TD>2C</TD><TD>2D</TD></TR>
```

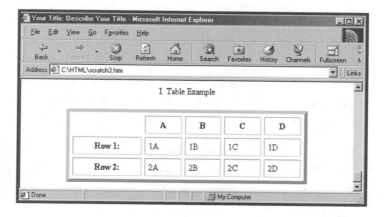

Figure 4.10

You can also add row headings to a table.

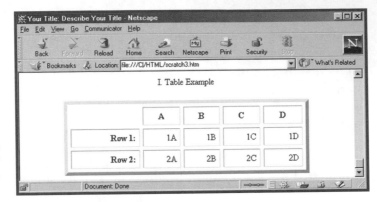

> **TIP** Besides using the ALIGN attribute in TR tags to horizontally align table rows, you can use it in TD and TH tags to horizontally align individual table cells.

Setting Column Widths

By inserting a WIDTH attribute in the top cell of a column, you can specify the width of the entire column. Column widths can be set in either percentages or pixels.

The columns of your table are fairly equal in width. Only the first column, where the row-header cells are, is somewhat wider than the other columns. A browser will expand or contract the columns depending on their contents (that's why the first column is wider, because its contents take up more horizontal space). In other words, you can't depend on any column remaining the same width once you've started to fill it in with real data.

Because the table has five columns, set each column to an equal width by inserting a WIDTH="20%" attribute in each of the TH tags in the top row of the table (see Figure 4.12):

```
<CAPTION>I. Table Example</CAPTION>
<TR><TH WIDTH="20%"></TH><TH WIDTH="20%">A</TH><TH
WIDTH="20%">B</TH><TH WIDTH="20%">C</TH><TH
WIDTH="20%">D</TH></TR>
```

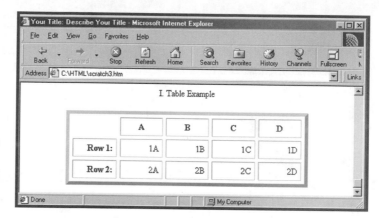

Figure 4.12

Each column of the table has been set to a width of 20 percent.

The percentage for setting equal column widths will depend on the total number of columns. If your table has six columns, you would set each to 16% (100 divided by 6).

Column widths set in percentages will expand or contract depending on the width of the browser window. Column widths set in pixels will remain the same width, regardless of the browser window width. Nothing stops you from setting the first column of a table in pixels and the remaining columns in percentages, the other way around, or in any other combination you want. However, if you do set all the columns to a fixed width using pixels, you should not set a percentage width in the TABLE tag.

Inserting an Image

You can insert an image inside a table cell. For this example, you'll be using a graphic, `one.gif`, that is included with the example graphics. Enter the following to insert an image inside the upper-left corner cell of your table (see Figure 4.13):

```
<CAPTION>I. Table Example</CAPTION>

<TR><TH WIDTH="20%"><IMG SRC="one.gif"></TH><TH
WIDTH="20%">A</TH><TH WIDTH="20%">B</TH><TH WIDTH="20%">C</TH><TH
WIDTH="20%">D</TH></TR>
```

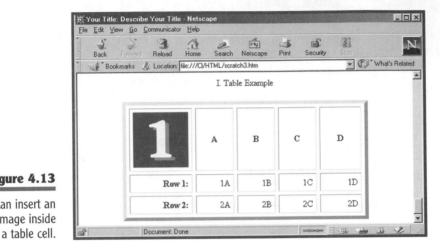

Figure 4.13

You can insert an
inline image inside
a table cell.

Vertically Aligning Cell Contents

You can also vertically align the contents of a table row (TR), a table heading (TH), or a table data cell (TD). `VALIGN="top"` will set top alignment, and `VALIGN="bottom"` will set bottom alignment (middle alignment is the default). Set the top row to be bottom-aligned (see Figure 4.14):

```
<CAPTION>I. Table Example</CAPTION>

<TR VALIGN="bottom"><TH WIDTH="20%"><IMG SRC="one.gif"></TH><TH
WIDTH="20%">A</TH><TH WIDTH="20%">B</TH><TH WIDTH="20%">C</TH><TH
WIDTH="20%">D</TH></TR>
```

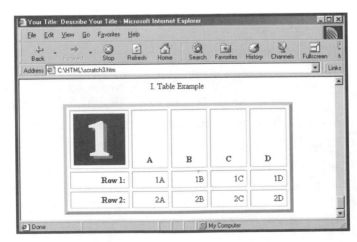

Figure 4.14

You can vertically
align cell contents.

Spanning Columns

The COLSPAN attribute lets you create cells that span across columns. Add a row to your table that includes three table head cells, the last two of which span across two columns each (see Figure 4.15):

```
<TR><TH VALIGN="bottom" WIDTH="20%"><IMG SRC="one.gif"></TH><TH
WIDTH="20%">A</TH><TH WIDTH="20%">B</TH><TH WIDTH="20%">C</TH><TH
WIDTH="20%">D</TH></TR>
```

```
<TR><TH></TH><TH COLSPAN="2">A & B</TH><TH COLSPAN="2">C &
D</TH></TR>
```

```
<TR><TH ALIGN="right">Row
1:</TH><TD>1A</TD><TD>1B</TD><TD>1C</TD><TD>1D</TD></TR>
```

To span additional columns, specify the number with the COLSPAN attribute. Just make sure you don't exceed the total number of columns in the table. For instance, this example amounts to three cells spanning five columns (1 + 2 + 2 = 5).

Spanning Rows

You can use the ROWSPAN attribute to span rows. This can be a little tricky because you need to remove any spanned cells from any following

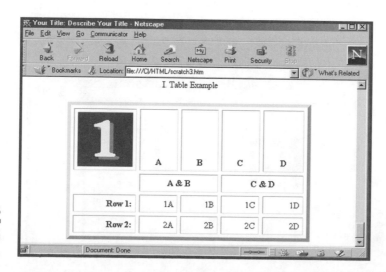

Figure 4.15

Table cells can span columns.

rows included in the span. Enter the following example (the cell you need to delete is struck through):

```
<CAPTION>I. Table Example</CAPTION>
<TR VALIGN="bottom"><TH ROWSPAN="2" WIDTH="20%"><IMG
SRC="one.gif"></TH><TH WIDTH="20%">A</TH><TH
WIDTH="20%">B</TH><TH WIDTH="20%">C</TH><TH
WIDTH="20%">D</TH></TR>
<TR><TH></TH><TH COLSPAN="2">A & B</TH><TH COLSPAN="2">C &
D</TH></TR>
```

As Figure 4.16 shows, the cell with the graphic of the number 1 in it now spans two rows.

Changing Font Sizes and Colors

You can change the font size and color of the contents of a table cell by inserting a FONT tag bracketing the text you want to be affected. The following example sets the font size to 7 and the color to blue for one of the cells (see Figure 4.17):

```
<CAPTION>I. Table Example</CAPTION>
<TR><TH ROWSPAN="2" WIDTH="20%"><IMG SRC="one.gif"></TH><TH
WIDTH="20%"><FONT SIZE="7" COLOR="blue">A</FONT></TH><TH
WIDTH="20%">B</TH><TH WIDTH="20%">C</TH><TH
WIDTH="20%">D</TH></TR>
```

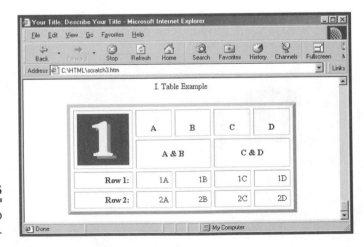

Figure 4.16

Table cells can also span rows.

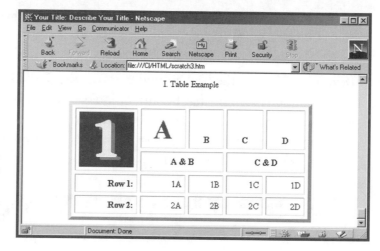

Figure 4.17

You can assign different font sizes and colors to text inside table cells.

Assigning Background Colors

You can assign a background color to an entire table, a row within a table, or a single cell. For instance, a table can be made more readable by assigning different background colors to distinguish row-heading cells and table-data cells.

Assigning a Background Color in the TABLE Tag

Navigator and Internet Explorer do not handle assigning a background color to an entire table in the same fashion. In fact, the most recent version of Internet Explorer doesn't even handle this the way earlier versions of Internet Explorer did. Navigator displays the background color only in the table's cells, not in the borders between the cells. Internet Explorer fills in the borders with the background color. Earlier versions of Internet Explorer also fill in a table caption with the background color. In other words, if you want to ensure your table is displayed at least similarly in both of these browsers, you should probably avoid setting a background color in the TABLE tag altogether. To see what it does, use the BGCOLOR attribute to set a background color in the TABLE tag (see Figures 4.18 and 4.19):

```
<TABLE BGCOLOR="aqua" ALIGN="center" BORDER="6" CELLSPACING="6"
CELLPADDING="6" WIDTH="75%">
<CAPTION>I. Table Example</CAPTION>
```

If you want to set the background color in the TABLE tag, that's okay.
However, don't assume that because it looks one way in Internet Explorer it's going to look the same way in Navigator or vice versa. If you want your table to look the same in both browsers, you should set background colors in the TR, TH, and TD tags, as shown next.

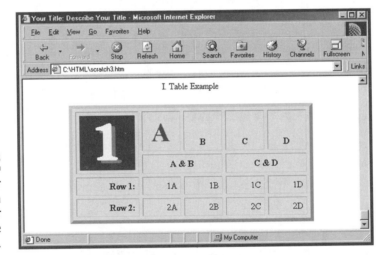

Figure 4.18

Internet Explorer displays a background color behind the whole table.

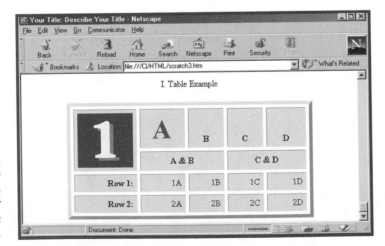

Figure 4.19

Navigator displays a background color only within the table's cells.

Assigning a Background Color in the TR, TH, and TD Tags

You can assign background colors to individual table rows (TR tags), as well as to individual table-heading (TH) and table-data (TD) cells. The following code will assign a lime color to the top row, red to the top-left TH cell (the one with the image in it), olive to the second row, and yellow to the bottom two rows (notice that BGCOLOR="aqua" should be deleted):

```
<TABLE BGCOLOR="aqua" ALIGN="center" BORDER="6" CELLSPACING="6"
CELLPADDING="6" WIDTH="75%">

<CAPTION>I. Table Example</CAPTION>

<TR BGCOLOR="lime"><TH BGCOLOR="red" WIDTH="20%" ROWSPAN="2"><IMG
SRC="one.gif"></TH><TH WIDTH="20%"><FONT SIZE="7"
COLOR="blue">A</FONT></TH><TH WIDTH="20%">B</TH><TH
WIDTH="20%">C</TH><TH WIDTH="20%">D</TH></TR>

<TR BGCOLOR="olive"><TH COLSPAN="2">A & B</TH><TH COLSPAN="2">C &
D</TH></TR>

<TR BGCOLOR="yellow"><TH ALIGN="right">Row
1:</TH><TD>1A</TD><TD>1B</TD><TD>1C</TD><TD>1D</TD></TR>

<TR BGCOLOR="yellow"><TH ALIGN="right">Row
2:</TH><TD>2A</TD><TD>2B</TD><TD>2C</TD><TD>2D</TD></TR>
```

As shown in Figure 4.20, different background colors appear behind one of the table cells, as well as behind the top, the second, and the last two table rows. You'll need to hop over to your Web browser, though, to really see what this looks like.

Removing Borders and Cell Spacing

You might think that you can get rid of the spacing and borders between cells just by removing the BORDER and CELLSPACING attributes in the TABLE tag. Not so. To get rid of them completely, you have to set these attribute values to zero, like this (see Figure 4.21):

```
<TABLE ALIGN="center" BORDER="0" CELLSPACING="0" CELLPADDING="6"
WIDTH="75%">

<CAPTION>I. Table Example</CAPTION>
```

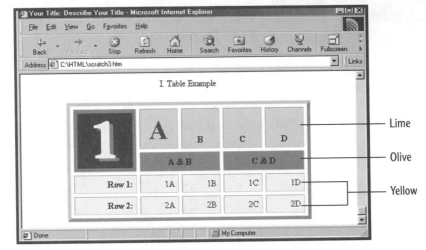

Figure 4.20

You can set different background colors for rows or individual cells.

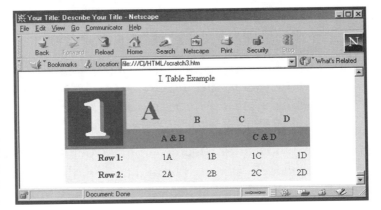

Figure 4.21

You have to set the BORDER and CELLSPACING values to zero to completely get rid of the borders and spacing between cells.

Using Background Images

You can also use background images in tables via the BACKGROUND attribute. However, this gets just a bit tricky because Navigator and Internet Explorer don't work the same way:

❖ As was the case with a background color, Internet Explorer displays a background image set in the TABLE tag behind the entire table, including behind the cell spacing. Navigator puts it only behind the individual cells.

✿ Internet Explorer does not recognize background images specified in the TR tag, but Navigator does. To specify a background image for a table row that will show up in both browsers, you need to specify it for each individual cell (TH or TD) in the row.

✿ In Navigator, a background image specified in the TABLE tag takes precedence over any background colors set in the rows, heading cells, or data cells; but in Internet Explorer, it's the other way around. Therefore, if you want to specify a background image in the TABLE tag that will display identically in both browsers, get rid of any BGCOLOR attributes elsewhere in the table.

The BACKGROUND attribute for the table tags is actually not a standard HTML attribute (in either HTML 3.2 or 4.0), unlike the BGCOLOR attribute (most likely because of the wide variance between how the two main browsers interpret it). Still, background images in tables can give a very nice effect, so I wouldn't necessarily avoid using this attribute just because it doesn't have the official stamp of approval yet. Just be careful how you use it, as detailed above. To check out what a BACKGROUND attribute set in the TABLE tag looks like, specify a background image in the TABLE tag, reset the BORDER and CELLSPACING attributes as shown, and delete any BGCOLOR attributes, like this (see Figures 4.22 and 4.23):

```
<TABLE BACKGROUND="backgrnd.gif" ALIGN="center" BORDER="6"
CELLSPACING="6" CELLPADDING="6" WIDTH="75%">

<CAPTION>I. Table Example</CAPTION>

<TR BGCOLOR="lime" VALIGN="bottom"><TH BGCOLOR="red" ROWSPAN="2"
WIDTH="20%"><IMG SRC="one.gif"></TH><TH WIDTH="20%"><FONT
SIZE="7" COLOR="blue">A</FONT></TH><TH WIDTH="20%">B</TH><TH
WIDTH="20%">C</TH><TH WIDTH="20%">D</TH></TR>

<TR BGCOLOR="olive"><TH COLSPAN="2">A & B</TH><TH COLSPAN="2">C &
D</TH></TR>

<TR BGCOLOR="yellow" ALIGN="right"><TH>Row
1:</TH><TD>1A</TD><TD>1B</TD><TD>1C</TD><TD>1D</TD></TR>

<TR BGCOLOR="yellow" ALIGN="right"><TH ALIGN="right">Row
2:</TH><TD>2A</TD><TD>2B</TD><TD>2C</TD><TD>2D</TD></TR>

</TABLE>
```

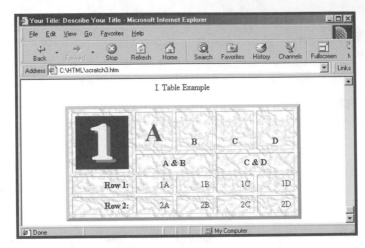

Figure 4.22

A background image in Internet Explorer is displayed behind the whole table.

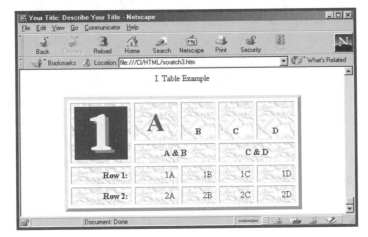

Figure 4.23

A background image in Navigator is displayed only behind the table cells.

Take a Break?

Wow, if you've been at it all day, you're definitely a long-distance runner! If your eyelids are drooping and your fingers cramping up, feel free to call it a night—I'll see you bright and early tomorrow morning, when you'll start planning your first Web page. You can always come back later to complete this tutorial. However, if you're not entirely out of breath, take a breather, if you want, and I'll see you back here in ten minutes or so, when you'll learn to use the new HTML 4.0 table tags and create fancy 3-D icon bullet link lists using tables.

Defining Table Head, Body, and Foot Sections

The HTML 4.0 tags covered in this section are currently supported in only Internet Explorer 4.x/5.x. If you're using Netscape Navigator as your Web browser, feel free to skip ahead to the next section.

HTML 4.0 has three new table tags: THEAD, TBODY, and TFOOT. You can use them to define different sets of rows as the head, body, and foot of your table. Actually, by themselves, these tags do absolutely nothing. To get them to strut their stuff, you have to define a style sheet that will specify how the sections of the table nested in these tags are to be displayed.

NOTE THEAD, TBODY, and TFOOT are supported only by Internet Explorer, version 4.0 or greater. No version of Netscape Navigator recognizes these tags.

Defining the Style Sheet

FIND IT ON ▶
THE WEB

The following sample style sheet will give you some idea of the possibilities. To find out where you can learn more about using style sheets, see my Web Links site at **www.callihan.com/weblinks/**—just click on Features, and then on Styles, in the sidebar menu. To create the style sheet, nest the following code in the HEAD element:

```
<HTML>
<HEAD>
<TITLE>The Table Tutorial</TITLE>
<STYLE type="text/css">
<! —
THEAD {font-family: sans-serif; font-style: bold; font-size:
200%; color: maroon; background-color: yellow}
TBODY {font-family: monospace; font-style: bold; font-size: 125%;
color: navy; background-color: aqua}
TFOOT {font-family: sans-serif; font-style: italic; color: white;
background-color: #FF8000}
 — >
```

```
</STYLE>
</HEAD>
```

TIP You can also include the style sheet codes in a linked style sheet. Just save the codes in your style sheet (from THEAD to TFOOT) as a text file, **table.css**, in C:\HTML. Then replace the whole STYLE tag with this:

```
<LINK rel=stylesheet HREF="table.css" TYPE="text/css">
```

You should realize, however, that a bug in Netscape Navigator 4.0+ causes it not to recognize a linked style sheet that is not in the same folder as the HTML file linking to it.

Using TBODY as the Default

If no THEAD or TFOOT sections are included in a table, the TBODY start and end tags may be omitted. In this case, all you have to do is define TBODY in your style sheet to have its properties automatically applied to your table.

As shown in Figure 4.24, the TBODY properties defined in the style sheet (here a bold, monospaced font set to navy and scaled up 125 percent in size) are applied to the entire table, even though the TBODY tag has been omitted.

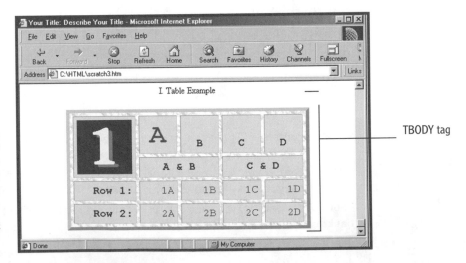

Figure 4.24

TBODY style properties will be applied to the whole table, even though THEAD, TFOOT, and TBODY are absent.

Actually, this beats using the FONT tag to assign font colors within a table, which you have to set within *every* cell where you want it to take effect. That's a bit laborious, in other words, if all you want to do is reset the font size and color for all the cells. (Too bad this only works in Internet Explorer 4.0+.)

Using THEAD, TBODY, and TFOOT Together

To have one or more rows in your table show up with the properties defined in the style sheet, just nest them in the THEAD, TBODY, or TFOOT tags. The following example nests the first two rows inside the THEAD tag and the second two rows inside the TBODY tag; a fifth row has also been added and nested inside of the TFOOT tag. Just add the THEAD, TBODY, and TFOOT tags, as shown (see Figure 4.25):

```
<TABLE BACKGROUND="backgrnd.gif" ALIGN="center" BORDER="6"
CELLSPACING="6" CELLPADDING="6" WIDTH="75%">

<CAPTION>I. Table Example</CAPTION>

<THEAD>

<TR VALIGN="bottom"><TH ROWSPAN="2" WIDTH="20%"><IMG
SRC="one.gif"></TH><TH WIDTH="20%"><FONT SIZE="7"
COLOR="blue">A</FONT></TH><TH WIDTH="20%">B</TH><TH
WIDTH="20%">C</TH><TH WIDTH="20%">D</TH></TR>

<TR><TH COLSPAN="2">A & B</TH><TH COLSPAN="2">C & D</TH></TR>

</THEAD>

<TBODY>

<TR ALIGN="right"><TH>Row
1:</TH><TD>1A</TD><TD>1B</TD><TD>1C</TD><TD>1D</TD></TR>

<TR ALIGN="right"><TH ALIGN="right">Row
2:</TH><TD>2A</TD><TD>2B</TD><TD>2C</TD><TD>2D</TD></TR>

</TBODY>

<TFOOT>

<TR><TD COLSPAN="5" ALIGN="center">This is the table
foot.</TD></TR>

</TFOOT>

</TABLE>
```

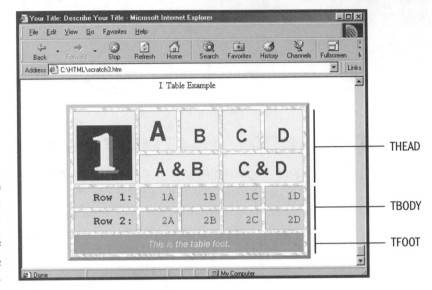

Figure 4.25

You can define styles that will render the head, body, and foot of your table in the format you prefer.

TIP

You can define as many TBODY sections as you want within a table. The only requirement is that a TBODY section must have at least one table row in it. (You should not define more than one THEAD or TFOOT section, however.)

Other HTML 4.0 Table Tags

The FRAME, RULES, COLGROUP, COL, and CHAR tags have been added to HTML 4.0. Of these, only the FRAME and RULES tags are supported, by Internet Explorer 4.0+. Navigator doesn't yet support any of these tags. The COLGROUP and COL tags allow you to specify formatting for column groups and individual columns, somewhat similar to how the TBODY, THEAD, and TFOOT tags specify formatting for rows or row sections. The CHAR tag, in conjunction with the COLGROUP or COL tags, allows vertical alignment within a column on a decimal point, which would definitely be a handy feature. Internet Explorer also supports other table tags—BORDERCOLOR, BORDER-COLORDARK, and BORDERCOLORLIGHT—that have not yet been included in HTML 3.2 or 4.0.

Saving Your Work

Save the HTML file you just created. You can use it later as a reference. When you first saved it, you named it `scratch3.htm`. If more than one person is going to be doing this tutorial and you want to make sure it doesn't get overwritten, you might want to give it a new name; you could use your initials in the file name (`jm-scratch3.htm`, if your name is Judy Monroe or Jimmy Mack, for instance). Once you've saved your scratch pad file, exit Notepad.

For your reference, a file, `tutor3.htm`, has been included with the example files that you installed from the CD-ROM. It includes all the previous code examples broken out into separate tables, so you can have a reference for each of the features covered here. Feel free to pull it up into Notepad or check it out in your browser.

Creating Icon Link Lists Using Tables

In the Intermediate HTML Tutorial, I showed you how to create indented icon link lists using left-aligned bullet images. That method works fine, except it was limited to indenting only two lines of text. In the following exercise, I'll show you how to create an indented icon link list using tables. Though this method is perhaps a bit more difficult to implement than using left-aligned bullet images, the lack of limitation on the number of indented lines compensates for it.

Loading Your Starting Template

You should start here with a fresh Notepad window. Restart Notepad to get a new empty Notepad window; then load the starting template you saved this morning, `start.htm` in C:\HTML. It should look like the following (if you didn't save the template, just retype it now):

```
<HTML>
<HEAD>
<TITLE>Your Title: Describe Your Title<'TITLE>
</HEAD>
```

```
<BODY>
</BODY>
</HTML>
```

Saving Your Scratch Pad File

Save your scratch pad file you'll be using in this brief lesson. In Notepad, select File, Save As. Change the folder where you're going to save your file to C:\HTML and then save your file as `scratch4.html`.

Creating the Icon Link List

In the following example, I've used the same hypertext links and link descriptions that you used in the Basic HTML Tutorial and the Intermediate HTML Tutorial. Feel free to copy and paste these from either `scratch.htm` or `scratch2.htm` (if that's what you named your scratch pad files for those two tutorials).

To create an icon bullet link list using tables, enter the following HTML (see Figure 4.26):

```
<BODY>
<TABLE WIDTH=100%>
<TR VALIGN="top">
<TD WIDTH="20"><P><IMG SRC="redball.gif" VSPACE="3"> </TD><TD><A
HREF="http://pages.nyu.edu/~tqm3413/yoyo/index.htm">Tomer's Page
of Exotic Yo-Yo</A> Dedicated to the "little-known, original,
unusual, difficult, or otherwise interesting tricks." This is one
of the more entertaining and fun Yo-Yo sites you can find on the
Web.</TD></TR>
<TR VALIGN="top">
<TD><P><IMG SRC="redball.gif" VSPACE="3"> </TD><TD><A
HREF="http://www.socool.com/socool/yo-yo.html">Just Say YO!!!</A>
Features the Web's first Yo-Yo animation.</TD></TR>
<TR VALIGN="top">
<TD WIDTH="20"><P><IMG SRC="redball.gif" VSPACE="3"> </TD><TD><A
HREF="http://www.pd.net/yoyo/">American Yo-Yo Association</A>
Read past issues of the AYYA Newsletter.</TD></TR>
```

```
<TR VALIGN="top">
<TD><P><IMG SRC="redball.gif" VSPACE="3"> </TD><TD><A
HREF="http://www.socool.com/socool/yo_hist.html">The History of
the Yo-Yo</A> All you want to know about Yo-Yo
history.</TD></TR>
</TABLE>
```

In this example of creating an indented icon link list using tables, you should pay attention to a number of things:

○ The TR tags include VALIGN="top" to set the vertical alignment. Without this, the icon bullet images would be middle-aligned, which is not what you want. You could also set this attribute value in the TD tag containing the icon bullet graphic.

○ A WIDTH attribute value of 20 pixels is set in the first cell of the top row to specify the width of the first column. This width can be increased or decreased to suit your taste.

○ A P tag is inserted in the first cell of each row, and a space is inserted at the end of the same cell. This makes allowance for older Web browsers that don't support displaying tables. The P tag will cause a non-supporting browser to display the table row as a separate line, and the space will be inserted between the icon graphic and the following text. Note that adding the P tag and inserting the space will not affect the display of the table in a tables-capable Web browser.

Figure 4.26

Using tables, you can create an indented icon link list with no limit on the number of indented lines.

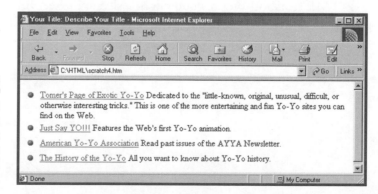

☼ The IMG tags for the icon bullet graphics include a VSPACE (vertical space) attribute of 3 pixels. Rarely will an icon bullet line up evenly with a following line of text. You can add or subtract pixels in the VSPACE attribute in the IMG tag to adjust the position of the icon bullet relative to following text.

Saving Your Work

Save the HTML file you just created. You can use it later as a reference. When you first saved it, you named it `scratch4.htm`. If more than one person is going to be doing this tutorial and you want to make sure this file doesn't get overwritten, you might want to give it a new name; you could use your first initial and last name for the file name (`jmiller4.htm`, for instance, if your name is John Miller).

Wrapping Up

You should now be comfortable including tables in your Web pages. If you completed the whole tables tutorial, you not only learned everything you need to know to create effective tables, but you also learned how to use some of the latest HTML 4.0 table tags in conjunction with a snazzy style sheet. And you also learned how to create fancy 3-D icon bullet link lists with tables.

If you managed to do all three Saturday tutorials, you're definitely a super HTML hotshot! Get a good night's sleep. I'll see you tomorrow, when you'll plan and create your first Web page.

Planning Your First Web Page

- ✿ Defining your objective
- ✿ Doing an outline
- ✿ Choosing a model
- ✿ Assembling your materials
- ✿ Creating a mock-up

Before you actually start creating your first Web page, you need to do some planning. You only have one morning for this, so what you'll be doing here is a kind of short planning session. It is intended to give you a taste of what a real planning process might be like; it is not presented as the one and only way to plan a Web page. I've broken down the planning process into a series of stages or steps that you can follow. These stages are largely practical—before you can set off on the yellow brick road, you've got to get the horse before the cart, and pointing in the right direction!

To make things easier for you, and to help you narrow down some of the possibilities, I'll provide you with three generic example Web pages. I'll ask you to select one as a guide for planning and organizing your own material. Then, this afternoon, you'll use that example Web page as a guide or template for creating your first Web page.

You won't actually be working with the Web page example files in this session, but when you get around to selecting the Web page you want to use as a model, you will want to pull them up in your browser and take a closer look at them. I'll also present screen grabs for easy reference—but paper never captures the feel of looking at a live screen. You'll want not only to see what the example pages look like, but also to check out how they work.

Installing the Example Web Pages

On the CD-ROM, I've included example Web pages, along with attendant graphic files, for you to use in this planning session, as well as in the creating session that follows this afternoon. You can use the interface on the CD-ROM to automatically install the example Web pages.

NOTE

If you don't have a CD-ROM drive, or don't have access to this book's CD-ROM, all the example Web pages and their attendant graphic files are available for download from this book's Web site at **www.callihan.com/create3/**. Just use WinZip (or any other unzipping utility) to unzip the files into the working folder (C:\MyPages) you're using to hold your Web pages.

To install the example Web pages (and create your working folder), just do the following.

1. Insert the CD-ROM in your CD-ROM drive.

2. If Prima Tech's user interface doesn't automatically run, do the following:

   a) Click on the Start button, and then select Run.

   b) In the Open text box, type *d*:\CDInstaller.exe (where *d* is your CD-ROM's drive letter), and then click on OK.

3. Read the license agreement and click on I Accept to accept its terms.

4. In the left windowpane, expand the contents (click the "+" button to the left) of Create Your First Web Page In a Weekend.

5. Expand the contents of Book Examples, and then click on Example Web Pages. Click on the Install button.

6. At the WinZip Self-Extractor window, click Unzip to unzip the example files to C:\MyPages. (Note: Do not change the Unzip to Folder content.)

7. Click on OK when the Web page example files have been unzipped, and then click on the Close button (the "x" button). To exit the CD interface, click on the Close button.

All of the Web page examples that are used in this and the following session should now be installed to a folder, C:\MyPages, on your hard drive. In planning and creating your first Web page, you'll be using this folder, rather than C:\HTML, as your working folder.

What You'll Be Doing This Morning

I've organized the planning process into a number of stages. It is important to realize that these stages are not sacrosanct but simply one approach that you can follow in planning a Web page. Here's a quick rundown on the planning stages I'll be covering:

○ **Defining an objective.** If you don't already have a pretty good idea of what you want to do, you can follow some of the brainstorming suggestions provided here to help you get pointed in the right direction.

○ **Doing an outline.** You'll break down your objective into its constituent parts, helping to define the basic structure of your page.

○ **Choosing an example Web page.** You'll choose one of the three basic example Web pages you installed earlier to use as a model for planning and creating your first Web page.

○ **Assembling your materials.** You'll pull together the materials that will compose your Web page. This can involve the following:

   ○ **Writing some text.** You'll write some text for your page, including a title, level-one heading, and an introductory paragraph.

   ○ **Gathering some URLs (optional).** You can follow one or more of the suggested techniques to gather some URLs (Web addresses) to include in a link list for your page. Optionally, you can use the sample link list included in the first example Web page.

- ✿ **Choosing or creating some graphics (optional).** You can choose or create a banner graphic for your page at this point, just to help personalize your first page. You can also choose and convert any other images you want to use (such as scanned snapshots, your company logo, and so on). Optionally, you can use the sample banner graphic as a placeholder until you create your own. (I'll be covering creating a banner graphic and other Web images in much more depth in the Sunday Evening bonus session, "The Graphics Tutorial.")

- ✿ **Creating a mock-up file.** In Notepad, you'll pull together in a single mock-up text file the elements you want to include in your Web page, placed in the rough position and order in which you want them to appear, including any text, references to any graphics, and URLs for any hypertext links.

- ✿ **Drawing a map (optional).** You don't need to do this the first time through, but when you get around to planning and creating a multiple-page Web site, this section may come in handy. Drawing a map can help you visualize not only the static structure of your site, but also the dynamic relationships that exist within and between your pages. This can be a big help in optimally organizing your site to ensure that all your pages are easily navigable and accessible from any point within your site.

What You Need to Get Started

You won't need anything special to begin planning your first Web page. You can start out working on a yellow legal pad, in your word processor, or continue to use Notepad. Work in whatever medium you feel most comfortable with.

TIP
Planning a Web page or Web site doesn't have to be a one-person affair. If you're part of a work group that wants to create a Web page or Web site, you may want to bring everybody into the act. A great way to do this is to start out working on butcher paper taped to the walls of your meeting room or on a white board.

Defining an Objective

First, you should define what you want to do. One way is to try to boil it down to an objective: the purpose of your undertaking. (This is sometimes called a mission statement, but that seems a bit too formal for this activity.)

In the following, you'll find some suggestions on how to brainstorm your objective. Even if you think you already know what you want to do, doing some brainstorming at this point can make a big difference in the quality, appropriateness, and success of your end result. *Don't assume that you already know your objective.* Even worse than thinking you know all the answers is thinking you know all the questions!

I've broken down the process of brainstorming your objective into a series of questions: Why? Who? What? and How?

NOTE
Because you have only a single morning to plan your first Web page (if you're following our schedule, that is), don't get bogged down here. As mentioned earlier, this is a short planning session for creating a single Web page and isn't intended as a full-fledged planning session for a whole Web site (which could easily take all day or even all weekend, if you want to do it right). For this session, don't take more than ten minutes on any of the brainstorming questions.

Why Do You Want to Create a Web Page?

Make a list of all the reasons you want to create a Web page. These are the factors that really motivate you to create a Web page. Don't just stop at the first answer. Try to be fairly general at this point, focusing on your motivations rather than on specific end results. For instance, you may decide that you just want to express yourself, learn and grow, or just have some fun! Or you may decide that you want to communicate, share information, get feedback, and so on about your favorite hobby, a political issue, or a social cause. Or you may want to advance your career, expand your company's markets, or network with colleagues and associates.

TASK   Come up with at least three reasons, preferably more, why you want to create a Web page. Once you have your list, prioritize it, numbering from the most to the least important.

Who Do You Want Your Page to Reach?

Think of the people you most want to reach with your page. This might be your customers, potential clients, friends and family, the public at large, professional or academic colleagues, or others sharing your same hobby, interest, or political, social, or cultural passion.

TASK   Come up with at least three groups of people you'd like your page to reach. Once you have your list, prioritize it, numbering from the most to the least important.

What End Results Do You Want Your Page to Achieve?

With the top three answers to your Why and Who questions in mind, think up as many end results as you can that will satisfy both your Why and your Who. For instance, if one of your basic motivations is just to

express yourself, spell out in more detail what you want to express through your page, keeping in mind who you want to express yourself to. For instance, you might want to display your artwork, show photos, or publish your writings to others who you think will enjoy or appreciate your efforts. If you want to advance your career, make a list of specific end results that will help achieve your goal. For instance, you might want to make contacts with others in your field or profession, describe your history and experience to potential employers or customers, demonstrate your skills and abilities to those who might want to make use of them, and so on. If you're primarily concerned with selling a product or offering a service, to accomplish that you may want to get feedback from customers or clients, help stimulate repeat business, cut down the cost of providing after-sale support, and so on.

▼ ▼

 TASK   Come up with at least three end results that you'd like your Web page to achieve. Once you have your list, prioritize it, numbering from the most to the least important.

▼ ▼

How Do You Want Your Page to Implement Your Why, Who, and What?

Here you want to think of specific ways in which your page can implement your Why, Who, and What. These should be much more specific, detailing the actual form or forms your Web page or pages might take to achieve your ends. This can be fairly simple—your own personal page so you can share your snapshots of your latest vacation with friends, relatives, and co-workers, for instance. Or an informational page on a hobby, subject of interest, or field of expertise, along with a list of links to related resources on the Web. Here are just some of the other forms that your page might take: a newsletter (to provide breaking news and information about your company or organization); a catalog of your products and prices; a brochure describing your services; a glossary of technical terms in your field; an FAQ (Frequently Asked Questions) page; a book review or academic paper; a collection of poems or a gallery of your artwork; an album of your favorite snapshots; a résumé detailing your experience and background; a genealogy page on your family history; a page of your favorite links; and so on. These are just some of the possibilities. Feel free to combine different possibilities or think up entirely new ones. If you want to take the time (not too much, though), get up on the Web and do searches at Yahoo! (**www.yahoo.com** or AltaVista **www.altavista.com**) to check out what kinds of things other people are doing with their Web pages.

TASK Come up with at least three possible ways by which your page can more specifically implement your desired objectives. Once you have your list, prioritize it, numbering from the most to the least important.

Wrapping Up Your Objective

This is the fun part. While keeping your prioritized answers to your Why, Who, What, and How questions in mind, try to boil it all down into a single statement that succinctly expresses your overall objective.

Don't spend so much time creating an objective that you end up being hesitant to change or alter it later in response to changing realities—which is why I've chosen to call it an objective here, rather than a mission statement. Don't get too hung up on formulating an absolutely final and definitive objective. Try to make it an aiming point, a working hypothesis, not a stone around your neck. Feel free to change it as you go.

Remember, right now you're only creating an objective for one page. You probably would come up with a different objective if it were for an entire Web publishing enterprise or undertaking. Tie that into the mission statement of your company, organization, or agency, and you'll probably come up with yet another objective.

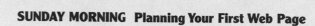

TASK

▼ ▼

Review the answers that you've prioritized to your Why, Who, What and How questions. To create your objective, write a single sentence that summarizes your answers.

▼ ▼

Doing an Outline

Whereas an objective expresses the intentions, purposes, and goals of your project as a whole, an outline organizes it into divisions and subdivisions, establishing the hierarchy and sequence of the material you want to present.

Your outline doesn't have to be complicated or even complete, but it should at least break down your objective into its basic components, even if only A, B, and C. As with your objective, your initial outline should not be carved in stone. It may not take full form, for instance, until you've further pulled together and created the actual materials that'll compose your page. Some people prefer to create an outline right off the bat. Others need to sketch out their ideas first, from which they can then distill their outline.

▼ ▼

TASK

Using your objective as the top level of your outline, break out beneath it the parts that you see as composing it. Try to arrange these in a logical order. These components define how you want to execute your objective, providing a structure for the information you're going to want to present to a viewer of your Web page. If you want, write a brief description of each component.

▼ ▼

Choosing an Example Web Page

I've placed this step here to help you visualize the Web page you are going to plan and create today. At the start of this session, you installed three example Web pages from the CD-ROM to your working folder (C:\MyPages). This afternoon, you'll be using one of these as a template or guide as you create your first Web page. This morning, you won't actually be working with the files themselves, but you should pull them up and review them in your browser. I'll also show you each Web page example in figures that you can use for easy reference while planning your Web page.

Once you become more adept at designing your own Web pages, you can skip this step. Think of the Web page examples presented here as training wheels that you can dispense with once you learn how to ride on your own. Following are the Web page examples that you can choose from:

- **A Web page using a link list.** This is the simplest of the three example Web pages. It includes a list of external links connecting to other pages out on the Web.

- **A Web page using subsections.** This example Web page is a little more complex, providing a table of contents (a *menu*) of internal links that jump to different subsections within the same page.

- **A Web site using subpages.** You should use this example Web page only after trying one of the first two. It provides a menu of external links that functions as an index to a multi-page Web site, allowing the user to jump to different subpages.

In the following sections I describe these Web page examples more fully. I've also included figures that show what these pages look like in a Web browser. Feel free, however, to open these example Web pages in your own browser to check out not only what they look like, but also how they work. Starting out, I recommend that you choose one of the first two Web page examples to use as a model for your first Web page; save the third example for when you want to create your first multi-page Web site.

▼ ▼

TASK   Read the following sections describing the three Web page examples, opening them in your Web browser to check out how they work. Select the example Web page you'd like to use as a model, leaving it open in your browser for easy reference. (For your first Web page, select either the first or second example Web page.)

▼ ▼

Example #1: A Web Page Using a Link List

This Web page example includes a banner graphic, a level-one heading, an introductory paragraph, a list, and an address block. The list can either be a list of particulars or a link list to other Web pages. An example of using this with a plain list (no links) would be to create a "business card" where you describe your business in the introductory paragraph, then follow that with a list of products, services, or qualifications. An example of a page using a link list that links to other pages on the Web would be a page that describes a hobby, professional expertise, or area of interest, followed by a list of links to other related pages on the Web. (See Figure 5.1.)

Go ahead and pull this up in your browser to get a closer look. If you copied the example Web page files at the start of this session, you should find it as `basic-1.htm` in your working folder (C:\MyPages).

Figure 5.1

The first Web page example, best for a relatively simple page, contains a banner graphic, a level-one heading, an introductory paragraph, a link list, and an address block.

Example #2: A Web Page Using Subsections

This is a more complex example, but it's still just a single page. Like the first Web page example, it includes a banner graphic, a level-one heading, and an introductory paragraph. However, the link list here, instead of linking to other Web pages, functions as a table of contents that jumps to the subsections of the document, using internal rather than external links. You probably want to use this example if your outline is more complicated. Think of the subsections as corresponding to the subsections of your outline. (See Figure 5.2.)

Pull this up in your browser to get a closer look. Test-drive the table of contents, jumping to the different subsections. You should find it as `basic-2.htm` in your working folder (C:\MyPages).

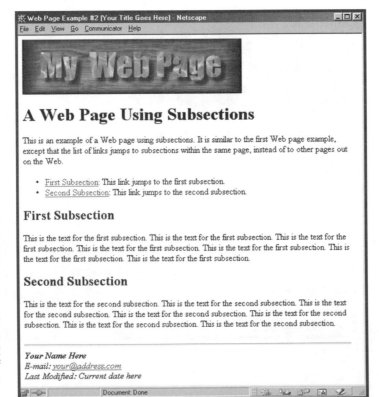

Figure 5.2

The second Web page example, best for a more complex page, contains a banner graphic, a level-one heading, an introductory paragraph, a table of contents that jumps to a series of subsections, and an address section.

Example #3: A Web Site Using Subpages

I don't recommend that you use this Web page example the first time through. Get your feet wet with one of the two earlier Web page examples; then, when you feel ready, come back and try using this example. Generally, if the material you want to present is extensive, you should consider breaking the page's subsections into separate subpages. Anytime a page extends beyond three or four screens, you should consider breaking it up into more than one page.

One of the advantages of breaking up a long Web page into a main page and subpages is that visitors to your Web site need only load the home page and the particular subpage they're interested in seeing, rather than wait for the whole document—along with any inline images—to load before they get at the part they want to read.

On the other hand, breaking up a long document into pieces can penalize visitors who want to view the whole thing, forcing them to reconnect to the server to retrieve each subpage. Another disadvantage is that a Web document that's broken up into a main page and subpages can't be printed in a single operation. Each subpage must be printed separately. You may want to try to strike a happy medium, still breaking an especially long Web document into subpages but limiting their number so only a few print operations will be required to print the whole document.

A compromise that you see fairly frequently on the Web is to do both— that is, to break up the site into subpages but include a link to another version that is all in one page and uses subsections.

You might also want to create a home page linked to subpages if you've created a number of different loosely related or unrelated Web pages that you want to link together through an index page. It's fairly common on the Web to see personal pages done this way, linking to and serving as indexes for other more specialized pages possibly created for business or other purposes.

See Figure 5.3 for an example of a home page linked to a number of subpages.

Figure 5.3

The third Web page example, best for an even more complex multi-page Web site, contains a banner graphic, a level-one heading, an introductory paragraph, and an "index" link list that jumps to a series of subpages.

Pull this up in your browser to get a closer look. You should find it as `basic-3.htm` in your working folder (C:\MyPages). Test-drive the menu, clicking on the first link to jump to an example subpage.

Figure 5.4 shows the example subpage that is included with the Web page example files.

I've only shown one example subpage here, but you probably want to use several subpages. Use this one as a model for any other subpages you want

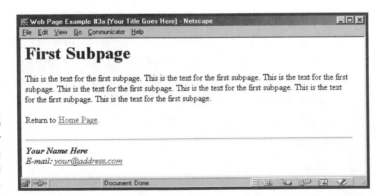

Figure 5.4

This subpage is for the Web site introduced in Figure 5.3.

to create. I haven't included a banner or logo graphic with this example. Because a subpage is just a Web page, you can use either of the first two example Web pages as a model for creating your subpages.

Notice that the subpage example includes a loop-back link at the bottom of the page that returns viewers to the home page. Check it out to see how it works. When you create subpages, it is always a good idea to include a loop-back link to your home page. Visitors don't necessarily come through your home page to get to a subpage. If they have the URL on their hotlist or bookmark list or have gotten it from a search engine, they go directly to your subpage. Without a loop-back link they would have no way to get to your home page—hitting the Back button won't work.

You should find this subpage as `basic-3a.htm` in your working folder (C:\MyPages). Feel free to pull it up in your browser directly. However, you'll get a better idea of how it works if you click on the link to it in the main page.

NOTE You may notice that I've included two example subpages, `basic-3a.htm` and `basic-3b.htm`. The second example is included so you can test both of the subpage links in the main page—otherwise, however, except for their titles and level-one headings, they are identical.

Take a Break?

You've defined your objective, done your outline, and chosen the Web page example you want to use as a model—hey, that's a lot of brain work! Time for a break! If you haven't eaten anything yet, you might want to get a bowl of cereal or some other sustenance because there's plenty more to do if you want to plan *and* create your first Web page today. So, give the noggin a rest and grab a late-morning snack if you're hungry. I'll see you back in five or ten minutes, when you'll assemble your materials and pull together your mock-up text file.

Assembling Your Materials

In this stage, you should start to pull together the different materials that will actually compose your Web page. I've broken this stage into three sections, covering writing the text for your page, gathering any URLs that you want to use in hypertext links in your page, and creating a banner graphic. At minimum, you should do the first section to write a title, level-one heading, and introductory paragraph. I also encourage you to do the second section to gather some URLs to use for hypertext links in your page, although you can use the sample link list included with the first example Web page for this if you're running short on time. This is also the point at which you would want to start creating any graphics, such as a banner graphic, that you plan to use in your page. If you want, you can take the time to create a banner graphic to help personalize your Web page, although I recommend you wait until after you've created your first Web page this afternoon before you put a whole lot of effort into doing this. The Sunday Evening bonus session, "The Graphics Tutorial," covers using Paint Shop Pro 5 to create eye-catching Web art special effects that can help to visually accent your page.

Writing Some Text

It is a good idea to write at least a title, level-one heading, and introductory paragraph before you actually start creating your Web page. Putting some thought and effort into this, right up front, can actually end up paying some big dividends in the future. That's because many search engines give special weight to these when they index your page. Many search engines also will display your title, level-one heading, and at least the start of your introductory paragraph when listing your page.

You may want to start out writing your title, level-one heading, and introductory paragraph directly in a Notepad window. (If you're using Windows 95 or Windows 3.1, be sure to turn on Word Wrap.) If you feel more comfortable starting with another medium, such as a yellow legal pad or your favorite word processor, that's okay too.

Writing a Title

The title of your page will be displayed in the title bar of a Web browser. The title of your page is very important. Every Web page should have a title that is informative and descriptive for a couple of reasons. Search engines place more weight on the contents of your title than on anything else in your page when indexing and listing your page. Search engines and other Web directories also use your title as their link to your page when they list you—if your title isn't informative and descriptive, prospective visitors may skip visiting your site, even if it is listed.

TIP

Try to think of keywords or key phrases that you think desirable visitors to your page might likely use when doing a Web search. Include at least one such keyword or key phrase in the title of your page, preferably closer to the start rather than toward the end of your title (search engines place more weight on words at the start of your title). This will greatly increase the likelihood that your page will get listed by a search engine when someone does a search using one of the keywords or key phrases you've included in your title.

TASK

In Notepad, in your favorite word processor, or on a yellow legal pad, compose a title for your page that is both informative and descriptive. Try to include at least one keyword or key phrase, preferably toward the start of your title. Try to keep it relatively short—fewer than thirty characters—if you can.

Writing a Level-One Heading

It is a good idea to include a level-one heading at the top of your page. This serves as the title for your page that will be displayed at the top of your page (rather than just in the title bar, as was the case with the title you created in the previous section).

You may want to use the same text, or close variants, in both places (for your title and your level-one heading). You should probably try to keep your level-one heading to fewer than 20 characters, however; your title might be longer. It is also a good idea to include at least one keyword or key phrase in your level-one heading that you think prospective visitors to your page might use when doing a Web search. If your page is about model railroads, for example, then make sure that "Model Railroad" is included in your level-one heading.

▼ ▼

Below the title you composed previously, compose a level-one heading for your page. This can be the same text that you used for your title, or a close variant of it, but you should try to keep it to fewer than 20 characters. To help snag search engines, try to include at least one relevant keyword or key phrase.

▼ ▼

Writing an Introductory Paragraph

An introductory paragraph does what it says—it introduces visitors to your page, letting them know what you're doing, why you're doing it, who you are, what they'll find, and so on. An introductory paragraph can be your opportunity to add personality and set the tone and style for your page.

If you're using the first example Web page, your introductory paragraph may serve as an introduction to your list of links, or it may stand on its own, being a kind of short essay (or even a longer one, if you like) or a soapbox. Also, many first-time Web publishers use their introductory paragraph to describe what they're planning on doing in the future, near or far.

▼ ▼

Below the level-one heading you just composed, write an introductory paragraph for your page. The length is up to you, although you may want to keep it to less than a browser screen (or two browser screens, at the most). Don't think you have to write a masterpiece—you'll have plenty of opportunities to change and improve it later. To help snag search engines, however, try to include several relevant keywords or key phrases in the first three or four sentences.

▼ ▼

CAUTION With the possible exception of headings, you should avoid using text in ALL CAPS. Doing so is generally considered to be impolite and poor etiquette (or *netiquette*). That's because it is generally considered to be the equivalent of shouting. If you want to emphasize text, you should bold or italicize it (using the B or I tag) instead.

Gathering Some URLs (Optional)

The first example Web page includes a list of links to other pages on the Web. Even if you're using the second example Web page, using a menu of links to jump to subsections, you may still want to include one or more lists of links to other pages on the Web. You may also want to include in-context links, which are links inserted directly into the text of your page.

NOTE This section and the following one, "Choosing or Creating Some Graphics," are optional. If you don't want to take the time this morning to gather your own URLs, you can use the sample link list included in the first example Web page, if you want. Also, feel free to use any of the URLs that I've included in Appendix A, "Web Resources." I've also included a sample banner graphic in each of the example Web pages that you can use as a placeholder until you get around to creating your own.

So, if you're running short on time, feel free to skip ahead to the next main section, "Creating a Mock-Up File."

The following sections cover methods you can use to gather the URLs you'd like to place in your Web page, including gathering URLs while you surf and using Navigator's bookmarks or Internet Explorer's favorites.

▼ ▼

TASK   Using any of the methods described in the following sections, assemble a list of at least a half-dozen URLs, along with the text you want to use for each link and the text you want to use to describe each link. If you've already started working in Notepad, you can paste your URLs into the same text file where you wrote your title, level-one heading, and introductory paragraph. If the text for your page is still on a yellow legal pad, just open a new Notepad file to hold your URLs.

▼ ▼

Gathering URLs as You Surf

The easiest way to gather your URLs is simply to connect to the Web, go to the Web page you want to link to, copy its URL, and then paste it into Notepad for safekeeping. You should also type or paste in any other text you want to include for the link text and the link description.

Here's a quick rundown on how to snag URLs while you browse:

1. Open the Notepad window into which you want to paste your URLs.

2. Connect to the Internet and run your Web browser.

3. Display the Web page you want to link to in your Web browser (see the following tip for using Yahoo! to find links).

4. Right-click on the URL (in the Location box in Navigator or in the Address box in Internet Explorer). This should highlight the URL and open a drop-down menu. Select Copy.

5. Hop over to Notepad and press Ctrl+V to paste in the URL you just copied.

6. Following the URL you just pasted, type in the title of the Web page you are linking to (you can copy and paste this from the Web page, if it is available there). Optionally, type in additional text describing the Web page. These will later form the link text and descriptive text for your link list.

7. Repeat these steps for any other URLs you want to include in your Web page. When finished, you should have a list of URLs in your

Notepad file, along with titles for the links and, optionally, text describing each link.

■ ■

TIP You may not have the foggiest notion of what links you want to include in your page. That's okay—hey, you're only starting out! A quick and easy way to find lots of links for a particular subject or area is to go to Yahoo! and do a search using a relevant keyword or key phrase describing your area of interest. Yahoo! will return a listing of categories and pages that match your search criteria.

■ ■

Using Your Bookmarks or Favorites to Get URLs

If you have been surfing the Web using Navigator or Internet Explorer, you probably have collected a pretty good selection of bookmarks in Navigator or favorites in Internet Explorer. Your bookmarks or favorites list can be an excellent source for URLs that you might want to include in your Web pages. The following is a quick rundown on how to use Navigator's bookmarks or Internet Explorer's favorites to gather URLs.

Using Navigator Bookmarks

If you use Netscape Navigator as your Web browser, the bookmarks list can be a great place to get URLs for your Web pages. To gather URLs using Navigator's bookmarks, just do the following:

1. Open the Notepad window into which you want to paste your URLs.

2. Run Navigator (no need to log on to the Internet). Click on the Bookmarks button, and then select Edit Bookmarks.

3. Right-click on a bookmark that you want to use, and then select Copy Link Location.

4. Hop back over to Notepad and press Ctrl+V to paste in the bookmark's URL. Following the URL, type in a title for the URL that you want to use as the link text (you may want to hop back over to

Navigator and check out what is listed for the bookmark). You can also add some description text for your link.

5. Repeat these steps until you have all the URLs you want to use, plus the link text and description text you want to include with each URL.

■■

Navigator stores its bookmarks in an ordinary HTML file, `bookmark.htm`. You can open this file in your browser, then easily copy and paste both the URLs and the link text into your Notepad file. Different versions of Navigator may store this file in different locations. (To find out where your `bookmark.htm` is, in Windows 95/98, click on the Start button, then select Find, Files or Folders. In Windows 3.1, run File Manager and select File, Search.) Once you have opened `bookmark.htm` into Navigator, just right-click on the link, select Copy Link Location, then hop over to Notepad and press Ctrl+V to paste in the URL. You can also click and drag to copy the link text from the bookmark file, and then paste it into your Notepad file.

■■

Using Internet Explorer Favorites

If you use Internet Explorer as your Web browser, you can use its favorites to get URLs for your Web pages. To gather URLs using Internet Explorer's favorites, just do the following:

1. Open the Notepad window into which you want to paste your URLs.

2. Run Internet Explorer (no need to log on to the Internet). Select Favorites, Organize Favorites. Open one of the folders (Cool Sites or Links, for instance).

3. Right-click on one of the favorites listed, then select Properties. In Internet Explorer 4.x, select the Internet Shortcut tab; the URL should already be highlighted in the Target URL box. In Internet Explorer 5.x, the URL should already be highlighted in the URL box. Just press Ctrl+C to copy the URL to the Clipboard.

4. Hop back over to Notepad and press Ctrl+V to paste in the URL. Following the URL, type a title for the URL that you want to use as the link text (you may want to hop back over to Internet

Explorer and check out what is listed for the favorite). You can also add some descriptive text.

5. Repeat these steps until you have all the URLs you want to use, plus the link text and description text you want to include with each URL.

NOTE

• •

It used to be considered bad netiquette to link to someone else's page without asking permission. That was because most Web host accounts way back when came with very skimpy traffic allowances. With more liberal traffic allowances now the norm, I don't know of anyone who doesn't want all the links he or she can get, so you should feel free, I believe, to link to others' sites without asking for permission. If someone wants you to first ask permission, he or she should say so on the site. (You should, of course, *never* link to someone else's images or other media files unless you have permission.)

It is not a bad idea, however, to let people know that you've linked to their page. Let them know the URL you've linked to, and let them know that you think their page is informative, well-designed, or just plain great—most Web authors are gluttons for appreciation. So don't be afraid to butter them up. And then ask if they'd like to link back to you—getting reciprocal links is an excellent way to build your own Web traffic. Of course, if they say they don't want you to link to their site, remove your link.

When I link to a page that is internal to another's site, I like to also include a link to that site's main page. I also like to include a reference to the site's author or owner.

• •

Choosing or Creating Some Graphics (Optional)

While assembling materials, you should also start pulling together any image files you want to include in your page. You may already have an image that you might want to use as a banner graphic, or you may have other pictures or images you want to include.

You can also take the time, if you want, to create a simple banner graphic to help personalize your first Web page. However, if time is running short, feel free to skip selecting or creating a banner graphic for now—

I've included a sample banner graphic with the example Web pages that you can use as a placeholder until you choose or create your own. If you have time and energy left after creating your first Web page this afternoon, I've scheduled a special bonus session for you this evening, "The Graphics Tutorial," that will show you some of the tricks of the trade when it comes to creating banner graphics.

If you want to create a quick and dirty banner graphic to give your page more of a personal touch, go ahead. You can use any image editor (an evaluation version of Paint Shop Pro 5 is included on the CD-ROM). Try to keep it smaller than 500 pixels wide x 150 pixels high. You might try, for instance, re-creating your level-one heading as a banner graphic but using a fancy "display" font while playing around with different color combinations—whatever looks good to you. Don't spend forever on it, however (you can perfect it or create a better one later). When done, save it as a GIF or JPEG image in your working folder (C:\MyPages).

If you have other pictures you'd like to display on your page (such as pictures of yourself, your family, your pets, and so on), then you might want to quickly look through them at this point to see which ones you'd most like to use. If they aren't already in electronic form, you'll need to scan them or have them scanned later—just make a note at this point of which ones you'd like to use.

TASK

▼ ▼

If you want to take the time at this point, you can create a quick and dirty banner graphic for your page using an image editor that saves GIF or JPEG images (an evaluation version of Paint Shop Pro 5 is included on the CD-ROM). Keep it to 500 pixels wide x 150 pixels high or smaller. Try setting your level-one heading in a fancy "display" font and experimenting with different color combinations. When done, save your image in your working folder (C:\MyPages) as either a GIF or JPEG image (`mybanner.gif` or `mybanner.jpg`, for instance).

▼ ▼

Creating a Mock-Up File

At this point, you'll be creating what I call a "mock-up text file," which will include at least a reference to everything you want to include in your Web page: any text you have written (such as your title, introductory paragraph, or other text); file names of any graphics you want to use; any URLs you want to include, either as in-context links or as a list of links; and an address section including your name, company name (if applicable), and e-mail address. You may already have created or gathered a good part of this while doing the previous tasks.

Some of this may still need to be determined, such as the file name for a graphic you have yet to scan or create. Some of it may still be scrawled on that yellow legal pad—or on a café napkin—and will finally need to be typed in. The basic idea here is to pull everything together in one file, in the rough order in which you want it to appear in your Web page. Use the outline you created and the example Web page you chose as guides for how to organize these different elements in your mock-up text file.

My recommendation is that you create your mock-up text file in Notepad—just make sure you turn on Word Wrap if you're using the Windows 95 version. If you've already created a Notepad text file that contains the text for your page (title, level-one heading, and introductory paragraph) and any URLs you've gathered, feel free to use that text file for your mock-up text file. If you took the time to gather your own URLs, you can use that text file for your mock-up text file. If the text for your page is still on a yellow legal pad and you're planning on using the sample URLs included in the first example Web page, then you'll need to open a new Notepad window to create your mock-up text file.

You can also use your favorite word processor for this, if you want. You'll need to save your final result as a text file, rather than in your word processor's native format, so you can pull it into Notepad when you create your Web page this afternoon.

As you gathered your materials, you may have found that your outline, or even your objective, has changed. A creative process is a fluid one. Feel free to change your course. Sometimes, not until you're pulling all the pieces together do you realize what you really want. A large part of any planning process involves a good amount of brainstorming, soul-searching, and research; and as an e-mail signature I once saw said, "If you know what you're doing, it isn't research!"

What you want to end up with here is a somewhat fleshed-out draft that at least has everything put roughly into place, even if it's in the form of "To be determined," "Need to create logo graphic," "Get photo of dog," "Write product description," "Create chart of sales figures," or similar notations.

You should include references (including file names, if available) to any graphics you want to display as inline images. These references should be inserted in your mock-up text file roughly relative to where you want them to be displayed in your Web page. For instance, below your title but above your level-one heading, you may want to insert a reference to a banner graphic ("Insert mybanner.jpg," for instance, or "Insert sample banner," if you want to use the sample banner graphic I provide).

Don't worry at this point about any purely decorative graphics, such as bullet icons, graphic rules, or background images, you may be thinking of using—you'll deal with those, if you wish, in this afternoon's creation process.

You'll also want to include any URLs you've gathered to use as links. If you're using them for a link list, you should also include the text you want to use for each link, as well as descriptions. (Feel free to use the sample link list from the first Web page example, if you wish.) For any URLs that you want to use as in-context links, you should insert them inside brackets within the paragraphs where you want them displayed, along with text for the link. When inserting notations for your links, to make tagging these later a lot easier, you should do so in this order: URL, link text, link description.

You'll also want to include, at the bottom of your mock-up text file, any contact and address information that you want to be part of your page. If you're creating a non-business page, you may want to include your name and e-mail address. If you're creating a business page, you may also want

to include your business or organization name, a mailing address, and phone and fax numbers.

If you're using the second Web page example, you will also need to include any subsection headings and text you want to use. Also, you may want to include separate link lists in one or more of your subsections. If you've gathered the URLs for these, you'll need to break them out, along with their link text and link descriptions, and arrange them under the subsections where you want them to appear.

TASK

▼ ▼

Create a text file (using Notepad or your word processor) containing all of the elements that will be included in your page. Include your title, level-one heading, introductory paragraph, link list URLs (with link text and link descriptions), references to inline images, and your contact and address information. Put in everything *except* the HTML codes (or at least as much as you can pull together at this point) in the rough order and position in which you want the different elements to appear in your page. Don't worry about the code—just focus on the content and organization of your Web page. When done, save your file as a text file (as `mockup.txt`, for instance) in your working folder (C:\MyPages). (If you used Word 97 or 2000, save your file as a "Text Only" file.)

▼ ▼

If you are using the third Web page example (meaning this is at least your *second* Web page!), you should create a separate mock-up text file for each page you are creating (your main page and your subpages). Feel free to use either the first or second Web page example, or both, as models for your subpages.

Drawing a Map (Optional)

You only need to work through this section if you're creating a multi-page Web site. You can create a map for a single Web page, but in most cases it won't be complex enough to be worthwhile. So, if you are not creating a multi-page Web site and are running short on time, feel free to skim or skip this section.

An outline defines the static structure of your document but does little to highlight and define any dynamic interrelations within your document. This is fine for paper, which doesn't do interrelations very well anyway. However, the advantage of a hypertext document is that it is dynamic, allowing many different ways to approach and peruse the information you provide. Your map may closely mirror your outline, or it may sharply diverge from it, opening up links between sections that might otherwise remain separate from each other.

This map can be a simple chart like an organizational chart, using boxes and lines. It can be a flow chart or a storyboard. Whatever approach you choose, you'll want to try to capture in it the dynamic relationships within and between parts of your Web site.

The map of one multi-page site can take many forms. The important thing is to be able to visualize the layout and relationships in your site.

As the first example, you might map your site in the form of an organizational chart, as shown in Figure 5.5

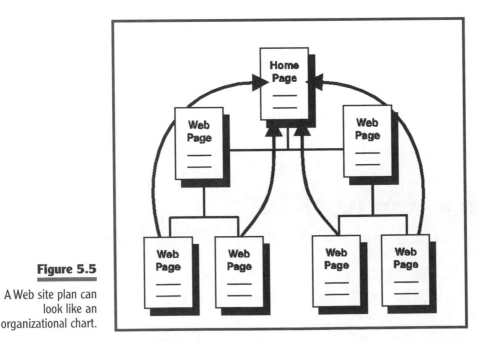

Figure 5.5

A Web site plan can look like an organizational chart.

Or, if you're a technical type, you might want to do a flowchart. Another kind of map can be described metaphorically as a train. A train map might be a good approach for something that uses sequential chapters. In this type of map, your Web pages are like a string of boxcars, as shown in Figure 5.6.

Another approach is to have your home page be the hub of a wheel, with the subpages along the rim, as shown in Figure 5.7.

And if you want to create a more complex site, you might want to create a more elaborate map, resembling a tree—with a trunk, branches, and sub-branches—like the one pictured in Figure 5.8.

Figure 5.6

A Web site plan can be organized like a train.

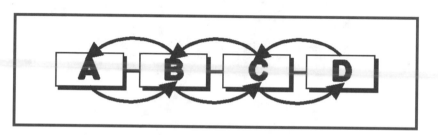

Figure 5.7

A Web site plan can take the form of a wheel.

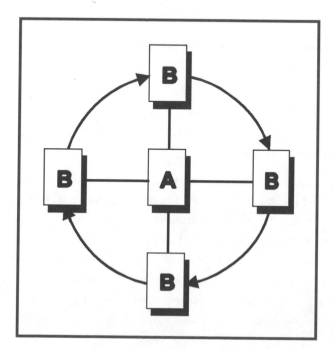

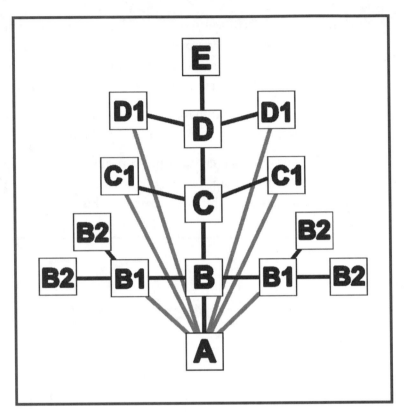

Figure 5.8

A more complex
Web site plan
might be laid out in
the form of a tree.

You could conceivably visualize your Web site map in many other ways. The last few figures represent only a handful of the possibilities, and in quite broad terms.

In planning your first Web page, you probably don't need to draw up a map. Maps are most useful for creating more elaborate, multi-page Web sites. Still, even if you're only creating a single page, you might want to try to visualize the kinds of dynamic interrelationships you can activate through links. For instance, if you're creating a Web page using subsections—as in the second example—in addition to the table of contents linking to the different subsections, you can include a loop-back link at the end of each subsection to return the reader to the table of contents.

Additionally, at the bottom of the page you might provide a link back to the top of the page. You can also include in-context links within the paragraph sections that will jump to different subsections.

▼▼

If you're creating a multi-page Web site, draw a map of your site. Don't just settle on the first map you think up. Try to picture two or three possible maps, and don't just stick to the examples shown here—you want a map that really suits the site you want to create. Visualize, in other words. Use different color pens to help distinguish the different relationships between your pages: one color to map out any hierarchical (top-down) or static relationships, and another color to map out any dynamic relationships between pages that are not explicit in your hierarchical plan. Alternatively, use another color pen (if you have one!) to draw in any loop-back links you want to include. The idea is to be able to see how your Web site will be structured both statically and dynamically.

▼▼▼

Be prepared to reorganize! Seeing the dynamic interactions within your Web site almost always leads to at least one forehead slap ("Of course!"). Don't be afraid to redo your outline to match your visualization. Try to simplify, making sure that everything that is important in your site is only a hop, skip, and jump away. Don't bury that price list ten levels deep! And don't be surprised if you end up redefining your objective—in many ways, you don't really know what you are doing until you can visualize it.

Wrapping Up

Before moving on to this afternoon's session, you should have defined an objective, done an outline, and gathered and organized your materials. The latter includes writing the text for your Web page, as well as possibly creating a banner graphic and gathering any URLs you want to use. The end product of this process should be a mock-up text file that contains the text you want to include in your Web page, references to the file names of any graphics you want to use (probably just a banner graphic), as well as any URLs inserted in the positions where you want them to appear. You'll use this mock-up this afternoon as the raw material for the Web page you create.

The first time through, for the purposes of this book, your mock-up should closely match one of the basic Web page example formats. The actual content, however, is entirely subject to your discretion. You can copy it out of the encyclopedia, if you want, just for the sake of practice, or you can come up with something original.

Is it lunchtime? Or pretty close? Take a break and grab a bite to eat. Because you've done a lot of brain work this morning, try to get something nourishing. I'll see you back in a half hour or so for the Sunday Afternoon session, when you'll create your first Web page!

Creating Your First Web Page

- ⚙ Choosing your approach
- ⚙ Creating the top section of your page
- ⚙ Creating the middle section of your page
- ⚙ Creating the bottom section of your page
- ⚙ Adding color and pizzazz to your page

I know you want to jump right in and see your own stuff on a Web page—and you should be ready by now, assuming you completed at least the Basic HTML Tutorial on Saturday morning and the Web page planning session this morning. If you missed those sessions, you should return and pick them up before starting to create your first Web page.

Are You Ready?

In this morning's planning session, you should have:

- Chosen one of the Web page examples to use as a model for planning and creating your first Web page. For the first time through, you should have chosen one of the first two Web page examples, either a Web page with a link list or a Web page with a menu and subsections. If you haven't decided yet which Web page example you'll use as a model for creating your first Web page, you should return to this morning's session and review the "Choosing an Example Web Page" section.

- Created a mock-up text file, basing at least its rough structure on the Web page example you selected. This can be fairly simple, if you want, including just a title, an introductory paragraph, and any contact info (name, e-mail address, and so on) that you want to include in your address block. It can be more complex, containing any other text you want to include (such as subheadings and

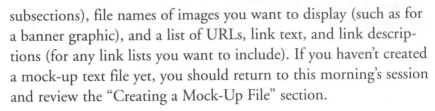

subsections), file names of images you want to display (such as for a banner graphic), and a list of URLs, link text, and link descriptions (for any link lists you want to include). If you haven't created a mock-up text file yet, you should return to this morning's session and review the "Creating a Mock-Up File" section.

If you have chosen the example Web page you'll use as a model and have created and saved your mock-up text file, then you're all ready to get started creating your first Web page!

Choosing Your Approach

You can take many approaches to create a Web page. Nothing says you can't, for instance, fold together the planning and creating processes, working directly in HTML from the start. For anything other than a fairly simple Web page, however, such an approach tends to be impractical. HTML works by defining structural elements that are common to all Web pages—the more logically organized and structured the material you want to tag, the better.

For this session, you'll be using the example Web page you selected as a model for planning your Web page this morning. You have the option of using your example Web page as either a template or a guide. Using it as a template involves replacing the sample text with your own, and using it as a guide involves copying its HTML tags and applying them directly to your mock-up text file. For now, just think of the example Web page you're using as a set of training wheels—once you get your balance, so to speak, you can dispense with the assistance and ride on your own.

If the page you planned this morning matches fairly closely the example Web page you selected, you might want to try the template approach, transferring your text and other content from your mock-up text file to your example Web page.

If the page you planned only roughly matches, or significantly differs from, the example Web page you selected, you might want to try the guide approach, using the example Web page as a guide for applying or copying the HTML codes to your mock-up text file.

Getting Started

In this morning's session, you should have selected an example Web page and created and saved your mock-up text file. Both of these files should be located in your working folder (C:\MyPages). To get started creating your first page:

1. Run Notepad and open the example Web page you selected this morning. If you selected the first example Web page, open `basic-1.htm`; for the second example Web page, open `basic-2.htm`. Note: To see the `*.htm` or `*.html` file extension when opening an HTML file in Notepad, change the file type from "Text Documents" to "All Files (*.*)."

2. Run a second copy of Notepad and open the mock-up text file you created this morning (`mockup.txt`, if you followed my naming suggestion).

3. If you're using your example Web page as a template, save it now as the HTML file you'll use to create your Web page. If you're using your example Web page as a guide, save your mock-up text file as the HTML file you'll use to create your first Web page. Save your HTML file as `index.html` (if you're using Windows 3.1, save it as `index.htm`) in your working folder (C:\MyPages).

4. Arrange the two Notepad windows so you can easily view the contents of both.

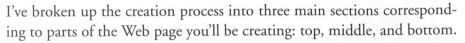

I've broken up the creation process into three main sections corresponding to parts of the Web page you'll be creating: top, middle, and bottom.

The top section (the banner graphic, level-one heading, and introductory paragraph) and the bottom section (the address block) of all three example Web pages are identical. You would probably include these elements on virtually any Web page you might create, except maybe for the banner graphic.

The middle section of an HTML file is the part that gets interesting. Basically, you can place anything you can dream up and format in HTML in this middle section. However, we need to limit the possibilities somewhat, or this session will probably end up looking more like a pretzel than a road map. That's why you should use one of the example Web pages as a model for organizing and planning the material for your Web page—to try to keep things from getting too complicated too fast. The following isn't the only way to go about creating a Web page—it's just the best way that I've been able to come up with to create your first Web page in a single weekend.

I've included the codes for all three example Web pages (plus one example subpage) in sidebars that are interspersed through the following pages, just so you can have an easily accessible hard-copy reference. You can also use these to type in the codes yourself from scratch, if you wish.

A WEB PAGE USING A LINK LIST (BASIC-1.HTM)

If your Web page is fairly simple and doesn't include subsections, you should use this Web page example as a template or guide.

```
<HTML>
<HEAD>
<TITLE>Web Page Example #1 (Your Title Goes Here)</TITLE>
</HEAD>
<BODY>
<P><IMG SRC="webpage.gif"></P>
<H1>A Web Page Using a Link List</H1>
<P>This is an example of a basic web page.  It contains a banner graphic,
level-one and level-two headings, an introductory paragraph, a short list
of links, a horizontal rule, and an address block.  The address block con-
tains the name of the author of the page, a Mailto
e-mail link, and a date reference.</P>
<H2>A List of Links</H2>
<UL>
<LI><A HREF="http://www.callihan.com/create3/">Create Your First Web Page
in a Weekend (3rd Edition)</A>: HTML is for everyone!
<LI><A HREF="http://www.w3.org/">World Wide Web Consortium</A>: Find out
the latest about the Web and HTML.
<LI><A HREF="http://www.infohiway.com/faster/homebcs.htm">The Bandwidth
Conservation Society</A>: Save bytes — don't be a bandwidth hog!
</UL>
<HR>
<ADDRESS>
<STRONG>Your Name Here</STRONG><BR>
E-mail: <A HREF="mailto:your@address.com">your@address.com</A><BR>
Last Modified: Current date here
</ADDRESS>
</BODY>
</HTML>
```

A WEB PAGE USING SUBSECTIONS (BASIC-2.HTM)

If your Web page is more complicated, with a number of subsections under subheadings (level-two headings), you should use this example Web page as a template or guide.

```
<HTML>
<HEAD>
<TITLE>Web Page Example #2 (Your Title Goes Here)</TITLE>
</HEAD>
<BODY>
<P><IMG SRC="webpage.gif"></P>
<H1>A Web Page Using Subsections</H1>
<P>This is an example of a Web page using subsections. It is similar to the first
Web page example, except that the list of links jumps to subsections within the
same page, instead of to other pages out on the Web.</P>
<UL>
<LI><A HREF="#sub1">First Subsection</A>: This link jumps to the first subsection.
<LI><A HREF="#sub2">Second Subsection</A>: This link jumps to the
second subsection.
</UL>
<H2><A NAME="sub1"></A>First Subsection</H2>
<P>This is the text for the first subsection. This is the text for the first sub-
section. This is the text for the first subsection. This is the text for the first
subsection. This is the text for the first
subsection. This is the text for the first subsection. This is the text for the
first subsection.</P>
<H2><A NAME="sub2"></A>Second Subsection</H2>
<P>This is the text for the second subsection. This is the text for the second
subsection. This is the text for the second subsection. This is the text for the
second subsection. This is the text for the second subsection. This is the text for
the second subsection. This is the text for the second subsection.</P>
<HR>
<ADDRESS>
<STRONG>Your Name Here</STRONG><BR>
E-mail: <A HREF="mailto:your@address.com">your@address.com</A><BR>
Last Modified: Current date here
</ADDRESS>
</BODY>
</HTML>
```

A WEB SITE USING SUBPAGES (BASIC-3.HTM)

This is the third basic Web page example, the one that uses local links to subpages of your main page. Consider using one of the other pages to create your first Web page. After you've done that, feel free to use this example as a template or guide for creating your first multi-page Web site.

```
<HTML>
<HEAD>
<TITLE>Web Page Example #3 (Your Title Goes Here)</TITLE>
</HEAD>
<BODY>
<P><IMG SRC="webpage.gif"></P>
<H1>A Web Site Using Subpages</H1>
<P>This is an example of a Web site using subpages. It is similar to the first two
Web page examples, except instead of a link list that jumps to other pages out on
the Web or that jumps to subsections
within the same page, it has a link list that jumps to subpages that are part of
the same Web site.</P>
<H2>Table of Contents</H2>
<UL>
<LI><A HREF="basic-3a.htm">First Subpage</A>: This links to the first subpage.
<LI><A HREF="basic-3b.htm">Second Subpage</A>: This links to the
second subpage.
</UL>
<HR>
<ADDRESS>
<STRONG>Your Name Here</STRONG><BR>
E-mail: <A HREF="mailto:your@address.com">your@address.com</A><BR>
Last Modified: Current date here
</ADDRESS>
</BODY>
</HTML>
```

EXAMPLE SUBPAGE (BASIC-3A.HTM)

Here are the codes for one of the example subpages used with the third example Web page. (I've also included a virtually identical second subpage example, `basic-3b.htm`, with the example Web page files.)

```
<HTML>
<HEAD>
<TITLE>Web Page Example #3a (Your Title Goes Here)</TITLE>
</HEAD>
<BODY>
<H1>First Subpage</H1>
<P>This is the text for the first subpage. This is the text for the first subpage.
This is the text for the first subpage. This is the text for the first subpage.
This is the text for the first subpage. This is the text for the first subpage.
This is the text for the first subpage.</P>
<P>Return to <A HREF="basic-3.htm">Home Page</A>.</P>
<HR>
<ADDRESS>
<STRONG>Your Name Here</STRONG><BR>
E-mail: <A HREF="mailto:your@address.com">your@address.com</A>
</ADDRESS>
</BODY>
</HTML>
```

NOTE If you skipped creating a banner graphic this morning, feel free to use the sample banner graphic included in the example Web pages. Also, if you skipped gathering a list of URLs, you can use the sample list of links from the first Web page example. Use these as placeholders until you can come back and create your own customized banner graphic, as well as gather a list of your own links.

I cover creating your own Web images in this evening's bonus session, "The Graphics Tutorial." To find additional URLs that you can use in your Web page, see Appendix A, "Web Resources."

Starting Your Web Page

If you're using your Web page example as a guide rather than as a template, you should insert the startup HTML tags into your mock-up text file now (if you're using the template approach, skip this):

```
<HTML>
<HEAD>
<TITLE></TITLE>
</HEAD>
<BODY>
```

Insert the following at the bottom of your mock-up text file:

```
</BODY>
</HTML>
```

In the remaining examples for this session, I'll be assuming that you're following the template approach—plugging in the text and other content from your mock-up text file into your example Web page. If you're doing it the other way around, using your example Web page as a guide for applying the HTML codes to your mock-up text file, you'll need to interpret the examples accordingly.

CAUTION ◆◆

Many of the features presented in this session as "extra options" require the use of an HTML 3.2-compliant Web browser. To preview these options in your Web browser, you should use Netscape Navigator 2.0 or higher or Microsoft Internet Explorer 3.0 or higher. You can also use the Opera or NeoPlanet browsers that are included on the CD-ROM, if you wish. If you want to make use of any extra options that use HTML 4.0 features, you should use Netscape Navigator 4.0 or higher or Microsoft Internet Explorer 4.0 or higher.

◆◆

Creating the Top Section
(All Three Example Web Pages)

The following section applies to all three of the example Web pages. It covers creating a title, a banner graphic, a level-one heading, and an

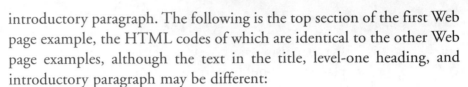

introductory paragraph. The following is the top section of the first Web page example, the HTML codes of which are identical to the other Web page examples, although the text in the title, level-one heading, and introductory paragraph may be different:

```
<HTML>
<HEAD>
<TITLE>Web Page Example #1 (Your Title Goes Here)</TITLE>
</HEAD>
<BODY>
<P><IMG SRC="webpage.gif"></P>
<H1>A Web Page Using a Link List</H1>
<P>This is an example of a basic web page.  It contains a
banner graphic, level-one and level-two headings, an introductory
paragraph, a short list of links, a horizontal rule, and an
address block.  The address block contains the name of the
author of the page, a Mailto e-mail link, and a date
reference.</P>
```

Creating Your Title

You should have decided on a title for your Web page when planning your Web page this morning. If you still haven't decided on a title, just put in a provisional one for now. It is a good idea to include a short description with your title (try to keep both together to fewer than thirty-five characters, however). Try to include a keyword or key phrase in your title that you think someone might use to search for a page like yours.

Delete the sample text from within the TITLE tag, and then plug in the title text you want to use from your mock-up text file (or just type it):

```
<HTML>
<HEAD>
<TITLE>Insert your title</TITLE>
</HEAD>
```

Inserting a Banner Graphic

If you created a banner graphic this morning to help personalize your page, you should insert it as an inline image at the top of your page. If you haven't yet created a banner graphic, that's okay—you can use the sample included with the Web page example as a placeholder until you create your own.

NOTE If you want some practice inserting a banner graphic, rather than just using the one already in the example Web page, you can use the banner graphic shown in the figure illustrations. Just insert `dummy.gif` as the name of the banner graphic.

If you have created a personalized banner graphic, replace "webpage.gif" in the example with the name of the GIF or JPEG file you want to use (see Figure 6.1).

```
<BODY>
<P><IMG SRC="Insert the file name of your banner graphic"></P>
```

NOTE Be sure to frequently check out what your page looks like in your browser. Resave your HTML file (File, Save), and then run your browser and open your HTML file. Use the Alt+Tab method to hop back and forth between your HTML file and your browser, saving your HTML in Notepad and pressing Ctrl+R to reload or refresh the display of your Web page in your browser.

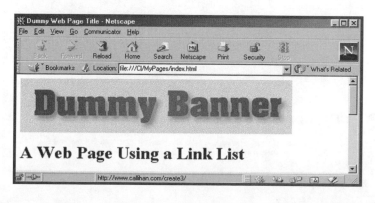

Figure 6.1

A banner graphic is a good way to make your Web page more visually appealing.

Creating a Level-One Heading

The level-one heading is actually a title. You should have only one level-one heading on your page, and you probably have already thought of one during this morning's planning session. If you haven't decided on a level-one heading yet, just put in a provisional one—you can always change it later. Try to keep it fewer than thirty characters. Insert your level-one heading as follows (see Figure 6.2):

```
<BODY>
<P><IMG SRC="The name of your banner graphic"></P>
<H1>Insert Your Level-One Heading</H1>
</BODY>
```

Creating Your Introductory Paragraph

During this morning's planning session, you probably created an introductory paragraph for your Web page. An introductory paragraph isn't absolutely essential—skipping it doesn't violate any laws. Having an introductory paragraph is a good idea, however, and helps viewers of your page decide whether they want to linger. Also, including keywords and key phrases in your introductory paragraph will help search engines to index your page. If you have created an introductory paragraph, insert it as follows (see Figure 6.3):

Figure 6.2

Here is an example of a level-one heading.

```
<BODY>
<P><IMG SRC="The file name of your banner graphic"></P>
<H1>Your Level-One Heading</H1>
<P>Insert your introductory paragraph text</P>
```

Extra Options for the Top Section

To further enhance or alter the appearance of your Web page, you might want to try some of the following options in the top section. You don't have to use any of these options to create your first page—feel free to skip them entirely. If you do choose to experiment with them, you might want to save your current Web page file, and then save another version for experimentation. If you find an effect you like, reload your original Web page file and incorporate the effect into it.

NOTE Many of these extra options use features that were covered in the Intermediate HTML Tutorial on Saturday afternoon. If you haven't done that tutorial, or you're running short on time, you might want to skip ahead to the discussion of creating the middle section of your Web page that relates to the Web page example you are using. You can come back and experiment with some of these suggested extra options later, after you've done the Intermediate HTML Tutorial.

Figure 6.3

It's a good idea to start your Web page with an introductory paragraph.

Introductory paragraph

Extra Option: Set the Width and Height Dimensions of Your Banner Graphic

It is a good idea to set the WIDTH and HEIGHT attributes for any inline images other than small bullet icons. That way, surrounding text will appear on the screen without waiting for your image to finish downloading. To set these dimensions, you need to know the actual dimensions of your image. If you have created your own custom banner graphic, you can find what its dimensions are in Paint Shop Pro by clicking on View and Image Information. If you are using the sample banner graphic, `webpage.gif`, provided with the example Web pages, you should set WIDTH=`"400"` and HEIGHT=`"100"` in the IMG tag. If you are using the dummy banner graphic, `dummy.gif`, displayed in the figure illustrations, you should set WIDTH=`"500"` and HEIGHT=`"100"` in the IMG tag, as shown here:

```
<P><IMG SRC="dummy.gif" WIDTH="500" HEIGHT="100"></P>
```

Extra Option: Center Your Banner Graphic and Level-One Heading

Most current Web browsers support centering headings and paragraphs. You can center an inline image by centering the paragraph in which it is nested. The best way to center headings and paragraphs (and nested inline images) is to insert an ALIGN=`"center"` attribute in a paragraph or heading tag, like this (see Figure 6.4):

```
<P ALIGN="center"><IMG SRC="The file name of your banner
graphic"></P>
<H1 ALIGN="center">Your Level-One Heading</H1>
```

You also could center-align your introductory paragraph by inserting ALIGN=`"center"` inside its paragraph tag. To right-align any of these elements, just insert ALIGN=`"right"` instead.

Extra Option: Add a Custom Horizontal Rule

For an additional touch, you can insert a horizontal rule between your level-one heading and your introductory paragraph. If you want to further

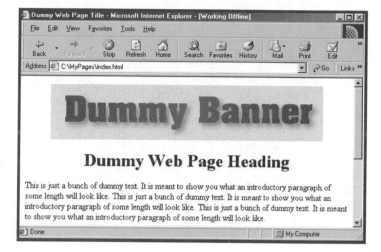

Figure 6.4

You can center-align both your banner graphic and your level-one heading.

customize it, you can set its width to a percentage of the browser window—it'll be automatically centered because that's the default horizontal alignment for horizontal rules. (This will look best if you've also center-aligned your banner graphic and level-one heading.) To insert an unshaded horizontal rule that is 10 pixels thick and extends across 66 percent of the browser window, you would do this (see Figure 6.5):

```
<P ALIGN="center"><IMG SRC="The file name of your banner
graphic"></P>
<H1 ALIGN="center">Your Level-One Heading</H1>
<HR SIZE="10" WIDTH="66%" NOSHADE>
```

 NOTE You also can set the width of your horizontal rule in actual pixels by leaving off the percent sign (%) at the end of the WIDTH attribute value.

Extra Option: Use a Graphic Rule

For an even nicer touch, you can use a graphic rule. By setting the HEIGHT and WIDTH attributes in the IMG tag, along with placing it in a center-aligned paragraph, you can get an effect similar to what you

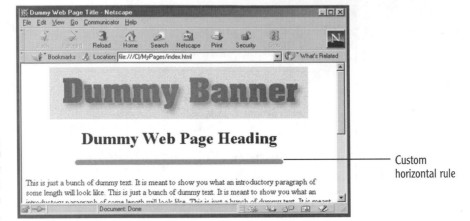

Custom horizontal rule

Figure 6.5

A strategically placed horizontal rule can add a nice touch.

could achieve using the horizontal rule, except that you get to add some extra color to your page. If you want, you can experiment with the sample graphic rule, `rain_lin.gif`, that was used in the Intermediate HTML Tutorial on Saturday afternoon—I've included `rain_lin.gif` with the Web page example files you installed this morning. For instance, you might substitute it for the horizontal rule that was used in the previous example, like this (see Figure 6.6):

```
<P ALIGN="center"><IMG SRC="The name of your banner graphic"></P>
<H1 ALIGN="center">Your Level-One Heading</H1>
<P ALIGN="center"><IMG SRC="rain_lin.gif" WIDTH="66%"
HEIGHT="10"></P>
```

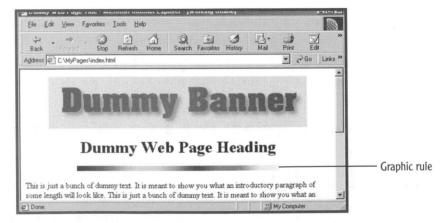

Graphic rule

Figure 6.6

A graphic rule is a good way to add extra color and visual appeal to your Web page.

NOTE

FIND IT ON ▶
THE WEB

Check out the Web art collections included on the CD-ROM for additional graphic rules that you can use to dress up your page. Also check out this book's Web site at **www.callihan.com/create3/** for even more Web art collections, including lots of graphic rules, that you can download and use. See also Appendix A, "Web Resources," for more links to where you can find and download Web art.

Extra Option: Wrap Your Heading around a Logo Graphic

You don't have to settle for a banner graphic and level-one heading, centered and stacked on top of each other. If your company has a logo, you can wrap your level-one heading around it to get a side-by-side look. For an extra touch, right-align your level-one heading. Because I don't expect you to have a logo graphic all ready and handy (and in GIF format to boot), I've included a sample logo graphic, `logo.gif`, with the example Web page files that you can use just to see how this works. If you want to use your own customized logo graphic, just create a GIF or JPEG image that is about 150 pixels wide by 100 pixels high. (In the following example, I've also changed the percentage width of the graphic rule to `100%`.)

If you want to try this without incorporating it into your Web page, you may want to make the code changes in a second copy of the HTML file you're working on. First, in C:\MyPages, save your original file, `index.html`, and then save your copy, `index2.html`. When finished checking out the example, just reopen `index.html` in Notepad.

To try this example, add the following (see Figure 6.7):

```
<P><IMG SRC="logo.gif" ALIGN="left"></P><BR>
<H1 ALIGN="right">Your Level-One<BR> Heading<BR
CLEAR="left"></H1>
<P ALIGN="center"><IMG SRC="rain_lin.gif" WIDTH="100%"
HEIGHT="10"></P>
```

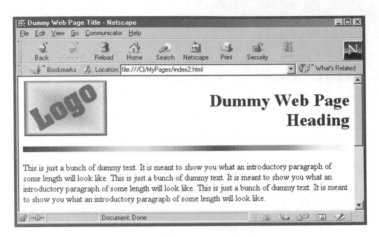

Figure 6.7

Instead of a centered banner and heading, you can wrap your heading around a logo graphic.

In the previous example, the IMG tag's `ALIGN="left"` attribute causes the following level-one heading to wrap around the right side of the image. The H1 tag's `ALIGN="right"` attribute causes the heading to be flush right. The BR tag on the first line causes the following heading to start wrapping closer to the middle, rather than the top, of the image. (Remember, you can't both left-align and middle-align an image, only one or the other.) Depending on the size of the logo graphic you use, you may need to add one or more additional BR tags here to move the heading down to a position that suits you. (Yes, I know that earlier, in the Basic HTML Tutorial, I said *not* to use multiple BR tags, but this is a case where nothing else can really do the trick.) Note also the `<BR CLEAR="left">` tag and attribute—this is inserted to make sure that the following elements don't also wrap around the image.

To do this the other way around, wrapping your heading around the left side of a right-aligned image, just reverse the relative positions of the image and the heading: insert `ALIGN="right"` in the IMG tag, delete `ALIGN="right"` from the H1 tag (left alignment is the default), and change to `CLEAR="right"` in the second BR tag.

Extra Option: Change the Color and Size of Your Level-One Heading

A good way to add more of a decorative flair to your page is to use the FONT tag to reassign the color and size of text in your page. The following example changes the color of your level-one heading to teal while increasing its size one level (see Figure 6.8):

```
<H1 ALIGN="center"><FONT COLOR="teal" SIZE="7">Your Level-One
Heading</FONT></H1>
```

Extra Option: Change the Font Face of Your Level-One Heading

In addition to changing the font color and size, you can use the FONT tag's FACE attribute to specify a single font face or a list of font faces. Specifying a list of font faces is preferred because it increases the chance that one of the font faces listed will be present on a viewer's system. Because Postscript fonts don't always display very well on Windows systems, you should always list one or two TrueType fonts before any Postscript fonts. Also, you should avoid specifying font faces that may be less commonly present on others' systems, even if they are present on your own.

Figure 6.8

You can increase the size and change the color of your level-one heading.

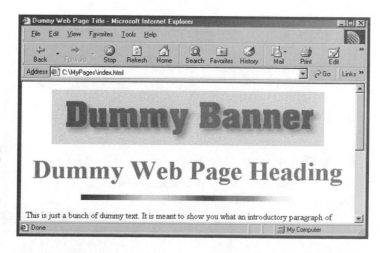

Apply a list of sans serif font faces (Verdana, Arial, and Helvetica) to your level-one heading (delete the `SIZE="7"` attribute while you're at it) (see Figure 6.9):

```
<H1 ALIGN="center"><FONT FACE="verdana, arial, helvetica"
COLOR="teal" SIZE="7">Dummy Web Page Heading</FONT></H1>
```

I had you delete the `SIZE="7"` attribute because I wanted you to see what this looks like using the default level-one heading size (equivalent to a size 6). Also, some font faces take up more horizontal space than others, possibly causing the heading to wrap when you don't want it to, if the largest font size (7) is set.

Extra Option: Use a Drop Cap Image

No tag exists for creating a drop cap, but you can create a graphic of the first letter of your paragraph and then insert it in place of that letter. Set left alignment in the IMG tag, and the following text will wrap around the graphic. I've included a sample drop cap graphic, `drop-t.gif`, with the example Web page files that can be used to insert a drop cap "T" at the start of the introductory paragraph (see Figure 6.10):

```
<P><IMG SRC="drop-t.gif" ALIGN="left" VSPACE="2" WIDTH="45"
HEIGHT="50">Your introductory paragraph text.</P>
```

Figure 6.9

You can change the font face, to a sans serif font, for instance, by including a list of font faces in the FONT tag.

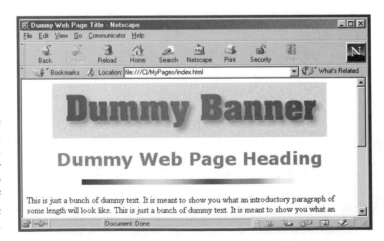

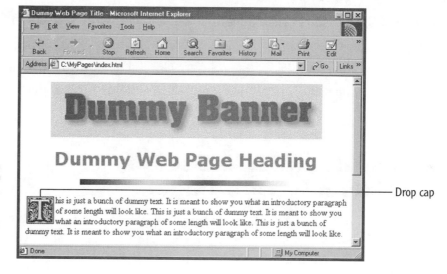

Figure 6.10

Adding a drop cap graphic is a good way to spice up the first paragraph in your Web page.

Drop cap

The example drop cap image was originally taken from a collection of decorative letters that is available for download from this book's Web site at **www.callihan.com/create3/**. I pulled it into Paint Shop Pro 5 and resized it and added some color. You can easily create your own drop cap images in Paint Shop Pro 5 or any other image editor that can save GIF or JPEG images. Adjust the width of your image to suit the letter you want to use (wider for a "W" and narrower for an "I"). You should try to align the bottom of your drop cap letter fairly closely with the bottom of the image. To further adjust the vertical position of the drop cap, adjust the VSPACE attribute up or down.

FIND IT ON ▶
THE WEB

Take a Break?

You can see how this is starting to work, and you may want to rush right on to the guts of the page. But it might be a good idea to stop and stretch, touch your toes, and get your energy level up for the next section. Scratch your cat, if you have one. Water your plants. I'll see you back in ten minutes or so.

Creating the Middle Section of Your Page

Though the top section was the same for all three example Web pages, their middle sections differ. The following three sections cover creating the middle portion of your page—choose the one that corresponds to the example Web page you're using.

Creating the Middle Section (First Example Web Page)

If you have selected the first example Web page (a Web page with a list of external links) as your guide or template for creating your Web page, you should proceed with this section—skip to the next section if you're using the second Web page example. The middle section of the Web page example file you've chosen (basic-1.htm) contains a level-two heading and a link list:

```
<H2>A List of Links</H2>
<UL>
<LI><A HREF="http://www.callihan.com/create3/">Create Your First
Web Page in a Weekend (3rd Edition)</A>: HTML is for everyone!
<LI><A HREF="http://www.w3.org/">World Wide Web Consortium</A>:
Find out the latest about the Web and HTML.
<LI><A HREF="http://www.infohiway.com/faster/homebcs.htm">The
Bandwidth Conservation Society</A>: Save bytes — don't be a
bandwidth hog!
</UL>
```

Adding a Subheading

The example includes a level-two heading (H2). Right now, the text simply indicates that a list of links follows the heading. You can exclude this or you can insert the specific subheading that you want. If you're creating a Web page focused on your favorite hobby, such as stamp collecting, then the subheading here might read "Philatelist Links" or something like that. If you're including a level-two heading, insert it like this (see Figure 6.11):

```
<H2>Insert Your Level-Two Heading</H2>
```

Although I haven't provided one in the example Web page, you can optionally insert a text paragraph following your level-two heading, if you feel the heading alone doesn't sufficiently describe your list of external links.

Creating a List of External Links

The example template uses a list of hypertext links to other pages on the Web. You might want to create a list of your favorite links, or a list of links related to an interest, hobby, or personal expertise. If you haven't yet gathered your own URLs, feel free to use the sample link list for now that is included in the example Web page. You can also find additional URLs in Appendix A, "Web Resources," that you can use here instead, if you want.

Actually, you don't have to include a list of any kind—you can completely eliminate it. Nothing says your Web page can't include just a banner graphic, a level-one heading, one or more paragraphs of text, and your address block. Nothing says you can't insert your links, in context, within your paragraph text. You might just want to include a list without links, or you might want to list the links without explanatory or descriptive text. Or you might want to include explanations for some links but eliminate them from others that you feel are largely self-explanatory.

If you're like most people, however, you'll *want* to include a link list that connects to other pages on the Web. In many ways, the Web is like a giant relay race—pass the baton, in other words.

The following is an example for creating a link list with descriptions. (If you only want to create a list here, eliminate the links and link text. If you want to create a link list without descriptions, eliminate the link descriptions.) Add as many additional link list items as you want. Follow this example to create a link list with descriptions (see Figure 6.11):

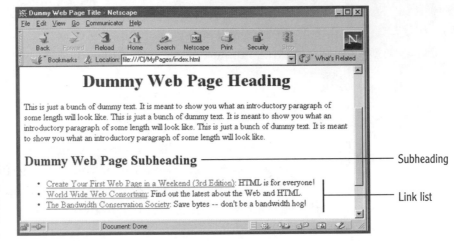

Figure 6.11

You can use a
level-two heading
to help identify a
list of links.

Subheading

Link list

```
<UL>

<LI><A HREF="Insert the URL of your first link">Insert the link
text</A>: Insert the link description.

<LI><A HREF="Insert the URL of your second link">Insert the link
text</A>: Insert the link description.

<LI><A HREF="Insert the URL of your third link">Insert the link
text</A>: Insert the link description.

</UL>
```

Extra Options for the Middle Section (First Example Web Page)

Here are a couple of extra options you might want to try for the middle section of your page if you're using the first example Web page.

Extra Option: Change the Color and Font Face of Your Level-Two Heading

If you used the extra options for the top section to change the color and font face of your level-one heading, you may want to do the same for the level-two heading in the middle section. The following example changes the color of your level-two heading to brick red (#CC0000) and provides

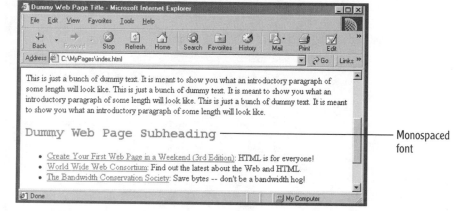

Monospaced
font

Figure 6.12

The color and font
face of the level-
two heading can be
changed.

a list of monospaced font faces that can be displayed if available (see Figure 6.12):

```
<H2><FONT COLOR="#CC0000" FACE="courier new, courier">Your Level-
Two Heading</FONT></H2>
```

Extra Option: Center Your Level-Two Heading and Link List

You can center both your level-two heading and your link list by nesting them inside of a CENTER tag (see Figure 6.13):

```
<CENTER>

<H2><FONT COLOR="#CC0000" FACE="courier new, courier">Your Level-
Two Heading</FONT></H2>

<UL>

<LI><A HREF="http://www.callihan.com/create3/">Create Your First
Web Page in a Weekend (3rd Edition)</A>: HTML is for everyone!

<LI><A HREF="http://www.w3.org/">World Wide Web Consortium</A>:
Find out the latest about the Web and HTML.

<LI><A HREF="http://www.infohiway.com/faster/homebcs.htm">The
Bandwidth Conservation Society</A>: Save bytes — don't be a
bandwidth hog!

</UL>

</CENTER>
```

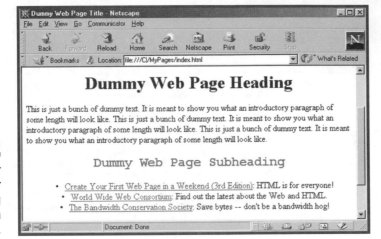

Figure 6.13

You can center elements on your page by nesting them inside of a CENTER tag.

Creating the Middle Section (Second Example Web Page)

If you have selected the second example Web page (a Web page using subsections) as your guide or template for creating your Web page, you should proceed with this section. The example Web page file you've chosen, `basic-2.htm`, includes the following list of internal links, which acts as a table of contents for the following subsections:

```
<UL>
<LI><A HREF="#sub1">First Subsection</A>: This link jumps to the
first subsection.
<LI><A HREF="#sub2">Second Subsection</A>: This link jumps to the
second subsection.
</UL>
<H2><A NAME="sub1"></A>First Subsection</H2>
<P>This is the text for the first subsection. This is the text
for the first subsection. This is the text for the first
subsection. This is the text for the first subsection. This is
the text for the first subsection. This is the text for the
first subsection. This is the text for the first subsection.</P>
<H2><A NAME="sub2"></A>Second Subsection</H2>
```

```
<P>This is the text for the second subsection. This is the text
for the second subsection. This is the text for the second
subsection. This is the text for the second subsection. This is
the text for the second subsection. This is the text for the
second subsection. This is the text for the second subsec-
tion.</P>
```

Creating a Table of Contents

This Web page example uses a link list as a table of contents for the following subsections. Although the example includes descriptions for each link, nothing says you can't use a link list here without descriptions. Feel free to eliminate the descriptions or to include descriptions only where you feel they are necessary. Use the following HTML code list as a guide in creating a link list to serve as a table of contents for the following subsections:

```
<UL>

<LI><A HREF="#sub1">Insert the link text</A>: Insert the link
description.

<LI><A HREF="#sub2">Insert the link text</A>: Insert the link
description.

</UL>
```

Although the example contains only two items, you should include as many link-list items as you have subsections to which you want to link. Just duplicate either of the list items for as many additional links as you need to add, then edit them to add new anchor names, link text, and link descriptions. Note also that the "sub1" and "sub2" anchor names correspond to the same anchor names used to create the "target" links in the subheadings for the subsections. When creating additional list items in your table of contents, be sure that each hypertext anchor has a unique anchor name ("sub3," "sub4," and so on).

Creating the Subsections

Next, you need to create the subheadings and subsections that correspond to the list items in your table of contents (see Figure 6.14):

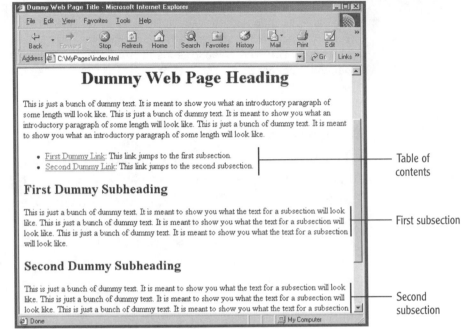

Figure 6.14

A table of contents, also called a link menu, can jump to as many subsections as you want to include in a Web page.

```
<H2><A NAME="sub1"></A>Insert First Subheading</H2>
<P>Insert text for the first subsection . . .
<H2><A NAME="sub2"></A>Insert Second Subheading</H2>
<P>Insert text for the second subsection . . .
```

To create additional subsections, just duplicate the second subsection example as many times as you need. Make sure, however, that each sub-heading has a unique anchor name that corresponds to the anchor name used in your table of contents ("sub3," "sub4," and so on).

Extra Options for the Middle Section (Second Example Web Page)

The following extra options apply specifically to the second basic Web page example. Later in the session, I'll give you an additional option that allows you to create an icon link list rather than a regular link list when you're using any of the three Web page examples.

Extra Option: Use a Definition List to Format Your Subsections

You can give your subsections a slightly different look by using a definition list (DL), also called a glossary list. Using a definition list indents your subsection paragraph text instead of displaying it flush to the left margin. Just insert your subheading on the definition term (DT) line, and use definition data (DD) tags for any following paragraph tags, like this (see Figure 6.15):

```
<DL>
<DT><H2><A NAME="sub1"></A>Your First Subheading</H2>
<DD><P>The text for the first subsection . . .
<DT><H2><A NAME="sub2"></A>Your Second Subheading</H2>
<DD><P>The text for the second subsection . . .
</DL>
```

Extra Option: Add Loop-Back Links

If you're using more than just a few subsections or if your subsections are fairly long, you may want to include loop-back links. These links let viewers jump back to your menu list without having to scroll all the way back up to the top of your page after they finish reading a subsection (see Figure 6.16).

Figure 6.15

You can use a definition list to give your subheadings and subsections a different look.

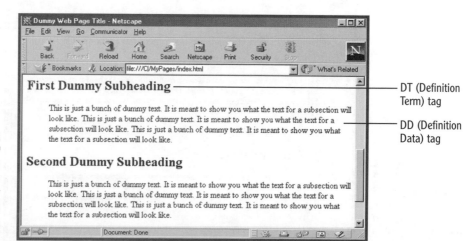

— DT (Definition Term) tag

— DD (Definition Data) tag

```
<UL><A NAME="toc"></A>
<LI><A HREF="#sub1">The link text</A>: The link description.
<LI><A HREF="#sub2">The link text</A>: The link description.
</UL>
<DL>
<DT><H2><A NAME="sub1"></A>Your First Subheading</H2>
<DD><P>The text for the first subsection . . .
<P>Return to <A HREF="#toc">Table of Contents</A>.</P>
<DT><H2><A NAME="sub2"></A>Your Second Subheading</H2>
<DD><P>The text for the second subsection . . .
<P>Return to <A HREF="#toc">Table of Contents</A>.</P>
</DL>
```

Creating the Middle Section (Third Example Web Page)

If you have selected the third example Web page (a Web page with sub-pages) as your guide or template for creating your Web page, you should

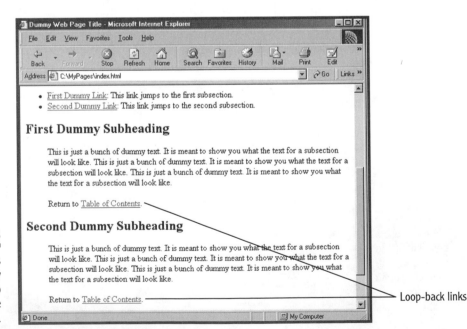

Figure 6.16

Loop-back links can make it easy for a viewer to return to your table of contents.

proceed with this section. The middle section of the Web page example file you've chosen, `basic-3.htm`, includes a table of contents that links to two example subpages (`basic-3a.htm` and `basic-3b.htm`).

This is the middle section of the third Web page example (`basic-3.htm`):

```
<H2>Table of Contents</H2>
<UL>
<LI><A HREF="basic-3a.htm">First Subpage</A>: This links to the
first subpage.
<LI><A HREF="basic-3b.htm">Second Subpage</A>: This links to the
second subpage.
</UL>
```

Creating a Table of Contents

Edit the table of contents of the third example Web page, inserting the file name, link text, and description text for each subpage you are linking to (see Figure 6.17):

NOTE   The file names for the subpages in the example are **basic-3a.htm** and **basic-3b.htm**. You need to substitute the actual names you want to use for your subpages, either variants of your main page's name or names that are more descriptive of the subpages. The only absolute requirement here is that the file name you include in the link menu below exactly match the actual file name of the subpage to which you want to link (including any uppercase or lowercase letters, because MySub1.HTML and mysub1.html refer to two different files on a UNIX Web server).

```
<UL>
<LI><A HREF="Insert the file name of your first subpage">Insert
the link text</A>: Insert the link description.
<LI><A HREF="Insert the file name of the second subpage">Insert
the link text</A>: Insert the link description.
</UL>
```

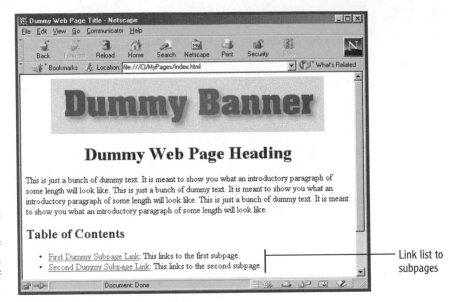

Figure 6.17

A main page uses a link list (table of contents) to link to a series of subpages.

Link list to subpages

NOTE   Just starting out, you're most likely storing all of your Web page files (HTML files and image files) in the same folder. By doing that, you only need to insert the file name as the URL when linking to another HTML file or inserting an inline image. Eventually, however, you'll want to start storing your Web page files in more than one folder. To do that, you'll need to use a relative URL (HREF="prices/index.htm", for instance). See "Using Relative URLs" in the Intermediate HTML Tutorial for more guidance on using relative URLs.

Creating Your Subpages

I've provided two example subpages, basic-3a.htm and basic-3b.htm, which are almost exactly the same. You can use either one as a template or guide for creating your subpages. The following are the codes for the first example subpage, basic-3a.htm.

```
<HTML>
<HEAD>
```

```
<TITLE>Web Page Example #3a (Your Title Goes Here)</TITLE>
</HEAD>
<BODY>
<H1>First Subpage</H1>
<P>This is the text for the first subpage. This is the text for
the first subpage. This is the text for the first subpage. This
is the text for the first subpage. This is the text for the
first subpage. This is the text for the first subpage. This is
the text for the first subpage.</P>
<P>Return to <A HREF="basic-3.htm">Home Page</A>.</P>
<HR>
<ADDRESS>
<STRONG>Your Name Here</STRONG><BR>
E-mail: <A HREF="mailto:your@address.com">your@address.com</A>
</ADDRESS>
</BODY>
</HTML>
```

Save a separate copy of the subpage example file for each subpage you want to create. I've sequentially named the example subpages, but you'll probably want to give your subpages names that'll help to identify their purpose or content (about.htm, prices.htm, contact.htm, and so on). The only requirement is that the file names match exactly (including uppercase and lowercase letters) what you use in the links for your table of contents on your main page.

Go ahead and edit your subpage, inserting a title, level-one heading, introductory paragraph, and loop-back link to your main page (see Figure 6.18):

```
<HEAD>
<TITLE>Insert a title for your subpage</TITLE>
</HEAD>
<BODY>
<H1>Insert a Level-One Heading</H1>
<P>Insert an introductory paragraph . . .
<P>Return to <A HREF="Insert the file name of your main
page">Home Page.</A>
```

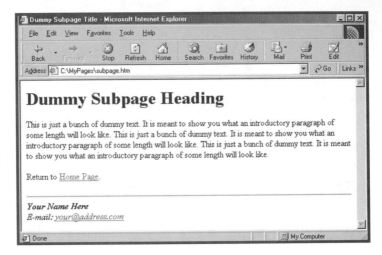

Figure 6.18

A subpage is a Web page linked from the home page of a multi-page Web site.

A subpage doesn't have to be this simple, of course. It can be a complete Web page, including a list of external links, as in the first Web page example, or a table of contents linking to internal subsections, as in the second Web page example. It could even link to subpages of its own!

In creating your subpages, feel free to use any of the three example Web pages as models, although you might use the first two examples first (before trying to create a site that links to subpages that link to further subpages).

For suggestions and directions for creating the bottom section (containing the address block) of your subpage, see "Creating the Bottom Section of Your Page (All Three Example Web Pages)" later in this session.

Extra Options for Subpages

You have several options for tying subpages more closely to the main page.

Extra Option: Add a Banner or Logo Graphic

The example subpage doesn't have a banner or logo graphic. Using a banner or logo graphic for your subpages can help tie them together,

however. A handy trick is to resize your banner graphic for display as a logo on your subpages. Normally, you wouldn't want to resize an image downward because you want images downloaded with your pages from the Web to be as small as possible. In this case, however, you only run into a bandwidth penalty if you end up getting a lot of visitors to your subpage who aren't coming to it by way of your main page. If that happens, you should probably use a second, smaller version of your banner graphic instead of resizing the original. Also, if there is a significant size difference between your full-size banner graphic and your resized logo graphic, it will probably take longer for your image to load into memory and be displayed than would be the case if you pulled it into your paint program to resize it.

The example shown here inserts and resizes `dummy.gif`, the dummy banner graphic that is included with the example Web page files. (If you are using `webpage.gif`, set the WIDTH to 200 instead of 250.) Just insert the following (see Figure 6.19):

```
<P><IMG SRC="dummy.gif" WIDTH="250" HEIGHT="50"></P>
<H1>Your Level-One Heading</H1>
```

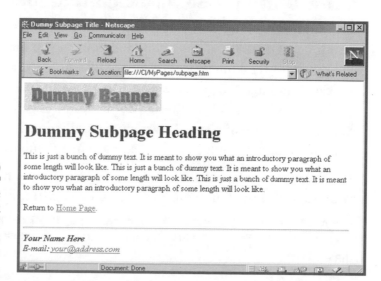

Figure 6.19

You can resize the banner graphic from your main page and use it as a logo graphic on your subpages.

If you are using a custom banner graphic here, you'll need to insert WIDTH and HEIGHT values that are proportional to the actual size of your graphic. For instance, if your banner graphic is 550 pixels wide by 150 pixels high, you might resize it here to 225 by 75 pixels.

You could also center-align both your logo graphic and your level-one heading, or you could left-align your logo graphic and wrap the level-one heading around it. See the extra options for the top section of all three example Web pages for more information on how to apply those features.

NOTE   The subpage example includes a loop-back link at the bottom of the page. This is a navigational device that lets the user get from the subpage to the home page. Including a loop-back link on subpages is important because you don't know how somebody is going to end up at a subpage—a visitor doesn't have to come through your home page to get to it but can jump in from anywhere as long as he or she has its URL. If someone comes to your subpage via a search engine, for example, pressing the Web browser Back button returns him or her to the search engine list, not to your home page.

Extra Option: Use a Navigational Icon

Navigational icons are a way to visually indicate a link without having to spell it out. Generally, an arrow or hand pointing up indicates that a link will return to the home page. An image of a house is also often used to indicate a link back to a home page. An arrow or hand pointing to the left indicates that a link will return to the home page or to the previous page in a sequence of pages. An arrow or hand pointing to the right indicates that a link will jump to the next page in a sequence of pages.

The following example uses an arrow pointing left as a navigational icon to indicate that the link returns to the home page (see Figure 6.20):

```
<P><A HREF="The file name of your main page"><IMG SRC="arr-
left.gif" HEIGHT="50" WIDTH="50" ALT="Home" BORDER="0"></A></P>
<HR>
```

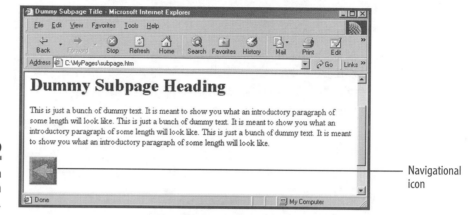

Figure 6.20

You can use a navigational icon as a loop-back link.

Navigational icon

TIP

If you're creating a series of subpages that visitors should view in sequence, you could use a right-pointing arrow or hand to indicate a link to the next subpage in the series. In that context, a left-pointing arrow would indicate a link back to the previous page. An up-pointing arrow could then indicate a link to the home page. A common navigational icon on the Web is the image of a house, indicating a link back to the home page. Besides the left-pointing arrow you've already seen (arr-left.gif), a right-pointing arrow (arr-right.gif) and an up-pointing arrow (arr-up.gif) have been included with the example Web page files.

The example uses the ALT attribute in the IMG tag to identify the navigational icon for people who can't see the image itself. You should always use an ALT attribute with navigational icons because a navigational icon offers no other indication of the graphic's purpose.

Creating the Bottom Section of Your Page (All Three Example Web Pages)

The bottom section of the example Web pages contains the address block. It is the same for all three example Web pages (as well as for the example subpages included with the third Web page example):

```
<HR>
<ADDRESS>
<STRONG>Your Name Here</STRONG><BR>
E-mail: <A
HREF="mailto:your@address.com">your@address.com</A><BR>
Last Modified: Current date here
</ADDRESS>
</BODY>
</HTML>
```

Creating Your Address Block

Edit the address block, inserting your name, e-mail address, and the current date (see Figure 6.21):

```
<ADDRESS>
<STRONG>Insert your name here</STRONG><BR>
E-mail: <A HREF="mailto:Insert your e-mail address">Insert your
e-mail address again</A><BR>
Last Modified: Insert the current date
</ADDRESS>
```

You can add additional contact information, if you wish, to your address block. For pages other than your home page, you might want to include a URL line with a link back to your home page. If your page is for your business, for instance, you might want to also include an 800 number, your fax number, and so on. Just add a <BR> tag to add another line.

Figure 6.21

Every Web page should have an address block telling a visitor how to contact you.

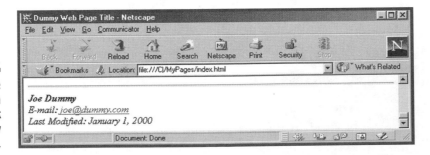

◆ ◆

If your page is going to be hosted on AOL, you may want to consider not including your e-mail address on your Web page at all. That's because AOL users tend to be targeted by spammers much more than those with pages hosted on non-AOL servers. One alternative is to use a guestbook, which will allow you to get messages from visitors to your site without having to reveal your e-mail address. AOL has a free guestbook that you can add to your page. Non-AOL users can check my Web Links site for links to where they can find a free guestbook for their pages—just go to **www.callihan.com/weblinks/** and click on Features in the sidebar menu.

Another alternative is to get a free Web mail account through Yahoo! Mail, MSDN Hotmail, Netscape WebMail, Mail.com, or others. (A Web mail account usually requires that you log in with your browser to check your mail, rather than downloading it with an e-mail program.) Create a contact page, with a mailto link to your Web mail address. That way, if you start getting too much spam, just switch to a new Web mail account—plus you'll only have to change your e-mail address on one page, your contact page. For lots of links to Web mail providers, check out Yahoo!'s list at **dir.yahoo.com/ Business_and_Economy/Companies/Internet_Services/Email_Providers/Free _Email/**.

◆ ◆

If you're creating a home page with subpages, you should create an address block for each page. Remember, you don't know how somebody is going to get to a particular page—a visitor can hop in from anywhere. Some search engines use robot agents (sometimes called *worms* or *spiders*) to scan and index the Web. These agents can pick up your subpages even when you didn't list them—and direct people to the depths of your site who have no idea where it is or what else might be on it.

It is also a good idea to include in your address block the date when the page was created or last updated, especially if your page includes information that may become outdated.

Extra Options for the Bottom Section

Following are some extra options you can use to dress up your address block in the bottom section of your Web page.

Extra Option: Vary the Height and Shading of the Horizontal Rule

You can change the height and shading of the horizontal rule. For instance, to use a 10-pixel unshaded rule as a separator between the rest of your Web page and your address block, do the following (see Figure 6.22):

```
<HR SIZE="10" NOSHADE>
<ADDRESS>
```

Extra Option: Use a Graphic Rule in Place of a Horizontal Rule

You can add more color and pizzazz to your page by using a graphic rule rather than a horizontal rule as a separator. The example here uses `rain_lin.gif`, the same graphic rule you saw in the extra option for inserting a graphic rule between the level-one heading and the introductory paragraph. The graphic rule is set in the following example at a width of 100% and a height of 10 pixels (see Figure 6.23):

```
<P><IMG SRC="rain_lin.gif" WIDTH="100%" HEIGHT="10"></P>
<ADDRESS>
```

Figure 6.22

To more emphatically separate your address block, increase the size of the horizontal rule and turn off the shading so you get a solid rule.

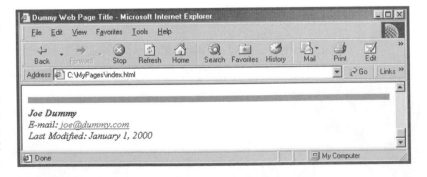

Figure 6.23

To even more emphatically separate your address block, use a multicolor graphic rule.

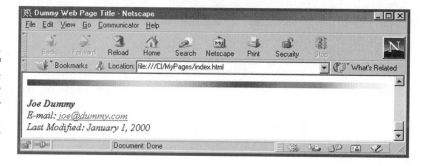

Extra Option: Center Your Address Block

The ADDRESS element is flush left by default. A nice touch can be to center your address block. To do this, just nest your address block inside a CENTER tag; and while you're at it, set the width of your graphic rule or horizontal rule to less than 100%, like this (see Figure 6.24):

```
<CENTER>
<P><IMG SRC="rain_lin.gif" WIDTH="75%" HEIGHT="10"></P>
<ADDRESS>
<STRONG>Your name here</STRONG><BR>
E-mail: <A HREF="mailto:Your e-mail address">Your e-mail address
again</A><BR>
Last Modified: The current date
</ADDRESS>
</CENTER>
```

Figure 6.24

Address blocks are often centered to make them stand out.

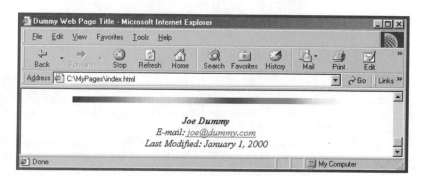

Adding Color and Pizzazz to Your Page

This section—which applies to all three example Web pages—contains a series of extra options that you can use to adjust the overall look and feel of your Web page. The options include setting font sizes and colors, creating an icon link list, changing the background and text colors, and using a background image.

Extra Option: Increase the Base Font Size

One thing you can do to make your page more readable is to increase the BASEFONT size a notch, from the default size of 3 to 4. The default base font size can be a little difficult to read at higher screen resolutions on less than bountiful monitor sizes (at 800 x 600 pixels on a 15- or 16-inch monitor, for instance). Also, the default base font size is even smaller on a Macintosh than on a Windows system. To give viewers of your page a break, insert the following at the top of your page (see Figure 6.25):

```
<BODY>
<BASEFONT SIZE="4">
```

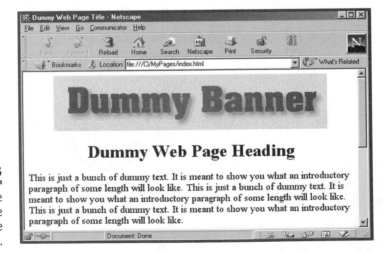

Figure 6.25

Increasing the base font size can make your page more readable.

Extra Option: Create an Icon Link List

Using an icon link list (instead of a plain unordered [bulleted] link list) is a good way to add color and visual appeal to your Web page. Because an icon link list doesn't use an unordered list, you need to first delete the UL start and end tags, and all the LI tags, so that the text for your link list looks like this:

 NOTE In the following, URL refers to the first basic Web page example, anchor name refers to the second basic Web page example, and subpage file name refers to the third basic Web page example.

```
<A HREF="The URL, anchor name, or subpage file name for your
first link">The link text</A>: The link description.
<A HREF="The URL, anchor name, or subpage file name for your
second link">The link text</A>: The link description.
<A HREF="The URL, anchor name, or subpage file name for your
third link">The link text</A>: The link description.
```

Now, to create an icon link list, you need to add three bits of code: a paragraph tag at the start of the list, a graphic icon bullet at the start of each list line, and a BR tag with the CLEAR="left" attribute value set. To do this, edit the text for your link list like this (see Figure 6.26):

ON THE

CD

The example that follows uses an icon bullet image, `icon.gif`, that I've included with the example Web page files. You can also check out the Web art collections included on the CD-ROM for even more icon bullets that you can use in your pages. A great way to check these out is to use Paint Shop Pro 5's Browse feature (select Open, Browse, and then open the folder you want to browse) to view thumbnails of all GIF or JPEG images in any folder on the CD-ROM, or on your hard drive, for that matter.

FIND IT ON ▶
THE WEB

You'll also find a collection of icon bullet images available for download from this book's Web site at **www.callihan.com/create3**.

```
<P><IMG SRC="icon.gif" ALIGN="left" HSPACE="8" VSPACE="4"><A
HREF="The URL, anchor name, or subpage file name for your first
link">The link text</A>: The link description.<BR CLEAR="left">

<IMG SRC="icon.gif" ALIGN="left" HSPACE="8" VSPACE="4"><A
HREF="The URL, anchor name, or subpage file name for your first
link">The link text</A>: The link description.<BR CLEAR="left">

<IMG SRC="icon.gif" ALIGN="left" HSPACE="8" VSPACE="4"><A
HREF="The URL, anchor name, or subpage file name for your first
link">The link text</A>: The link description.<BR
CLEAR="left"></P>
```

If you did the Tables Tutorial on Saturday evening, you might also try creating an icon link list here using a table. That will allow you to indent an unlimited number of following lines.

Extra Option: Set Background, Text, and Link Colors

You can add significant impact to your Web page just by changing the background and text colors. The text colors here include not only the text color (TEXT), but also the color of links (LINK), visited links (VLINK), and activated links (ALINK), which are links where you have pressed but not released the mouse button. If you've set the font colors for your level-one and level-two headings, you'll want to adjust those colors so they'll work in conjunction with the background color you set in the BODY tag.

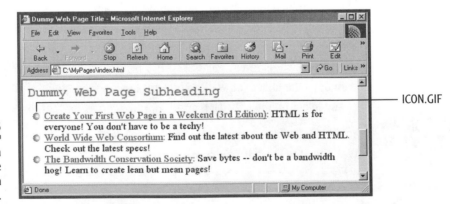

Figure 6.26

An icon link list is a good way to give your Web page a whole new look.

The following example sets colors for the background, text, links, visited links, and activated links, as well as for the level-one and level-two headings (see Figure 6.27):

```
</HEAD>
<BODY BGCOLOR="#004080" TEXT="#FFFFCC" LINK="#00F00"
VLINK="#99CC99" ALINK="#F0099">
<P ALIGN="center"><IMG SRC="Your banner graphic"></P>
<H1 ALIGN="center"><FONT COLOR="#FF6699">Your Level-One
Heading</FONT></H1>
<P>Your introductory paragraph....
<H2><FONT COLOR="#FF9900">Your Level-Two Heading</FONT></H2>
```

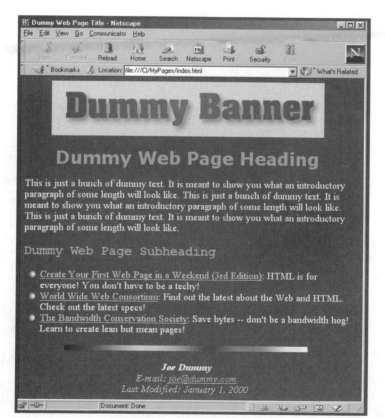

Figure 6.27

To give your Web page a completely different look, assign colors to the background, text, links, and headings.

ON THE

CD

I've included an HTML file, `colors.html`, with the Web page example files that shows all 216 browser-safe colors and their corresponding RGB hex codes. Just open it in your browser (from C:\MyPages) to check it out. Feel free to play around with different color combinations to find just the right colors for your page. Remember, however, that finding the wrong color combination is easy; finding just the right one can take a while.

Extra Option: Use a Background Image

You can add a background image to your Web page by using the BACK-GROUND attribute in the BODY tag. This can help to give your page more of a 3-D look. To test this, insert the following background image (see Figure 6.28):

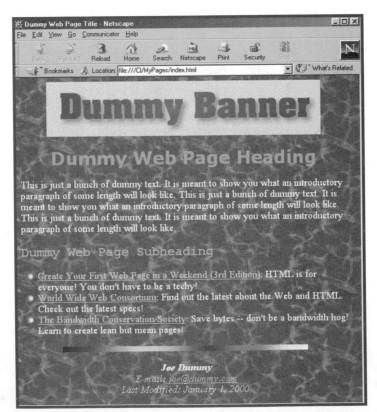

Figure 6.28

For a dramatic effect, use a background image.

```
<BODY BACKGROUND="pool.jpg" BGCOLOR="#004080" TEXT="#FFFFCC"
LINK="#00F00" VLINK="#99CC99" ALINK="#F0099">
```

Extra Option: Use a Transparent Banner Graphic Against a Background Image

One way to give your Web page a three-dimensional look is to use a banner graphic with its background color set to transparent against a background image. You haven't learned yet how to create transparent GIF images (I cover that in tonight's bonus session), so in the following I have you insert a sample transparent banner graphic, dummy_tr.gif, so you can see what this looks like. This transparent graphic works best when displayed against a background image in which the primary color is white. Replace your current BODY tag with what is shown below and change the name of your banner graphic to dummy_tr.gif (see Figure 6.29):

```
</HEAD>
<BODY BACKGROUND="backgrnd.gif" BGCOLOR="white">
<BASEFONT SIZE="4">
<P ALIGN="center"><IMG SRC="dummy_tr.gif"></P>
```

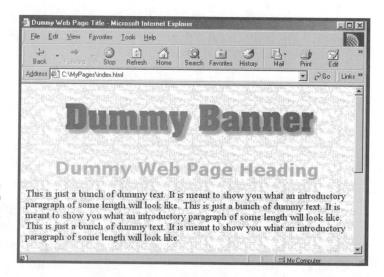

Figure 6.29

A transparent banner graphic can give your page a 3-D look.

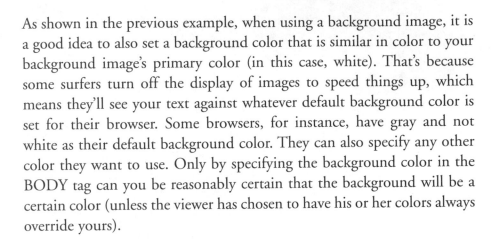

As shown in the previous example, when using a background image, it is a good idea to also set a background color that is similar in color to your background image's primary color (in this case, white). That's because some surfers turn off the display of images to speed things up, which means they'll see your text against whatever default background color is set for their browser. Some browsers, for instance, have gray and not white as their default background color. They can also specify any other color they want to use. Only by specifying the background color in the BODY tag can you be reasonably certain that the background will be a certain color (unless the viewer has chosen to have his or her colors always override yours).

Extra Option: Define a Style Sheet

I included some examples of using styles in the Saturday Afternoon and Evening sessions. We don't have enough time or space to devote to styles, but you don't have to be an expert in using Cascading Style Sheets to add some nice touches to your Web page. I've included an HTML file, style.htm, that uses a style sheet with the example Web page files. To check it out, just pull it up in your browser (see Figure 6.30).

The current versions of Internet Explorer and Netscape Navigator differ fairly significantly in how they display this file. Internet Explorer clearly offers the superior support for style sheets at this time. Undoubtedly, that will change rapidly because style sheets are the wave of the future.

If you want to find out more about using styles, read Eric Meyer's excellent introduction to the subject, "Creating Your First Style Sheet," at **webreview.com/wr/pub/97/10/10/style/index.html**. Then see the W3C's page on Cascading Style Sheets at **www.w3.org/Style/CSS/**, which has the full specifications for both Cascading Style Sheets, level 1 (CSS1) and Cascading Style Sheets, level 2 (CSS2). To double-check which styles will work in which browsers, see Web Review's Cascading Style Sheets Guide for compatibility charts at **webreview.com/wr/pub/guides/style/style.html**. For links to where you can find out even more about using styles, see my

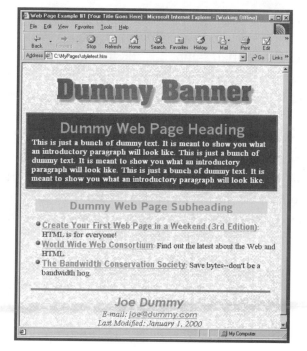

Figure 6.30

You can do things with styles that you can't do any other way.

Web Links site at **www.callihan.com/weblinks/** (click on Features and then Styles in the sidebar menu).

Wrapping Up

You should now have created your first Web page. Hooray! True, you may have stuck to creating a very basic Web page, which uses only tags and features from Saturday morning's Basic HTML Tutorial. Or you may have incorporated a number of the suggested extra options to jazz it up, most of which are based on tags and features from Saturday afternoon's Intermediate HTML Tutorial. You may also have used one of the example banner graphics or the example link list I provided as placeholders until you have time to create your own. A Web page tends to be a work in progress—never, ever finished, in other words. And one page tends to lead to another, and to another, and so on. The more you work at it, the better you get.

If you have managed to do everything I've put before you up until now, all in a single weekend, that's fantastic. Even if you've stuck to doing the Basic HTML Tutorial, skipped all the extra options when creating your first Web page, and used my sample banner and links, you've still accomplished a lot! Remember, it is the tortoise and not the hare that wins the race in the old fable because he keeps his eye on his final objective and is always making steady progress—not that the hare doesn't also get across the finish line. He just tends to get more easily distracted, runs in fits and starts, and takes more side trips and detours along the way. (Hey, that kind of sounds like me!) The point is to do it your own way; follow your own style of learning and working. And if you get frustrated because you're spinning your wheels, take a break!

So, what's next? If you haven't done the Intermediate HTML Tutorial or the Tables Tutorial that were scheduled for Saturday afternoon and evening, you might want to go back and do those tutorials first.

For those of you who have managed to finish everything so far and still have some time and energy left, I've got a final bonus session for you tonight, the Graphics Tutorial, that covers using Paint Shop Pro 5 to create some really neat graphics special effects. If you want to give that a try, first take a break, and have some dinner. Reintroduce yourself to your family while you're at it—they probably haven't seen you in a while! I'll see you back here in an hour or so.

On the other hand, you may be ready to call it a day! Feel free to come back and do the Graphics Tutorial—or any of the other tutorials that you've skipped—on another day, or another weekend!

The Graphics Tutorial

(BONUS SESSION)

- ⚙ Paint Shop Pro 5's layout
- ⚙ Creating transparent and interlaced GIFs
- ⚙ Creating drop shadow effects
- ⚙ Using color, pattern, and gradient fills
- ⚙ Creating 3-D buttons

It's Sunday evening! If you are on schedule, you planned your first Web page this morning and created it this afternoon. This evening, if you have the time and energy, I'll show you how to create some Web art special effects that you can use to dress up your Web page.

Installing and Running Paint Shop Pro 5

For this tutorial, you'll be using Paint Shop Pro 5, a great shareware image editor. A 30-day evaluation version of Paint Shop Pro 5 is included on the CD-ROM.

 NOTE Paint Shop Pro 5 requires a 32-bit version of Windows (95, 98, NT, or 2000). If you're using one of the 16-bit versions of Windows (3.1 or 3.11), you won't be able to install Paint Shop Pro and do this tutorial. Jasc, Inc. (**www.jasc.com**) does have a 16-bit version, Paint Shop Pro 3.11, that you can download, although it significantly differs in its capabilities and features from the version covered in this tutorial.

This tutorial is best done in a screen resolution of 800 x 600 pixels or greater. If your system is limited to a 640 x 480 screen resolution, you can still do the tutorial, although you might find it a bit cramped. All of the figures for this session were grabbed at 800 x 600.

You can install Paint Shop Pro 5 directly from Prima's interface for the CD-ROM. To install Paint Shop Pro 5, do the following:

1. Insert the CD-ROM. If Prima Tech's user interface doesn't automatically run, click on the Start button, select Run, type **d:\CDInstaller.exe** (where *d* is your CD-ROM's drive letter), and click on OK.

2. Click on I Accept to accept the Prima license terms. In the left windowpane, expand the contents of Create Your First Web Page In a Weekend, expand the contents of Multimedia, click on Paint Shop Pro, and then click on the Install button.

To run Paint Shop Pro 5, click on the Start button, then select Programs, Paint Shop Pro 5, and Paint Shop Pro 5 again.

Setting File Associations

When running Paint Shop Pro 5 the first time, you're prompted to specify the file types to associate with Paint Shop Pro. You might check the CompuServe Graphics Exchange and JPEG - JIF Compliant check boxes. That way, if you double-click on a *.gif or *.jpg file name in Windows Explorer or My Computer, for instance, the file will automatically be opened in Paint Shop Pro. To unselect a file type, just click on its check box so that it's unchecked. (You can easily change any of these associations later by selecting File, Preferences, and File Associations. If you later choose to uninstall Paint Shop Pro 5.03, the version on the CD-ROM, you'll be prompted to remove any file associations you've set.) To accept the current selections, just click on OK.

Using the Tip of the Day Dialog Box

By default, Paint Shop Pro pops up a Tip of the Day dialog box. If you find this to be more of a nuisance than a help, feel free to uncheck the Show Tips on Startup check box. To view an additional tip, click on the Next Tip button. To close the Tip of the Day dialog box, click on the Close button.

Turning Off or Moving the Layers and Controls Palettes

When you first run Paint Shop Pro, the Layers and Controls Palettes are displayed in the middle of Paint Shop Pro's window. Because I won't be covering Layers in this tutorial, feel free to turn off display of the Layers Palette. Select View and ToolBars from the menu bar, and then uncheck the Layers Palette check box. You'll be using the Controls Palette later, so just drag it out of the way, dropping it in the bottom-right corner of the window, for instance.

Creating a New Image

Before you can start using Paint Shop Pro 5, you need to either open an image you've already created or create a new image. To create a new image, follow these steps:

1. Select File, New.

2. In the New Image dialog box, set the Width to **450** and the Height to **125**.

3. For the Background color, select White. Leave the other options set as they are: Resolution, 72, and Image type, 16.7 Million Colors. (See Figure 7.1.) Click on OK.

NOTE Many of the special effects that you can create in Paint Shop Pro require a color palette of 16.7 million colors. If you don't set this at the New Image dialog box, you can increase the number of colors later, if you want.

Paint Shop Pro's Screen Layout

Pause for a moment and go over the Paint Shop Pro screen layout. This is important because throughout this section, I'll refer to different parts of Paint Shop Pro's screen by name instead of describing them in detail.

Figure 7.1

The New Image
dialog box defines
the dimensions,
background color,
and color depth of
a new image.

Tool Palette   Image window   Status bar

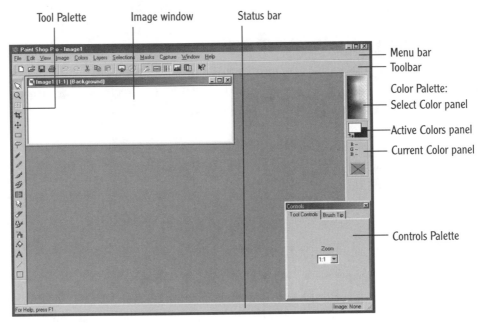

Menu bar
Toolbar
Color Palette:
Select Color panel
Active Colors panel
Current Color panel
Controls Palette

Figure 7.2

Paint Shop Pro's
screen layout.

As you go through the following exercises, you can use Figure 7.2 as a
quick reference to what is on the screen.

The following list describes the callouts to Figure 7.2:

○ **Menu bar**. This is the pull-down menu (File, Edit, View, and so
on) at the top of Paint Shop Pro's window.

○ **Toolbar**. This is the top row of buttons, which are primarily short-
cuts for operations that can be carried out using the menu bar. For

instance, instead of selecting File, New to create a new image, you can just click on the first toolbar button (New). It also has five buttons grouped at the right that let you toggle on and off the display of the Tool, Control, Color, Histogram, and Layer Palettes.

- **Tool Palette**. This is the row of buttons that runs down the left side of the window (unless you've dragged and dropped it somewhere else). The buttons allow you to zoom in or out, move your image in the image window, select part of the image, paint, erase, fill, add text, and so on.

- **Controls Palette**. This palette displays the controls that are available when any of the tools on the Tool Palette are selected. For instance, when the Flood Fill tool (the paint-bucket icon) is selected, you can select Fill Style, along with other controls, from the Control Palette.

- **Color Palette**. This is located on the right side of the screen. It has three parts: the Select Color, Active Colors, and Current Color panels. In this tutorial, you'll primarily be using the Active Colors panel, which is composed of two overlapped color swatches showing the currently assigned foreground and background colors.

- **Image window**. This is the window that contains the actual graphic you're creating. Note that you can have more than one image window open at a time, but only one of them will be the active image window.

- **Status bar**. This is the bar that runs along the bottom of Paint Shop Pro's window. It provides information about images, features, and operations. For instance, if you pass the mouse over an image, the dimensions of the image are displayed in the status bar.

Creating Special Effects with Paint Shop Pro 5

In this tutorial, I'll be showing you how to create a variety of special effects that are especially useful for creating images for Web pages. Of course, you're not going to be able to learn everything there is to know about using Paint Shop Pro 5 in a single evening, but hopefully this tutorial will give you a good head start. This tutorial covers the following features of Paint Shop Pro 5:

- Creating text effects
- Creating transparent and interlaced GIFs
- Creating drop shadow effects
- Using color, pattern, and gradient fill effects
- Creating 3-D buttons

Creating Text Effects

Creating text effects is a great way to give impact to your Web images. This can be especially useful for creating banner graphics. All of the special effects covered in this tutorial involve using text effects to one degree or another, although they can also largely stand on their own.

Selecting a Foreground Color

If you want your text to be a particular color, you should select it first. You can select a color two ways.

The first is to select a color from the Select Color panel. If you move the mouse cursor over the Select Color panel, you'll notice that the color under the cursor is shown in the Current Color panel. If you click the left mouse button, the current color is applied to the foreground color swatch in the Active Colors panel. If you click the right mouse button, the color is applied to the background color swatch.

The other way to select a color is to click directly on either the foreground-color or background-color swatch to open the Color dialog box. Use this method to assign a foreground color:

1. In the Active Colors panel, click on the foreground-color swatch. The Color dialog box opens (see Figure 7.3). The Color dialog box

provides you with a number of ways to select colors. You can select one of the Basic Colors, or you can select from the color matrix on the right. You can also specify the RGB or HSL values for a color, or you can specify an HTML Code for a color. You can also create a selection of custom colors so you can come back and reselect the same color later.

You can use the HTML Code box in the Color dialog box to help you select "browser-safe" colors for your images. As you may recall from the Intermediate HTML Tutorial, the browser-safe HTML color codes are composed of these hex codes: 00, 33, 66, 99, CC, and FF. Colors composed of only these hex codes will not be dithered on systems that can only display 256 colors. This is not as big of an issue as it once was because the number of 256-color systems in use is dwindling rapidly. If you do want to stick to using browser-safe colors, just make sure for any color you select that the hex code in the HTML Code box is only composed of the hex codes above.

The HTML Code box can be helpful in another way. You can use it to find the RGB hex code for any color, so you can then insert it into your HTML file as a font or background color. For instance, you might want to coordinate a color in your banner image with your Web page's background color.

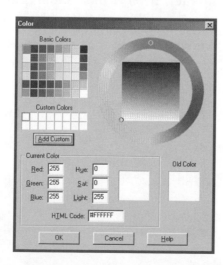

Figure 7.3

The Color dialog box can be used to select a foreground or background color.

2. For this example, click on the color red (the first color in the first column) under Basic Colors. You'll see your selection reflected in the color matrix on the right and in the Current Color area.

3. Click on OK. Notice that the foreground-color swatch has changed to red.

Inserting Some Text

Now that you've selected your text color, insert text into your image window:

1. Click on the Text tool (the "A" icon) on the Tool Palette, and then click in the middle of the image window.

2. In the Add Text dialog box, select Arial as the Name of your font, Bold as the Style, and 72 (points) as the Size. Leave the Antialias check box selected (to help smooth font curves and diagonals). Also, make sure the Floating check box is checked. Leave any other settings as they are.

◀◀◀◀◀◀◀◀◀◀◀◀◀◀◀◀◀◀◀◀◀◀◀◀◀◀◀◀◀◀◀◀◀◀◀◀◀◀◀

Anti-aliasing smooths out the edges of a font by fuzzing the pixels around the edge, alternating different color shades to give the appearance of a smoother contour.

◀◀◀◀◀◀◀◀◀◀◀◀◀◀◀◀◀◀◀◀◀◀◀◀◀◀◀◀◀◀◀◀◀◀◀◀◀◀◀

3. In the text box (Enter text here) at the bottom of the window, type **Headline**. (See Figure 7.4.) Click on OK.

4. Click and hold the mouse pointer on the text and drag it so it is roughly centered vertically and horizontally within the image window. Just lift off the mouse button to drop the text where you want it. (See Figure 7.5.)

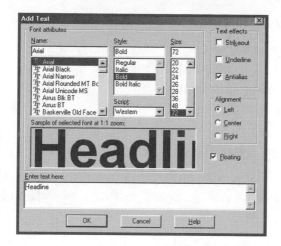

Figure 7.4

In the Add Text dialog box, the word "Headline" has been set as a 72-point bold Arial font.

Figure 7.5

When you add text to an image window, it appears in the current foreground color and is surrounded by a dotted line (indicating that the text is selected).

Creating Transparent and Interlaced GIFs

Using transparency and interlacing are handy tricks you can do with GIF images. With GIF images, you can set one color as transparent (usually the background color), and you can set the whole image to be interlaced. The first allows you to display a GIF image transparently against a Web page's background color or background image; the second uses several passes to paint the image, with each pass displaying only some of the lines of the image. This gives a viewer of the image over the Internet an idea of what the whole image is going to look like before it has been downloaded and displayed.

Creating Transparent GIFs

Creating a transparent GIF in Paint Shop Pro 5 is a two-step process. First, you need to assign the color you want to be transparent to the background-color swatch; second, you need to specify that you want the color to be transparent.

Assigning the Background Color

The current color in the background of your image is white. To be able to set it as transparent, you need to first assign the color white to the background-color swatch:

1. If the color assigned to the background-color swatch does not match the color in the background of the image window (white), click on the background-color swatch to open the Color dialog box.
2. Click on the white color (bottom-right corner of Basic Colors) to select it.

The main thing to realize here is that the color assigned to the background-color swatch has to match the color in your image that you want to be transparent (in this case, white). For instance, if you were to fill the background of the image with a black color, to turn that color transparent you'd need to first assign the color black to the background-color swatch.

Setting the Transparent Color

To set the color displayed in the background-color swatch (in this case, white) as transparent, just do the following:

1. Select Colors and Set Palette Transparency.
2. At the prompt telling you that the image must be reduced to one background layer and 256 colors, click on Yes.
3. In the Decrease Color Depth window, Optimized Median Cut and Error Diffusion should be selected. Leave the other options unchecked. Click on OK.

4. In the Set Palette Transparency window, select the second radio button (Set the transparency value to the current background color). (See Figure 7.6.) Click on OK.

Viewing the Transparency

To make sure that the color you want is transparent, do the following:

1. Click on Colors and View Palette Transparency.

2. The transparent background color is displayed in a checkerboard pattern (see Figure 7.7).

3. Repeat step 1 to turn off viewing the transparency.

Saving Your Transparent GIF

To save your image as a transparent GIF, you need to save it as a CompuServe Graphics Interchange Format (GIF) image. In the next section, where you'll learn how to save an interlaced GIF, I'll walk you through saving your file in this format.

Figure 7.6

You can turn transparency on or off in the Set Palette Transparency window.

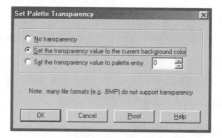

Figure 7.7

When View Palette Transparency is turned on, the transparent color is displayed in a checkerboard pattern.

NOTE Don't expect a transparent GIF to look different from any other GIF image when viewed with Paint Shop Pro 5 or another paint program or graphics viewer. The image will only appear transparent when viewed as an inline image with a Web browser.

Saving an Interlaced GIF

To save an interlaced GIF, you just need to select that option when saving your file:

1. Click on File and Save (or Save As).
2. To save your image in the working folder for your Web pages (C:\MyPages, for instance), click on the Save in box, and then click on the [C:] drive icon. In the folder window, double-click on your working folder (MyPages, or whichever folder you're saving your Web pages in).

TIP Although saving your GIF and JPEG images directly into your working folder for Web pages makes it easier to insert them inline in your HTML files (you need only to include the file name as the URL), you should consider saving your images into a separate folder, just to help keep them straight. For instance, create a new folder, images, inside of your working folder, and then save your images there (to C:\MyPages\images, for instance). In the Save As dialog box, click on the Create New Folder icon, type **images**, and hit Enter. Double-click on the images folder to open it.

Then to insert your image in an HTML file saved in your working folder, instead of using just the image file name as the URL, you would use a relative URL that includes both the folder name and the file name (<IMG SRC="images/headline.gif">, for instance).

3. Click on the Save as type box, and then scroll up and select CompuServe Graphics Interchange (*.gif).
4. In the File name box, type **headline.gif** as the name of your image.
5. Click on the Options button. Click on the Interlaced radio button. Leave the Version 89a radio button selected. Click on OK.

6. Click on the Save button to save `headline.gif` (to C:\MyPages\images, if you followed the tip, or C:\MyPages, if you didn't).

Checking It Out in Your Browser

To really see how the interlacing works, you'd have to include your image as an inline image in a Web page, transfer the Web page up onto the Web, and then view it in your browser. If you try to view it locally, the image will paint so fast that you won't really be able to see the interlacing effect.

There's no problem viewing the transparency effect on your local machine. You will need, however, to insert it as an inline image in an HTML file with a background color or background image set to be able to see the transparency. For instance, create the following HTML file in Notepad:

```
<HTML>
<HEAD>
<TITLE>Web page title</TITLE>
</HEAD>
<BODY BACKGROUND="backgrnd.gif">
<P ALIGN="center"><IMG SRC="images/headline.gif"></P>
</BODY>
</HTML>
```

NOTE The previous example assumes you're saving your images into an `images` folder inside of your working folder. If you're saving your images directly into your working folder (C:\MyPages), you should change the relative URL accordingly:

```
<P ALIGN="center"><IMG SRC="headline.gif"></P>
```

Save this file in your working folder (C:\MyPages) as `headline.htm`, for instance, and then open it in your browser (see Figure 7.8). Leave this file open in your browser because you'll be hopping back to it later.

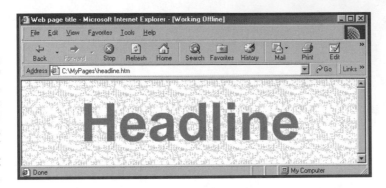

Figure 7.8

A Web page's background image (or background color) shows through the GIF image's transparent color.

Creating Drop Shadow Effects

A great way to set off your text (or any other object included in your image) is to create a drop shadow effect.

Applying a drop shadow effect, like many other of Paint Shop Pro's special effects, requires that you increase the number of colors in the image's palette back up to 16.7 million: Select Colors, Increase Color Depth, and 16 Million Colors (24 bit).

To create a drop shadow effect you need to first select the color you want to use for the effect, and then select the shadow effect parameters you want to use:

NOTE   If you don't know where any HTML files are, you can use the Find command to search for them. Just click on the Start button; select Find, Files and Folders; type `*.htm` or `*.html` in the Named box; then click Find Now.

1. Click on the foreground-color swatch. Choose any color (other than red) that you think might look good (for instance, try selecting the blue-green color, the fourth color down in the third column under Basic Colors). Click on OK.

2. Select Image, Effects, and Drop Shadow. In the Drop Shadow dialog box, select Foreground Color for the Color. Try setting 90 for the Opacity, 15 for the Blur, and 6 for both the Vertical and Horizontal offsets. (See Figure 7.9.) Feel free to experiment with other combinations—you can see the results in the dialog box's preview box.

3. Click on OK. You'll see the drop shadow effect added around your text. To get a better look at it, without the dashes around the text, choose Selections, and then Select None. (See Figure 7.10.)

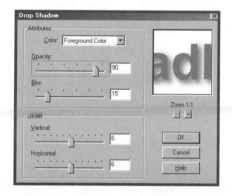

Figure 7.9

You can select the color, opacity, blur, and offsets of a drop shadow.

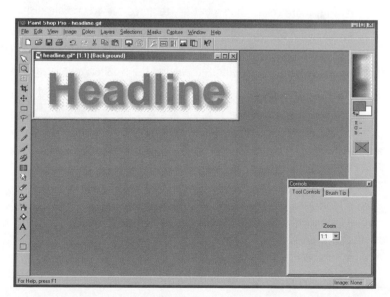

Figure 7.10

A drop shadow has been added to the text.

If you want to save your image as a JPEG image, you don't have to do anything more to it. However, if you want to save it as a regular or a transparent GIF image, you should do a couple of other things first. The next two sections cover creating an optimized color palette and setting the transparency tolerance level.

Creating an Optimized Color Palette

Because you're using a blur effect with your drop shadow effect, simply reducing the number of colors to 256 may not yield the optimum results for your image. To get better results, you should create an optimized color palette, which contains only colors already included in the image. To do that, do the following:

1. Select Colors, Decrease Color Depth, and X Colors [4/8 bit].

2. Select 256 as the Number of colors and Error diffusion as the Reduction method. Leave the other settings as they are. (See Figure 7.11.) Click on OK.

TIP

You can further optimize your GIF images by creating optimized color palettes that contain no more colors than what are required for acceptable display quality. To test your images, first create an optimized 256-color palette, make a copy of the image, and then create a 64-color palette, followed by a 32-color or 16-color palette, for instance. The fewer colors in your optimized palette, the smaller your image will be. For example, if you have a black and white image, reduce the number of colors to 2!

Figure 7.11

By decreasing the color depth to X colors (to anywhere from 2 to 256 colors), you create an optimized color palette composed only of colors already in the image.

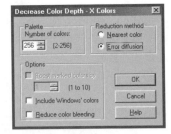

Setting the Transparency Tolerance Level

The next thing you need to do is set the transparency tolerance level. The original default setting is a level of 0, meaning that only one color will be made transparent. However, when using a blurred drop shadow effect, this can result in too much of a "halo" effect when displaying the image against a background image or against a background color that doesn't exactly match the image's transparent color. Adjusting the transparency tolerance level allows you to set a range of tonal gradations within the same color as transparent. Here's how to do that:

1. Select Selections, and then Select All.

2. Select Selections, Modify, and Transparent Color.

3. Select Background Color as the Transparent Color. Select 15 as the Tolerance. (See Figure 7.12.)

You'll notice a dashed line around the drop shadow. Everything outside of the dashed line will be rendered as transparent. By adjusting the tolerance level, you can draw a tighter or looser noose, so to speak, around your drop shadow. Set your tolerance level too low, and too many of the nearly white (in this case) blur colors will not be included in the transparency, giving your drop shadow a noticeable halo when displayed against a background image, even if its primary color is white. Set it too high, however, and you'll eliminate too much of the blur.

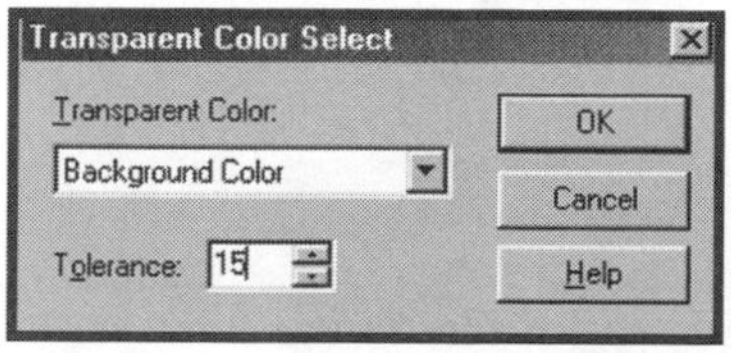

Figure 7.12

By increasing the transparency tolerance level, you can include a range of color gradations in your transparency.

Resetting the Transparent Color

When you increased the color depth to create the drop shadow effect, you lost your transparency. You'll need to set it again:

1. Select Colors and Set Palette Transparency.

2. Select the second radio button (Set the transparency value to the current background color). Click on OK.

3. To view the transparency, select Colors and View Palette Transparency. (See Figure 7.13.) Repeat to turn off viewing the transparency.

4. Select Selections, and then Select None.

Checking It Out in Your Browser

Save your image (select File and Save). If you left `headline.htm` open in your browser previously, just hop over to it and press Ctrl+R (or click on the Reload or Refresh button) to update the display of your graphic. If not, run your browser and open `headline.htm`. (See Figure 7.14.)

Displaying Transparent Drop Shadows against a Non-White Background Image

The image you just created has a transparent drop shadow, but it will only work well if it is displayed against a background image in which the primary color is white. If you want to display a drop shadow against a background image in which the primary color is not white, you need to set the color of your transparent background to match the predominant color in the background image as closely as possible.

Figure 7.13

The transparency (the checkerboard pattern) is closely skirting the drop shadow effect.

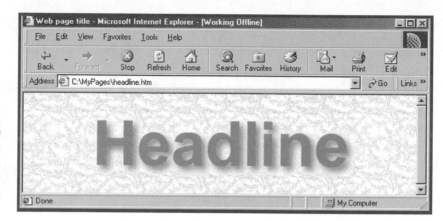

Figure 7.14

The drop shadow's blur effect displays transparently against the background image.

This is because a blurred drop shadow effect blurs to whatever color is present in your image's background. If the background is white, then the drop shadow also blurs to white (using shades of the drop shadow color that get progressively whiter). If you then display this in a Web page against a non-white background color or a background image in which the primary color is not white, you'll see what is sometimes called a halo or "cookie-cutter" effect.

If you want to check this out, just edit the example HTML file you created earlier (headline.htm) to substitute a background image in which the primary background color is not white (see Figure 7.15):

```
<HTML>
<HEAD>
<TITLE>Web page title</TITLE>
</HEAD>
<BODY BACKGROUND="3dgreen1.gif">
<P ALIGN="center"><IMG SRC="images/headline.gif"></P>
</BODY>
</HTML>
```

Actually, if you look around the Web, you'll have to look long and hard to find a transparent drop shadow effect that melds into a background image where the primary color is not white. Most Web publishers, even many so-called "pros," don't know how to do this.

Figure 7.15

Figure 7.15

If the background color of your image and your Web page don't match, a transparent drop shadow effect that uses a blur will display a very noticeable "halo" or "cookie-cutter" effect.

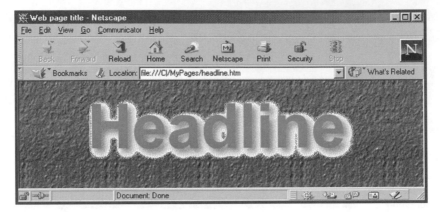

In this section I'll be showing you a technique that you can use to match a transparent drop shadow to virtually any background image. This can be very effective on a Web page and go a long way toward making your Web page really stand out.

Opening a New Image Window

For this example, you'll need to open a new image window and start fresh. Just leave `headline.gif` open in Paint Shop Pro (you'll be coming back to it a little later). Go ahead and open a new image window:

1. Select File, New.
2. Your previous settings should still be there (450 and 125 for the width and height, White for the background color, and 16.7 Million Colors). Just click on OK.

Opening the Background Image

You'll be picking a color out of the actual background image you'll be using in your HTML file, so you need to first open that image in Paint Shop Pro 5:

1. Select File, Open.

2. Open your working folder (C:\MyPages). (Click on the Look in menu and the [C:] icon, and then double-click on the MyPages folder.)

3. Double-click on `3dgreen1.gif` to open it in Paint Shop Pro 5.

Using the Dropper to Pick Up and Drop a Color

Next, you'll be using the Dropper tool to pick up a color out of the background image (as close to the primary color as you can manage) and drop it into the background-color swatch—you'll then be able to use the dropped color to fill the background of your new image. To do this, just do the following:

1. First, increase the zoom factor for the image to make it easier to pick out the color. Use the Controls Palette to increase the zoom factor to 2:1 (or select View, Zoom In, and 2:1).

2. Click on the Dropper tool in the Tool Palette. Now, if you pass the Dropper pointer over the background image, you'll see the color directly under the Dropper displayed in the Current Color panel. (See Figure 7.16.)

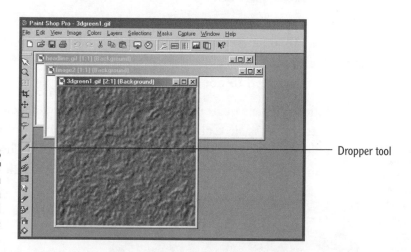

Figure 7.16

You can pick up a color from a background image using the Dropper tool.

Dropper tool

3. When you see a likely color (neither too dark nor too light) displayed in the Current Color panel, without moving the mouse cursor, right-click the mouse to pick up and drop the color into the background-color swatch.

Filling the New Image's Background

You now need to fill the background of your new image with the color you just picked up and dropped with the Dropper tool. To do this:

1. Click on the title bar of the blank image window you opened earlier to bring it to the foreground.

2. Click on the Fill tool (the paint-bucket icon) in the Tool Palette. Position the Fill cursor over the blank image window, and then right-click (*not* left-click) the mouse button to fill the image with the color assigned to the background-color swatch. (See Figure 7.17.)

You can also left-click the Dropper tool in the background image to pick up and drop a color into the foreground-color swatch, and then left-click the Fill cursor in the blank image window to fill it with the foreground color.

Adding the Text, Drop Shadow, and Transparency

Now you need to add the text for your banner graphic, as well as create the drop shadow and transparency effects. Because you've already done this once, here's a bit more of a truncated rundown, all in one set of steps, on what you need to do:

1. Click on the foreground-color swatch to select a new color for your text. From Basic Colors, select one of the lighter colors (any of the colors in the seventh column should do), so you'll have more of a contrast between it and the background color. Click on OK.

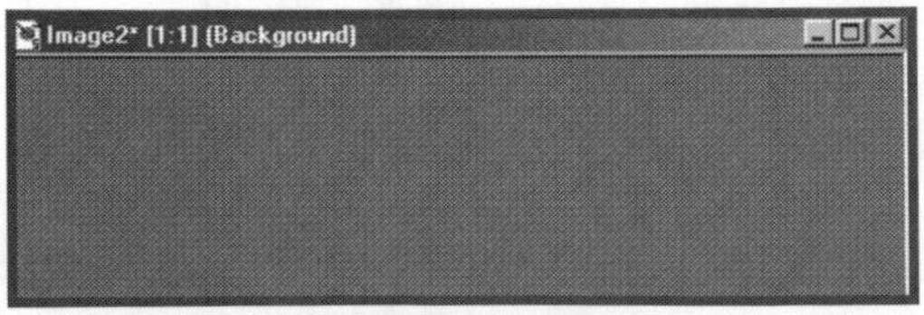

Figure 7.17

The new image's background is filled with the color that was picked up and dropped from the background image using the Dropper tool.

2. Click on the Text tool in the Tool Palette, and then click the mouse in the center of your image. Your previous settings should still be there (Arial, Bold, 72, and `Headline` as the text). Click on OK. Click and drag the text to position it in the center of your image.

3. Click on the foreground color to select a new color for your drop shadow effect. From Basic Colors, select a darker color that'll contrast with the background color (for instance, try the navy blue color, fifth down in the third column). Click on OK.

4. Select Image, Effects, and Drop Shadow. Your previous settings should still be there (Foreground Color, 90 and 15 for the opacity and blur, and 6 for the offsets). Click on OK.

5. Create an optimized color palette (this is important because the background color may not be present in the standard 256-color palette). Select Colors, Decrease Color Depth, and X Colors [4/8 bit]. At the message, just click on Yes (to okay reducing the image to a single layer). Your previous settings should still be there (256 as the number of colors, Error diffusion as the reduction method, and all check boxes unchecked). Click on OK.

6. Set the transparent color. Select Colors and Set Palette Transparency. Select the second radio button (to select the background color as the transparent color). Click on OK.

7. Set the transparency tolerance level. Because your drop shadow is still selected, you don't have to select Select All here. Just select Selections, Modify, and Transparent Color. Your previous settings should still be there (Background Color as the transparent color, and 15 as the tolerance value). Click on OK.

8. To see what your image looks like, select Selections, and then select Select None. (See Figure 7.18.)

Figure 7.18

A new banner graphic has been created using a color from a background image as its own background color.

9. Save your new image. Select File and Save (or Save As). If you haven't saved any other images in the meantime, the folder where you saved your first image (C:\MyPages\images) should still be open. (If it isn't, change to that folder now.) For the file type, select CompuServe Graphics Interchange (*.gif). Type **headlin2.gif** as the file name. Click on Save.

To check this out in your browser, just edit the example HTML file you created earlier (`headline.htm`). `3dgreen1.gif` should already be set as the background image. Edit the IMG tag to substitute the new banner graphic you just created (see Figure 7.19):

```
<HTML>
<HEAD>
<TITLE>Web page title</TITLE>
</HEAD>
<BODY BACKGROUND="3dgreen1.gif">
<P ALIGN="center"><IMG SRC="images/headlin2.gif"></P>
</BODY>
</HTML>
```

Figure 7.19

The drop shadow effect now transparently blends into the background image.

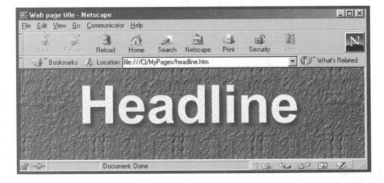

Displaying Transparent Drop Shadows against a Background Color

This works pretty much like displaying a transparent drop shadow against a non-white background image, except you don't have to go through the rigmarole of using the Dropper to pick up and drop the color you want to use.

You can set the background color hex codes in your HTML file and then define the same background color for your image in Paint Shop Pro 5; or you can do it the other way around, defining the background color first in Paint Shop Pro and then inserting the hex codes in your HTML file. Here's a brief rundown on doing the latter:

1. Open a new image (keeping the same settings you used previously).
2. Click on the background-color swatch. Select a color that you want to use for the background of your image (and your Web page). Note the HTML Code value (at the bottom of the dialog box) for the color you've chosen. Write it down. Click on OK.
3. Click on the Fill tool in the Tool Palette, and then right-click the mouse inside of the image window to fill it with the background color you just selected.

I'm not going to bore you with going through creating the text, drop shadow, and transparency effects all over again. You don't have to do this again just to check this out (unless you want to, of course). The main thing is that you understand the why and wherefore here.

Assuming that you have done all this, saving your new image as `headlin3.gif` to your C:\MyPages\images folder, for instance, then you only need to specify the background color and banner graphic in your HTML file. Here's an example (don't bother creating this because it's just for reference—unless you've gone to the bother of actually creating and saving `headlin3.gif`):

```
<HTML>
<HEAD>
<TITLE>Web page title</TITLE>
```

```
</HEAD>
<BODY BGCOLOR="HTML Code Value">
<P ALIGN="center"><IMG SRC="images/headlin3.gif"></P>
</BODY>
</HTML>
```

You'll need to substitute for "HTML Code Value" above the HTML code value you made note of when selecting the background color in Paint Shop Pro 5 ("#EED198", for instance).

Take a Break?

You've been at this *all* weekend. You deserve a break! Get up and stretch those muscles. Brew a cup of tea if you need a picker-upper. If you're all tuckered out, feel free to save the rest of this tutorial until later (just reopen headline.gif when you're ready to start up again). However, if you're all fired up to learn more about creating your own Web images, I'll see you back here in ten minutes or so.

Using Color, Pattern, and Gradient Fill Effects

You can also use a variety of different *fill effects*—effects you can create using the Flood Fill tool (the paint-bucket icon) on the Tool Palette.

For this section of the tutorial, you'll be using the first example image, headline.gif, as a base for trying some of the different fill effects you can apply in Paint Shop Pro 5. It should still be open in Paint Shop Pro 5's workspace (if not, just open it from C:\MyPages\images, or wherever you saved it). Click on its title bar to bring it to the foreground.

Your first example image, headline.gif, currently has a color depth of 256 colors. To get more colors to work with, increase the number of colors back up to 16.7 million:

1. Select Colors and Increase Color Depth.
2. Select 16 Million Colors [24 bit].

In the following sections, you'll be learning how to apply three kinds of fills: solid, pattern, and gradient.

Using Solid Fills

You've actually done this already, when you used the color from the background-color swatch to fill your image's background. In this section, I'll be covering a couple of other ways you can use solid color fills.

Filling Solid Color Areas

You can fill any solid color area in your image. For instance, fill the letter "H" with a new solid color:

1. Click on the foreground-color swatch to select a color for the fill.

2. Select any of the Basic Colors. For instance, select the bright blue color (fifth down in the first column). Click on OK.

3. Click on the Fill tool (if it isn't already selected) in the Tool Palette. Click the mouse on the "H" letter (the paint bucket's crosshairs should be positioned inside of the letter).

The primary limitation of doing it this way is that not all of the letter necessarily gets filled. You may see a noticeable red line still present at the top horizontal edges of the letter. This is because anti-aliasing was set when you created the text object. If you don't use anti-aliasing, this shouldn't be a problem. The way to fix the problem is to select the letter before filling it.

Filling a Selection

You'll often run into trouble trying to fill a whole letter when anti-aliasing has been used. The solution is to select the letter and then increase its size:

1. First, select Edit and Undo Flood Fill to get rid of the blue fill. To get a better look at what you're doing, change the zoom factor to 2:1 (View, Zoom In, and 2:1).

2. Click on the Magic Wand tool in the Tool Palette, and then click the pointer on the "H" letter to select it. You'll notice a dashed line around the letter, indicating that it is selected.

3. To expand the selection, select Selections, Modify, and Expand. Leave 1 as the number of pixels to expand the selection. This will expand the selection just enough to include the anti-aliasing along the edge of the letters in the selection. Click on OK.

4. Click on the Fill tool. In the Controls Palette, change the Match Mode value to None. Click the mouse pointer inside the "H" letter. You'll notice that the color has entirely filled the letter—there is no more red at the top edges of the letter (see Figure 7.20).

Using Pattern Fills

You can use a background image (such as 3dgreen1.gif, for instance) to create a pattern fill. You can actually use any image you have open in Paint Shop Pro 5, but background images work best because they're designed to seamlessly tile. Follow these steps to fill the "e" letter with a pattern fill:

1. Open in Paint Shop Pro 5 any background image that you want to use for a pattern fill. For this example, you'll be using 3dgreen1.gif, which you've already opened. (If you haven't opened it, just open it from your working folder, C:\MyPages, and then click on the title bar of headline.gif to bring it back to the foreground.)

2. Select the Magic Wand tool and click it on the "e" letter to select it, and then expand the selection by 1 pixel (Selections, Modify, and Expand).

Figure 7.20

An expanded selection has been filled with a bright blue color.

3. Select the Fill tool. In the Controls Palette, change the Fill Style to Pattern. Leave None as the Match mode.

4. Click on the Options button in the Controls Palette. From the third menu (New pattern source), select `3dgreen1.gif`. (See Figure 7.21.) Click on OK.

5. Click the mouse pointer inside the "e" letter. You'll see that the letter has been filled with the pattern (based on `3dgreen1.gif`). (See Figure 7.22.)

Using Gradient Fills

A gradient fill uses two colors with gradations of the colors blending between the selected colors. Paint Shop Pro 5 has a variety of gradient fills that you can apply to your image, including linear, rectangular, sunburst,

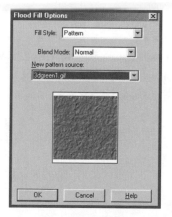

Figure 7.21

A pattern fill is selected in the Flood Fill Options dialog box.

Figure 7.22

The letter "e" is filled with the pattern fill.

and radial gradients. In the following, you'll apply a linear gradient to the last seven letters ("eadline"):

1. First, select Edit and Undo Pattern Fill. Select Selections, and then Select None.

2. Select the two colors for your gradient. Click on the foreground-color swatch and select a lighter color (one of the yellow colors, for instance). Click on OK. Click on the background-color swatch and select a darker color (one of the green colors, for instance). Click on OK.

3. Click on the Fill tool. In the Controls Palette, change the Fill Style to Linear Gradient. Leave the Match mode set at None. Click on the Options button in the Controls Palette. You could also change the angle of the gradient by pulling the Direction pointer around the circle or by typing in a degree. For this example, however, leave this as it is. (See Figure 7.23.)

NOTE Paint Shop Pro 5 retains settings in the Controls Palette. If you later want to fill a solid color area without using a selection, you'll need to return the Match mode setting to RGB.

Figure 7.23

The Flood Fill Options dialog box shows the gradient you've selected in the colors you've selected.

4. If you don't like how the gradient looks (it is easy to get some pretty icky color combinations), click on the Cancel button and select two new colors in the foreground- and background-color swatches. Then click on the Options button again to see what the gradient will look like. When you like the result, click on OK.

5. Click on the Magic Wand tool, and then click the mouse pointer inside the "e" letter. Select Selections, Modify, and Select Similar. You'll notice that all of the red letters are now selected.

6. To include the anti-aliasing in the selection, select Selections, Modify, and Expand. Leave the number of pixels set at 1. Click on OK.

7. Click on the Fill tool again, and then click the mouse pointer inside of the "e" letter. You'll notice that all of the selected letters are now filled with the gradient fill. (See Figure 7.24.)

8. To see what the whole unselected image looks like, change the zoom factor back to 1:1 and turn off the selection (Selections, Select None).

If you want to save your image as a GIF image, you should first create an optimized color palette for your image, as you did previously (Colors, Decrease Color Depth, X Colors). If you want to save it as a transparent GIF, first assign the color (white) of your image's background to the background-color swatch (they need to match), and then set the background color as transparent (Colors, Set Palette Transparency). The previous transparency tolerance level is still set, but you may want to adjust it up or down (Select, Select All, and then Select, Modify, Transparent

Figure 7.24

All of the selected letters have been filled with the linear gradient.

Color). Just select File and Save to save `headline.gif` or File and Save As to save it under another name.

The point of this section was to show you some of the more handy effects you can use in creating your own Web images. I didn't go into what are more strictly design issues involved in creating Web images (other than warning you about icky color combinations), simply because there isn't time or space available to do the subject justice. The example images that you've worked with so far were meant to illustrate how the effects work rather than be great design examples.

You should now have a good feel for how Paint Shop Pro 5's text, drop shadow, fill, and transparency effects work. You should also understand how to create an optimized color palette for your GIF images, which is key if you want to create really sharp-looking GIF images. Feel free to play around and experiment to create a banner graphic for your Web page. Try creating a banner graphic using your page's level-one heading, for instance, using some, or even all, of these effects. And don't think you have to stick just with what's covered here—branch out and explore (try a radial gradient, for instance). Don't worry about trying to become a design pro overnight (unless you're already a design pro, of course). For right now, just concern yourself with creating Web images that you like—it's your page, after all. The more practice you get, the better your results will be.

Take a Break?

Go ahead and take another break here if you feel you need it. It's been a long weekend, and, hey, you deserve it! Grab a soda from the fridge or brew that late night cup of tea you've been dying for.

If you're just plain out of gas, that's okay. You've done a lot! Feel free to call it a night. You can come back at any time to complete the rest of this tutorial. However, if you've still got fuel in your tank, I'll see you back here in fifteen minutes or so, when you'll learn how to create 3-D buttons.

Creating 3-D Buttons

For this example, you'll create a 3-D Home button. You can use this button as a navigational icon, an image link that hops back to your home page.

Just to clear the boards, close any image windows that you have open in Paint Shop Pro 5. Then do the following to create your new image:

1. Select File and New.

2. Type **150** as the Width and **75** as the Height. Leave the other settings as they are (72 for the Resolution, White for the Background color, and 16.7 Million Colors). Click on OK.

3. Because this is a fairly small image, increase the zoom factor to 2:1 (View, Zoom In, 2:1).

Creating a Diagonal Gradient Fill

What I call here a "diagonal gradient" fill is simply a linear gradient fill turned at an angle, so the gradient extends from the upper left to the lower right of the image, rather than just from the top to the bottom. This can be a handy technique to use when creating 3-D objects because it gives a more naturalistic lighting effect to the object. For this example I'll have you select a yellow color and a darker gold color to give your button a kind of burnished gold appearance. Just do the following:

1. Click on the foreground-color swatch and select one of the yellow colors. Click on OK.

2. Click on the background-color swatch. Click the mouse in the orange area of the color wheel on the right. Click the mouse inside the color square on the right until you come up with a color that looks like gold to you (see Figure 7.25). Click on OK.

3. Click on the Fill tool on the Tool Palette.

4. In the Controls Palette, select Linear Gradient as the fill style (if it isn't already selected). Leave the other settings as they are.

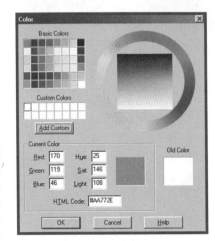

Figure 7.25

A gold color is selected using the Color dialog box's color wheel and color square.

5. Click on the Options button on the Controls Palette. Pull the Direction pointer to the right to 325 degrees, or just type **325** in the Degree box (see Figure 7.26). Click on OK.

6. Click the mouse pointer inside of the image window. You'll notice that the image has been filled with a linear gradient, from bright yellow to a darker gold color, running from the top left to the bottom right of the image (see Figure 7.27).

Figure 7.26

A "diagonal" gradient fill is defined in the Flood Fill Options dialog box.

Figure 7.27

The image window has been filled with the "diagonal" gradient fill.

Creating the Button Effect

Paint Shop Pro has a really neat special effect that you can use to create 3-D buttons. To add the button effect, do the following:

1. Select a different color for the button shadow. Click on the background-color swatch (which is used to set the button shadow color). On the color wheel, click the mouse in the red-orange area. In the color square, click the mouse until you have an orange color (your pick). Click on OK.

2. Select Image, Effects, and Buttonize.

3. Select the Transparent Edge radio button. Change the Height value to 15 and the Width value to 15. Leave the Opacity value set at 75. To sneak a peek at what your button will look like, click on the Proof button (see Figure 7.28). Click on OK.

The button effect has now been added to your image, as shown in Figure 7.29.

Figure 7.28

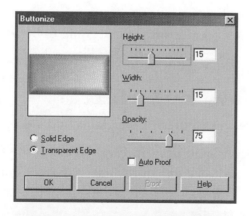

The Buttonize dialog box lets you change the settings for and proof your button.

Figure 7.29

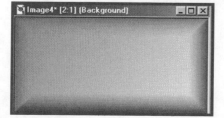

The image has been buttonized.

Adding the Home Text

Right now, you only have a button. If you want to use it as a navigational icon, you need to add some text to help identify its purpose. To do that, follow these steps:

1. Select a color for your text. Click on the foreground-color swatch. For instance, click on the aqua blue color (fourth color in the fifth column of Basic Colors). (You can always change this later by filling the text with another color or a gradient or pattern fill.) Click on OK.

2. Click on the Text tool in the Tool Palette, and then click the pointer inside your button image. Feel free to select any font name that you have available. For the example, I'll be sticking with Arial (because all readers should have that font). Leave Bold selected as the font style. Select 28 as the font size. In the text box, type **Home**. Click on OK.

3. Grab the text with the mouse and drag it so it is roughly centered on the button. (Feel free to position the text so it is just up and to the left of center because next you're going to be adding a drop shadow down and to the right.) (See Figure 7.30.)

Adding a Drop Shadow to the Text

To give your Home text more of a 3-D look, add a drop shadow effect:

1. Select a color for your drop shadow. Click on the foreground-color swatch and pick one of the darker colors. For instance,

Figure 7.30

The Home text has been added to and centered on the button.

Figure 7.31

A drop shadow effect is added to the Home text.

select the dark green color (fourth down in the second column). Click on OK.

2. Select Image, Effects, and Drop Shadow. Leave Foreground Color set as the color of the drop shadow. Set the Opacity at 100 and the Blur at 5 (or thereabouts). Set the Vertical and Horizontal Offset values at 2. Click on OK.

3. To see what your button looks like, select Selections, and then Select None. (See Figure 7.31.)

4. To see what your button looks like at normal size, change the zoom factor back to 1:1—just click on View and Normal Viewing (1:1).

Saving Your Button Image

Because you don't need this image to be transparent, you'll get the best result if you save it as a JPEG image. That's because JPEG images use a color palette of 16.7 million colors as opposed to 256 colors for GIF images. To save your button image, do the following:

1. Select File and Save (or Save As).

2. If you haven't saved any images in the meantime, the C:\MyPages\images folder should still be open. (If it isn't, use the Look in menu and the folder list to open it.)

3. For the file type, select JPEG - JIF Compliant [*.jpg, *.jif, *.jpeg].

4. In the File name box, type a name for your button, using *.jpg as the file extension (for instance, type **mybutton.jpg**, or something like that).

NOTE You can also save your image in Paint Shop Pro format (*.psp), which may make it a little easier to rework the image later, if you want. You can't display a Paint Shop Pro format image in a Web page, however. To do that, it has to be a GIF or JPEG image.

5. Click on the Options button. You can select the encoding type and the compression level. I recommend that you always select the Standard encoding radio button (many older browsers can't display progressive JPEGs). For now, change the Compression level to 1 (I'll show you more about using this setting in the next section). Click on OK, and then click on Save.

Optimizing JPEG Images

You can save a lot of bandwidth by optimizing your JPEG images. Here's the method I use:

1. First, save your JPEG image using a compression level of 1. You already did that in the last step of the previous section when you saved mybutton.jpg, so you don't need to do that again.

2. Select File and Save As to resave your JPEG image. Change the file name (to **mybutton2.jpg**, for instance). Click on the Options button and change the compression level to 20, for instance. (See Figure 7.32.) Click on OK, and click on Save.

Figure 7.32

A compression level of 20 is set for the JPEG image.

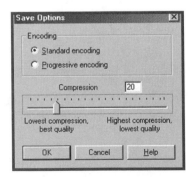

3. Repeat step 2, renaming the file each time (to **mybutton3.jpg**, **mybutton4.jpg**, and so on). For each new image increase the compression level (to 40 and 60, for instance).

4. Close the current image window, and then open all of the images you just saved. Arrange them side by side so you can easily compare them (see Figure 7.33).

5. Next, use Windows Explorer to check the actual file sizes of the images. Click on the Start button and select Programs and Windows Explorer (or just select Run, type **explorer**, and hit Enter). Change the folder view to the folder where you saved your images (C:\MyPages\images, if you've been following my suggestions).

As shown in Figure 7.34, Windows Explorer shows that the three images are 7, 3, 2, and 2 KB in size, respectively. Obviously, jumping from a compression level of 1 to 20 yielded a significant result, cutting the size of the image by more than half (from 7 KB to 3 KB). Jumping from a compression level of 20 to 40 also yielded a significant result, further cutting the size of the image by a third (from 3 KB to 2 KB). Jumping from a compression level of 40 to 60, however, didn't save any bytes. To my eye, the vote is for mybutton2.jpg, which yields a significant saving in bytes while showing a relatively small deterioration in the image quality compared to the two other images.

To do even more tests, try resaving your first uncompressed image (mybutton.jpg) at compression levels of 25, 30, and 35, for instance. If it can save you an extra byte, it might be worth it (or it might not).

Figure 7.33

All four button images, using different compression levels, are arranged side by side so they can be visually compared.

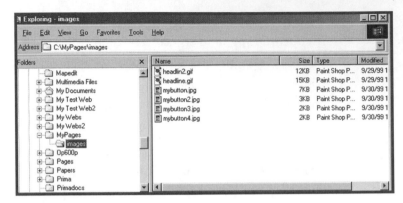

Figure 7.34

Use Windows
Explorer to
check your
savings in bytes.

Your button image is a fairly small image, so you should expect to see much larger differences in file sizes when you test larger JPEG images at different compression levels. Optimizing all of the JPEG images in a Web site that contains even a few JPEG images can make a big difference in speeding up the downloading and displaying of your pages. If you have a lot of images, it can make a huge difference. Optimize, optimize, optimize, in other words!

Finding Out More about Creating Your Own Web Images

In this session, you've only been able to scratch the surface of creating your own Web images. Hopefully, however, you've been able to get a grip on some of the key tricks that should be up the sleeve of every Web publisher. Don't expect to become a Web graphics pro in a single evening! Only by continuing to work at it can you expect to become reasonably proficient.

Learning More about Paint Shop Pro 5

The Web contains lots of resources for learning more about using Paint Shop Pro. Here are just a few:

❁ Paint Shop Pro Users Group at **www.pspusersgroup.com/psp.html**

- Web Graphics on a Budget at **mardiweb.com/web/**
- Paint Shop Pro Tips at **psptips.com**
- Paint Shop Pro 5 Layers and Other Tutorials at **www.grafxdesign.com/21psp.html**
- ZD University at **www.zdu.com/**

Image Editing Software Options

The version of Paint Shop Pro included on the CD-ROM is an evaluation version. You have 30 days to use the program, after which you'll need to register the program if you want to continue using it. When you read this, a new version of Paint Shop Pro should be available, Paint Shop Pro 6, which you should be able to download and try for another 30 days. The cost of registering Paint Shop Pro 6 will be $99. To find out more, visit Jasc Software's Web site at **www.jasc.com**.

Though Paint Shop Pro is a great image editor, you're not limited to using it for creating Web images. Here are some other very affordable image editors that won't break the budget:

- Adobe Photoshop 5.0 Limited Edition. This is a scaled-down and much less expensive version of Photoshop 5. The cost to order is $99, which is a real bargain. Though no trial version is available, Adobe Photoshop 5 has one. For more info, see **www.adobe.com/prodindex/photoshople/main.html**.

- ULead PhotoImpact 5. A full-feature image editor optimized for creating Web graphics. At $79, a real bargain. For more information and a trial download, see **www.ulead.com/pi/runme.htm**.

- Microsoft Image Composer 1.5. Many Web publishers swear by this image editor, and it can do a great job of creating Web images. It is, however, only available bundled with the stand-alone versions of FrontPage 98 or FrontPage 2000 ($149). For more information, see **www.microsoft.com/frontpage/**.

Wrapping Up

If you've learned Basic HTML, planned and created your first Web page, and completed this session's optional Graphics Tutorial, you've laid down a very solid foundation for your future Web publishing efforts! Feel free to come back at another time to do any of the optional tutorials that you may have missed this time around. You've come a long way!

If you've managed to complete *everything* this weekend, then you are well on your way to becoming a certified Web publishing whiz! Check out Appendix A, "Web Resources," for links to where you can find many additional Web publishing resources and tools.

ON THE

CD

Once you have your Web page finalized, check out Appendix D, "Putting It Up on the Web," for information on how to find a Web host for your pages and instructions on how to use WS_FTP LE, a great freeware FTP program (included on the CD-ROM), to transfer your Web page to a Web server.

Be sure to check out the Web site for this book at **http://www.calli-han.com/create3/** for additional information, downloads, and resources.

APPENDIX A

Web Resources

The world of HTML and Web publishing includes a great deal more than what can be covered in a single book, especially one that you are completing in just a few days. To really become a Web publishing pro will take much more time than that, although hopefully you've gotten a big leg up this weekend. This appendix is a short road map to where on the Web you can find out more about HTML and Web publishing. You'll find information about:

✪ Web publishing references, guides, and tutorials

✪ Windows Web publishing software tools

✪ Web graphics sources

✪ Web site promotion resources

 NOTE All of the URLs listed in this appendix omit the "http://" at the start. For most current Web browsers, typing in the "http://" is no longer necessary—the browser will automatically add it for you. Also, if you see a URL that doesn't start with a "www," don't add it because not all URLs start with "www".

Web Publishing References, Guides, and Tutorials

The World Wide Web Consortium at www.w3.org. This is where to find all the latest developments in HTML and other emerging Web standards, including Cascading Style Sheets (CSS), XML and XHTML, DOM, MathML, SMIL, and more. It includes the official specification for HTML 4.0.

Sizzling HTML Jalfrezi at vzone.virgin.net/sizzling.jalfrezi/. This is an excellent A to Z HTML reference.

Introduction to HTML by Ian Graham at www.utoronto.ca/webdocs/ HTMLdocs/NewHTML/htmlindex.html. It provides plain English explanations of the HTML 4.0 specification.

The HTML Guru! by Chuck Musciano at members.aol.com/htmlguru/. It is another excellent source for the inside dope on HTML and Web publishing.

The HTML Writers Guild at www.hwg.org. This is a great central stopping point for all things HTML.

Style Guide for Online Hypertext by Tim Berners-Lee at www.w3.org/Provider/Style/Overview.html. Here are wise words from the inventor of the World Wide Web.

WDVL: Web Developer's Virtual Library at www.stars.com. If you want to get serious about becoming a Web developer, this is a great place to start.

WebDeveloper.com at www.webdeveloper.com. This is a great repository of info for the serious Web developer.

Web Developer's Journal at www.WebDevelopersJournal.com. Contains lots of great info on Web publishing. Don't miss the "Wacky HTML" page.

Web Techniques at www.webtechniques.com. This is the online version of *Web Techniques* magazine. Read the current issue or browse the archives for lots of great articles on Web publishing.

DevEdge Online by Netscape at developer.netscape.com. This is Netscape's omnibus site for Web developers.

MSDN Online Web Workshop by Microsoft at msdn.microsoft.com/workshop/default.asp. This is Microsoft's omnibus site for Web developers.

HTML Goodies by Joe Burns at www.htmlgoodies.com. This is a great collection of tutorials on just about everything related to Web publishing; you'll find tutorials for creating frames, forms, tables, and much more.

Site Development Help and Tutorials (from Oregon State University) at osu.orst.edu/aw/tutorials/. Excellent collection of Web publishing tutorials.

Steve Callihan's Web Links at www.callihan.com/weblinks/. This is my Web site of Web publishing links.

Windows Web Publishing Software Tools

TUCOWS: The Ultimate Collection of Winsock Software at www.tucows.com.

Stroud's Consummate Winsocks Apps List at cws.internet.com/home.html.

PC Win Resource Center at pcwin.com.

Tudogs: The Ultimate Directory of Gratis Software at www.tudogs.com.

The WinSite Archive at www.winsite.com.

ZDNet Software Library at www.zdnet.com/swlib/.

www.32bit.com at www.32bit.com.

WinFiles.com at www.winfiles.com.

BHS.COM: Windows NT/2000 Resource Center at www.bhs.com.

Icon Shareware at www.iconshareware.com.

SHAREWARE.COM by C/NET at www.shareware.com.

Topdownloads.net at www.topdownloads.net.

TheFreeSite.com at www.thefreesite.com.

Steve Callihan's Web Tools at www.callihan.com/webtools/. This is my Web site of links to Web publishing software tools.

Web Graphics Sources

DiP: A Guide to Digital Pictures & More at DIPweb.com. This is a gold mine of tips and tricks for users of Photoshop, Painter, and Kai's Power Tools.

The Pixel Foundry by Tom Karlo at www.pixelfoundry.com. Here you'll find tips, tricks, and techniques for Photoshop and Kai's Power Tools. It also includes an archive of backgrounds.

The Bandwidth Conservation Society at www.infohiway.com/faster/. Here's lots of great info on how to optimize your Web images for faster download.

Creating graphics for the Web at www.widearea.co.uk/designer/. Covers creating interactive graphics using JavaScript, anti-aliasing, optimizing Web images with Photoshop, and creating GIFs and JPEG graphics.

Barry's Clip Art Server at www.barrysclipart.com. This is a big collection of clip art that you can download and use in your Web pages, including a large collection of animated GIFs.

Rose's Backgrounds Archive at www.wanderers2.com/rose/backgrounds. html. This has not just backgrounds, but lots of other Web art as well, including icons, arrows, and rules.

The Clip Art Connection by Eric Force at www.ClipArtConnection.com. This site includes tons of Web art images, including alphabets, arrows, buttons, and numbers.

Laurie McCanna's Free Art Site at www.mccannas.com/. Also includes tips for Photoshop, Corel, Painter, and Paint Shop Pro.

Backgrounds by NCSA at www.ncsa.uiuc.edu/SDG/Software/ mosaic-w/coolstuff/Backgrnd/. This is a nice collection of backgrounds from NCSA, developer of the Mosaic Web browser.

The Background Sampler from Netscape at home.netscape.com/assist/ net_sites/bg/backgrounds.html or www.baylor.edu/textures/.

AOLpress Clip Art Gallery at www.aolpress.com/gallery/. Here is an excellent collection of free Web art, including coordinated sets and themes, as well as sidebar background images.

Bryan Livingston's CoolText.com: Online Graphics Generator at www.cooltext.com. You can create your own eye-boggling text banner, in seconds, ready to download and insert in your page. Super cool, really.

MediaBuilder 3D Text Maker at www.3dtextmaker.com/. Another free online utility that will create a fancy animated 3-D text banner for you. Pretty neato.

Create Your First Web Page In a Weekend (3rd Edition) at www. callihan.com/create3/. Visit this book's Web site to find additional Web art collections that you can download and use.

Web Site Promotion Resources

Submit It! at www.submit-it.com. Submit your Web page to fifteen search engines and indexes by filling out only one form.

AllSubmit! at www.riffnet.com/all-submit/. This one won't submit your registration for you, but it has a nifty form-interface that'll take you directly to the registration pages for quite a few directories, search engines, award sites, and free-for-all link sites.

Web Marketing Today Info Center at www.wilsonweb.com/webmarket/. Links to bunches of articles on Web marketing.

META Tagging for Search Engines at www.stars.com/Search/Meta/ Tag.html. Covers how to use the META tag to snag search engines.

LinkExchange at www.linkexchange.com. A free service for exchanging banner ads.

FAQ: How To Announce Your New Web Site at www.ep.com/faq/ webannounce.html.

Promoting Your Pages at osu.orst.edu/aw/promote/. Tips on submitting your page to search engines, directories, and so on.

Promotion World at www.promotionworld.com. Lots of free Web site promotion info, including tutorials, articles, and more.

Search Engine Tutorial for Web Designers at www.northernwebs.com/set/. How to design your pages with search engines in mind.

APPENDIX B

Special Characters

The ISO 8859-1 character set is the official character set for Web pages, at least as far as Western languages (English, French, German, and so on) are concerned. It is an 8-bit character set, which allows for 256 code positions. The code positions 000 through 031 and 127 are assigned as control characters (line feed, space character, and so forth). Positions 032 through 126 correspond to the US-ASCII characters that you can type in at the keyboard. Code positions 128 through 159 are designated as "unused" in ISO 8859-1, although both the Macintosh and Windows systems assign characters to many of these positions.

The only characters that are officially specified by the ISO 8859-1 character set as okay to use in a Web page correspond to 160 through 255. Windows and UNIX systems display all of these characters because the ISO 8859-1 character set is also their native character set. However, fourteen of the officially sanctioned characters are missing from the Macintosh native character set (which is a different character set than the ISO 8859-1 character set).

In the following sections you'll find tables showing the reserved, unused, and special characters that are included in the ISO 8859-1 character set.

Reserved Characters

These are the numerical and named characters that are reserved for formatting HTML tags and codes.

You should only type "<" or ">" (left or right angle brackets) into your HTML documents to designate the start or end of an HTML tag; to use these characters as is, you need to type in the numerical or named entity code < and >.

Double quotations and ampersands, on the other hand, generally need only be replaced in an HTML file if they are part of an HTML code that you want to display as is.

Number	Name	Description	Character
"	"	Double quotation	"
&	&	Ampersand	&
<	<	Left angle bracket, less than	<
>	>	Right angle bracket, greater than	>

TABLE B.1 RESERVED CHARACTERS

NOTE When inserting character codes into an HTML file, you should in most cases stick to using the numerical entity codes (the left-hand column) if you want to ensure the widest compatibility with both old and new Web browsers. Versions of Netscape Navigator earlier than 4.0 will only display the characters corresponding to the named entity codes for the four reserved characters listed above, the copyright character, and the registered character (see the Special Characters table).

Unused Characters

Both Windows and the Macintosh assign characters to many of the code positions that the ISO 8859-1 character set designates as unused, and twelve of these extra characters are dissimilar on the two systems. *There is no guarantee that any of these characters will display on other platforms.* Generally, it is best to avoid using these characters in an HTML file, with the possible exception of the trademark symbol (™), which displays on Windows, Macintosh, and UNIX systems and is too useful to be ignored. (Its entity name, ™, should be avoided, however.)

TABLE B.2 UNUSED CHARACTERS

Number	Name	Description	Character
€		Unused	
		Unused	
‚		Single quote (low)	,
ƒ		Small Latin f	ƒ
„		Double quote (low)	„
…		Ellipsis	…
†		Dagger	†
‡		Double dagger	‡
ˆ		Circumflex	ˆ
‰		Per mile sign	‰
Š		S-caron	Š (not on Mac)
‹		Left angle quote	‹
Œ		OE ligature	Œ
		Unused	
Ž		Unused	
		Unused	
		Unused	
‘		Left single quote	'
’		Right single quote	'
“		Left double quote	"
”		Right double quote	"

Number	Name	Description	Character
•		Bullet	•
–	–	En dash	–
—	—	Em dash	—
˜		Small tilde	~
™	™	Trademark	™
š		s-caron	š (not on Mac)
›		Right angle quote	›
œ		oe ligature	œ
		Unused	
ž		Unused	
Ÿ		Y-umlaut	Ÿ

TABLE B.2 UNUSED CHARACTERS (CONTINUED)

Special Characters

The following characters, 160 through 255, are part of the ISO 8859-1 character set. They should generally be available on any operating system that uses the ISO 8859-1 character set, but fourteen of these codes display as different characters or not at all on the Macintosh (marked as "not on Mac").

TABLE B.3 SPECIAL CHARACTERS

Number	Name	Description	Character
		Non-breakable space	[ ] (brackets added)
¡	¡	Inverted exclamation	¡
¢	¢	Cent sign	¢
£	£	Pound sign	£
¤	¤	Currency sign	¤
¥	¥	Yen sign	¥
¦	¦	Broken vertical bar	¦ (not on Mac)
§	§	Section sign	§
¨	¨	Umlaut	¨
©	©	Copyright	©
ª	ª	Feminine ordinal	ª
«	«	Left guillemet	«
¬	¬	Not sign	¬
­	­	Soft hyphen	–
®	®	Registered	®
¯	&hibar;	Macron	¯
°	°	Degree	°
±	±	Plus/minus sign	±
²	²	Superscripted 2	² (not on Mac)
³	³	Superscripted 3	³ (not on Mac)
´	´	Acute accent	´

TABLE B.3 SPECIAL CHARACTERS (CONTINUED)

Number	Name	Description	Character
µ	µ	Micro sign	µ
¶	¶	Paragraph sign	¶
·	·	Middle dot	·
¸	¸	Cedilla	¸
¹	¹	Superscripted 1	¹ (not on Mac)
º	º	Masculine ordinal	º
»	»	Right guillemet	»
¼	¼	1/4 fraction	¼ (not on Mac)
½	½	1/2 fraction	½ (not on Mac)
¾	¾	3/4 fraction	¾ (not on Mac)
¿	¿	Inverted question mark	¿
À	À	A-grave	À
Á	Á	A-acute	Á
Â	Â	A-circumflex	Â
Ã	Ã	A-tilde	Ã
Ä	Ä	A-umlaut	Ä
Å	Å	A-ring	Å
Æ	Æ	AE ligature	Æ
Ç	Ç	C-cedilla	Ç
È	È	E-grave	È
É	É	E-acute	É

TABLE B.3 SPECIAL CHARACTERS (CONTINUED)

Number	Name	Description	Character
Ê	Ê	E-circumflex	Ê
Ë	Ë	E-umlaut	Ë
Ì	Ì	I-grave	Ì
Í	Í	I-acute	Í
Î	Î	I-circumflex	Î
Ï	Ï	I-umlaut	Ï
Ð	Ð	Uppercase Eth	Ð (not on Mac)
Ñ	Ñ	N-tilde	Ñ
Ò	Ò	O-grave	Ò
Ó	Ó	O-acute	Ó
Ô	Ô	O-circumflex	Ô
Õ	Õ	O-tilde	Õ
Ö	Ö	O-umlaut	Ö
×	×	Multiplication sign	× (not on Mac)
Ø	Ø	O-slash	Ø
Ù	Ù	U-grave	Ù
Ú	Ú	U-acute	Ú
Û	Û	U-circumflex	Û
Ü	Ü	U-umlaut	Ü
Ý	Ý	Y-acute	Ý (not on Mac)
Þ	Þ	Uppercase Thorn	Þ (not on Mac)

TABLE B.3 SPECIAL CHARACTERS (CONTINUED)

Number	Name	Description	Character
ß	ß	Sharp s (German)	ß
à	à	a-grave	à
á	á	a-acute	á
â	â	a-circumflex	â
ã	ã	a-tilde	ã
ä	ä	a-umlaut	ä
å	å	a-ring	å
æ	æ	ae ligature	æ
ç	ç	c-cedilla	ç
è	è	e-grave	è
é	é	e-acute	é
ê	ê	e-circumflex	ê
ë	ë	e-umlaut	ë
ì	ì	i-grave	ì
í	í	i-acute	í
î	î	i-circumflex	î
ï	ï	i-umlaut	ï
ð	ð	Lowercase Eth	ð (not on Mac)
ñ	ñ	n-tilde	ñ
ò	ò	o-grave	ò
ó	ó	o-acute	ó

TABLE B.3 SPECIAL CHARACTERS (CONTINUED)

Number	Name	Description	Character
ô	ô	o-circumflex	ô
õ	õ	o-tilde	õ
ö	ö	o-umlaut	ö
÷	÷	Division sign	÷
ø	ø	o-slash	ø
ù	ù	u-grave	ù
ú	ú	u-acute	ú
û	û	u-circumflex	û
ü	ü	u-umlaut	ü
ý	ý	y-acute	ý (not on Mac)
þ	þ	Lowercase Thorn	þ (not on Mac)
ÿ	ÿ	y-umlaut	ÿ

NOTE The latest versions of Internet Explorer for the Macintosh actually do display the "not on the Mac" characters listed above by substituting the "Western (Latin 1)" character set ("Latin 1" is another name for the ISO 8859-1 character set) for the native Macintosh character set. These characters, however, will not be displayed in any version of Netscape Navigator or in earlier versions of Internet Explorer for the Macintosh.

Completing Your Wish List

This appendix is a kind of grab bag that covers a number of oft-requested and popular features that you can add to your pages. Once you've done all of the HTML tutorials, planned and created your first Web page, and learned how to create eye-appealing Web images with Paint Shop Pro 5, then you might want to try to implement some of the features covered in this appendix:

- Adding background sounds
- Adding hit counters and guestbooks
- Adding GIF animations
- Adding Java applets
- Adding interactive animations
- Using image maps
- Using frames and forms

Adding Background Sounds

One of the most frequent questions I get from readers is how to add background sounds to their pages. The main difficulty with getting background sounds to work is that Internet Explorer and Netscape Navigator use different methods to do this. Internet Explorer uses the BGSOUND tag, which is a Microsoft extension to HTML, and Netscape Navigator uses the EMBED tag. In the following, I'll briefly cover how to use these two tags, plus how to get the two tags to work together on the same page.

Finding Sounds

Before you can add a background sound, you'll need to choose or create the background sound that you want to use. WAV (*.wav) sound files are pretty easy to find. You can probably find quite a few in different locations on your hard drive. Just click on the Start button, point to Find, and select Files or Folders. In the Named box, type *.**wav** and click on New Search. MIDI (*.mid) sound files aren't nearly as common as WAV sound files, but they can provide better audio quality, especially for music files, while taking up fewer bytes. It is also much more likely that visitors to your site will need to download and install a MIDI player before they'll be able to listen to your MIDI clips. To search for MIDI files on your hard drive, type *.**mid** in the Named text box.

Using the BGSOUND Tag

The BGSOUND tag is used to play background sounds in Internet Explorer. You can insert the BGSOUND tag either in the HEAD or in the BODY element. Here's an example (you'll need to substitute the file name of the actual sound file you want to use):

```
<BGSOUND SRC="mysound.wav">
```

In most cases, this should play the sound file, mysound.wav, once when your page is loaded, although some players may loop the sound clip indefinitely. It is a good idea to specifically set your sound clip to play only a set number of times. Here's an example of setting your background sound to play only once:

```
<BGSOUND SRC="mysound.wav" LOOP="1">
```

To make sure that your background sound loops indefinitely, just add a LOOP="infinite" attribute, although I don't generally recommend that you do this. (I personally find indefinitely looping background sounds to be just a bit irritating.)

Using the EMBED Tag

If you want to play background sounds in Netscape Navigator, you have to use the EMBED tag, not the BGSOUND tag. The EMBED tag will work in both Netscape Navigator and Internet Explorer. The EMBED tag is inserted in the BODY element. Here's an example of using the EMBED tag:

```
<EMBED SRC="mysound.mid" WIDTH="145" HEIGHT="60" BORDER="0"
AUTOSTART="true">
```

If you want to play your background sound indefinitely, just add a LOOP="true" attribute, like this:

```
<EMBED SRC="mysound.mid" WIDTH="145" HEIGHT="60" BORDER="0"
AUTOSTART="true" LOOP="true">
```

You can also set the sound clip to play a set number of times—LOOP="3", for instance, would set your clip to play three times.

You can also hide the player, which will cause your background sound to work the same as using the BGSOUND tag for Internet Explorer. If you do choose to hide the player, it is a good idea to set the LOOP attribute to a specific number rather than having the sound clip play indefinitely. Here's an example of hiding the player and setting the sound clip to play three times:

```
<EMBED SRC="mysound.mid" AUTOSTART="true" LOOP="3" HIDDEN="true">
```

NOTE Not every player will play a sound clip when the player is hidden. I've even run into one player that wouldn't play the sound if the player height and width dimensions were set to less than two pixels. One way around this is to insert the EMBED tag at the bottom of your page with **HEIGHT="2"** and **WIDTH="2"** attributes set while leaving out the **HIDDEN="true"** attribute.

Here's a rundown on the attribute values that can be assigned to the EMBED tag:

- **LOOP.** Values: true (for infinite loop), false (to not loop), or integer (to loop a set number of times)
- **ALIGN.** Values: top, right, left, middle, and bottom. To center, nest the EMBED tag inside of a CENTER tag
- **AUTOSTART.** Values: true and false
- **WIDTH and HEIGHT.** Values: integer; sets the width and height of the player console in pixels
- **VOLUME.** Values: 0 to 100; the default volume is 100

Using the BGSOUND and EMBED Methods Together

If you use both the BGSOUND and EMBED methods at the same time, Internet Explorer will actually use both to play the sound. This may cause some problems in some versions of Internet Explorer. The only way to handle this (other than using JavaScript to determine the browser being used and route a visitor to a Netscape-only or Internet Explorer-only page) is to embed the BGSOUND tag inside of a NOEMBED tag. This has the effect of forcing most versions of Internet Explorer to play the sound clip in the EMBED tag and ignore the one in the BGSOUND tag. Versions that do not recognize the EMBED and NOEMBED tags, however, will play the sound clip in the BGSOUND tag. With those provisos noted, here's an example of using the NOEMBED tag:

```
<NOEMBED>
<BGSOUND SRC="mysound.wav" LOOP="1">
</NOEMBED>
<EMBED SRC="mysound.wav" AUTOSTART="true" LOOP="1" HIDDEN="true">
```

Adding Hit Counters and Guestbooks

Hit counters and guestbooks are probably the two most popular things people want to add to their Web pages. The first place you should check is your Web space provider, many of which provide free hit counters and guestbooks that you can easily add to your pages. Just follow their instructions to add the proper code to your pages.

If your Web space provider does not provide a hit counter or guestbook that you can add to your pages, free hit counters and guestbooks are available on the Web. These usually involve some form of advertising that accompanies the hit counter or guestbook. Here are some places to check out:

- ✿ WebCounter at **www.digits.com**
- ✿ SuperStats at **v2.superstats.com**
- ✿ TheCounter.com at **www.TheCounter.com**
- ✿ LiveCounter Classic at **www.chami.com/counter/classic/**. This is a Java counter that displays up-to-the-minute hit counts, like an odometer.
- ✿ GuestWorld at **saturn.guestworld.tripod.lycos.com**
- ✿ Guestbook.com at **www.guestbook.com**
- ✿ Guestbook4free.com at **www.guestbook4free.com**

🜨 Dreambook at **www.dreambook.com**

🜨 Alx' Free Guestbook Service at **www.alxbook.com**

To find even more, do a search at Yahoo! (**www.yahoo.com**) for "hit counter" or "guestbook."

Adding GIF Animations

GIF animations are a great way to spice up your page. A GIF animation is just a regular GIF image file, except it contains several image frames instead of just one. You link to a GIF animation exactly the same way you would to a regular inline image. You can find GIF animations many places on the Web. Here are just a few:

🜨 Barry's Clip Art Server at **www.barrysclipart.com/**. Has a library of over 400 GIF animations to choose from.

🜨 Rose's Animated Gifs at **www.wanderers2.com/rose/animate.html**. Over 350 GIF animations to choose from.

🜨 Royal Frazier's GIF Animation on the WWW at **members.aol.com/royalef/gifmake.htm**. An excellent tutorial on creating your own GIF animations. Click on the "Gallery" link to check out the available GIF animations that you can download.

ON THE

CD

Look on the CD-ROM for three programs that will let you create GIF animations: GIF Construction Set, GIFmation, and Animation Shop (included with Paint Shop Pro 5).

Adding Java Applets

Java applets are another good way to spice up your page. A Java applet is a software program that is actually downloaded and run on your computer. Many kinds of Java applets are available on the Web, from relatively simple Java animations to more sophisticated full-feature applications.

◄◄

A *Java applet* is a small program (thus the word "applet") created in the Java programming language that can be downloaded with a Web page and executed by any Java-enabled browser. All current Web browsers should support running Java applets.

◄◄

Generally, the source of the Java applet should provide you with the HTML code required to insert the applet in your page, as well as all of the files and folders that compose the applet. In many cases you can just copy the source code for the applet and then paste it into your page. Here's an example of doing that:

1. View the applet's page source. In either Internet Explorer or Netscape Navigator, just right-click on the applet's Web page, and then click on View Source.

2. Highlight applet code (everything starting with `<applet>` and ending with `</applet>` and press Ctrl+C to copy the code. Use Ctrl+V to paste it into the HTML file where you want to use it.

3. You may need to edit the code slightly. For instance, if you are placing all the Java applet files in the same folder as the applet's HTML file, then you should delete any "codebase" attribute value included in the "applet" tag.

Places Where You Can Get Java Applets

You can find Java applets to download and use in your Web pages at lots of places on the Web. Here are some Web sites where you can find Java applets:

⚙ Applet Depot at **www.ericharshbarger.org/java/**

⚙ Gamelan: The Official Directory for Java at **www.developer.com/directories/pages/dir.java.html**

⚙ The Java Boutique at **www.javaboutique.internet.com**

Adding Interactive Animations

One way to really juice up your site is to create interactive animations. You can do this a number of ways without having to become a Java programmer.

There isn't the time or space to go into this thoroughly in this book, but here are some tools you can check out that allow you to create your own interactive animations for your Web site:

- Microsoft Liquid Motion at **www.microsoft.com/liquidmotion**. Creates DirectX animations for Internet Explorer 4.0/5.0 and Java animations for Java-enabled browsers (Netscape Navigator, Internet Explorer 3.0, and others). Free 45-day trial version available ($149 to purchase).

- Macromedia Flash at **www.macromedia.com/software/flash/**. The Flash player is built into Netscape Navigator 4.0+ and Windows 98, but some may have to download a plug-in to see the animations. Free 30-day trial version is available ($269 to purchase).

- MetaCreations' Headline Studio at **www.metacreations.com/ products/hls/**. Won't do interactive animations but has lots of other tricks up its sleeve. Creates animated headlines, banners, logos, and other Web objects; the final product is in the form of a GIF animation. Free 30-day trial version is available ($169 for online purchase; $199 for retail purchase).

NOTE I've written a book for Prima Tech, *Create Web Animations with Microsoft Liquid Motion In a Weekend*, that covers everything you need to know to create and implement Liquid Motion animations for your Web site. For more information and example animations, see my Web site for the book at **www.callihan.com/liquidmotion/**.

Using Image Maps

Another neat feature that can add great visual appeal to your site is an image map. This is beyond the scope of this book, but you'll definitely want to learn about using image maps once you've gotten your Web publishing feet wet, so to speak.

I don't recommend that you try to plot out all of the hot-spot coordinates for an image map by hand—it is much easier to use one of the handy image-map editors that are available. Several are included on the CD-ROM:

ON THE
CD

- Mapedit by Boutell.com at **www.boutell.com/mapedit/**. Just open the image you want to use, draw your hot spots, assign the links, and Mapedit will then add the image-map code to whatever page you designate. Thirty-day evaluation version available ($25 to purchase).

- CoffeeCup Image Mapper++ by CoffeeCup Software at **www. coffeecup.com/mapper/**. Shareware ($20 to purchase).

- Map This! A freeware image mapper that works very similarly to Mapedit. You have to manually insert the USEMAP attribute (USEMAP="#mapname", for instance) in the IMG tag to reference the name of the MAP element (Mapedit does this automatically). Available for download at various software archives, such as CWSApps at **cws.internet.com/32webimage2.html**.

Using Frames and Forms

Frames and forms are slightly more "advanced" features of HTML that, for reasons of space and time, just couldn't be covered in this book. They are, however, important parts of HTML that you'll very likely want to find out more about.

In the HTML templates that are included on this book's CD-ROM, you'll find two for creating framed Web sites. The first is for creating a fairly simple two-frame Web site, and the second is for creating a more sophisticated "nested" three-frame Web site (just like my Web site for this book). For more information on installing the HTML templates from the CD-ROM, see Appendix F, "What's on the CD-ROM."

ON THE
CD

You'll also find a great frames utility, Frame-It, on the CD-ROM. It can make creating sophisticated multi-frame Web sites a snap. Although Frame-It was released as freeware, a user name and code are still required to be able to continue to use it beyond its evaluation period—see Frame-It's info screen in the CD interface for the user name and code you need to enter.

Forms are even more of an advanced topic than frames. For beginning Web publishers, the best bet for adding forms to your site is to use a software tool that can automate the process for you. Several of the more full-feature Web authoring suites and HTML editors can automate the creation of forms. A couple of programs that specialize in creating forms are included on the CD-ROM that you might want to try:

ON THE

CD

✿ WebForms by Q & D Software Development at **www.q-d.com**. Creates both mailto and CGI forms (creates the CGI script for you) and retrieves and manages form responses. Shareware ($39.95 to purchase WebForms Pro).

✿ CGI*StarPro by Web Genie Software at **www.webgenie.com/ Software/Cspro/**. This one can create the form and the CGI script for you, or just the CGI script for a form you've already created. If your Web server doesn't support custom CGI scripts or you just don't want to go through the rigmarole of installing a CGI script on your Web server, you can use Web Genie's AutoCGI feature to use its CGI hosting facility (at an extra cost). Thirty-day trial version available ($99 to purchase; $169 per year for CGI hosting license).

For more links to online resources and tools for creating frames and forms, see my Web Links and Web Tools sites at **www.callihan.com/weblinks/** and **www.callihan.com/webtools/**.

Putting It Up on the Web

Now that you've created your first Web page, you're going to want to put it up on the Web so that the rest of the world can see your handiwork. This is really a two-part process involving the following:

○ Finding a Web host for your Web page

○ Using an FTP client to transfer your page up to your folder on a Web server

Finding a Web Host

The first step is to find a server to host your page. If you are a student, your school might be able to host your page. If you are a subscriber to one of the online services such as CompuServe or AOL, it also might provide some Web space. Your local access provider that connects you to the Internet might also provide Web space for free or at a nominal cost.

There are also Web space providers on the Web that will host your pages for free, generally in exchange for placing their ad banner on your page or having an extra pop-up window with advertising open when your page is accessed.

However, if you want to create a commercial Web page, expect to generate a considerable amount of traffic, or want to have access to a fuller range of features and services, you might want to consider finding a Web host that specializes in providing Web hosting services. Many Web hosting companies provide affordable Web hosting accounts.

FIND IT ON ▶   I've created a Web site, Steve Callihan's Web Hosts Page at **www.callihan.**
THE WEB   **com/webhosts/**, where you'll find links to lists of free, budget, and other Web hosting services.

Transferring Your Web Page to a Server

Your Web host should provide you with FTP access to your folder on its server. This means providing you with a user ID and a password, as well as assigning you a password-protected folder on its server where you can store your HTML and other files. You might also be assigned an account name, although usually not. This allows you to access your folder (and any folders you create within that folder) through FTP, copying files to or from it, while keeping everyone else out.

A Few Things You Need to Know

Your Web host should provide you with all the information you need to connect to your folder on its server using an FTP program. Here's a short rundown on the information you'll need to have:

- **Host name.** This is the name of your Web server. Generally, this is in the form of *server.domain.category* (srv2.yourhost.net, for instance). If you have a domain name, you may also be able to access your Web space folders by using your domain name (not all servers support this, however). Some servers may also let you use your Web address path (www.theirserver.com/yourfolder/, for instance) as the host name.

- **User ID.** This is your user name. If you have received your Web space from a local ISP or a commercial online service, this will very likely be the same as the user name you use to log on. If not, it will be the user name you requested and/or had assigned to you when you signed up for your account. (Your user ID is case sensitive.)

- **Password.** Your password will keep others from accessing your Web site folders. As with your user ID, if you have received your Web space from a local ISP or a commercial online service, your password will likely be the same as the password you use to log on to the Internet. If not, it will be the user name you requested and/or had assigned to you when you signed up for your account. (Your password is case sensitive.)

In the vast majority of cases, that is all you'll need to access your Web site folders on your Web host's server. You should be automatically switched to your Web site folder when you connect.

NOTE In very rare instances, a Web host may also provide an account name, in addition to your user ID, that you'll need to connect to its server. An occasional Web host won't automatically switch you to your Web site folder, in which case you'll need to know the remote directory path to your folder on its server. Your Web host should let you know if either of these is required.

If your Web site folder is located behind a firewall (most aren't), your Web host should let you know what other settings you'll need to connect to your site.

Using WS_FTP LE to Transfer Your Web Page Files

WS_FTP LE is a shareware FTP program that is free for qualified non-commercial users.

Setting Up WS_FTP LE

ON THE

CD

FIND IT ON ▶
THE WEB

The following covers using WS_FTP LE 5.06, included on the CD-ROM, to transfer your Web page files to your Web server folder. Earlier versions of WS_FTP LE should be quite similar, except the arrangement of the Properties and Options menus might be somewhat different. Other FTP programs should work similarly, although I can only speak here for WS_FTP LE.

If you don't have a CD-ROM drive, you can download WS_FTP LE or WS_FTP Pro directly from the Ipswitch Web site at **www.ipswitch.com**.

At this point, I am assuming that you have a connection to the Internet, that you have been provided or have rented some space on a Web server to store your Web pages, and that you have password-protected access to your directory. I'm also assuming that you know the information detailed earlier under "A Few Things You Need to Know" and that you have installed WS_FTP LE.

Connect to the Internet, and then run WS_FTP LE (Start, Programs, WS_FTP LE).

Figure D.1 shows the opening screen of WS_FTP LE, version 5.06, displaying the General tab section of the Session Properties window (earlier versions of WS_FTP LE might combine the General and Startup tab sections in one window).

Go through the following steps to define a new session profile.

The General Tab

1. In the Profile Name box, type a name for your session profile. This can be whatever you want. For instance, you might define "MySite" as your profile name. Just make it something you can remember.

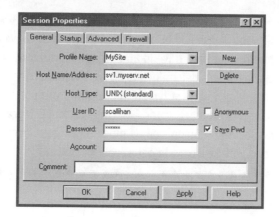

Figure D.1

The General tab section of the Session Properties window.

2. In the Host Name/Address box, type the host name of the Web host server where your Web space is located. This is a fully qualified Internet host name or IP address. This should be in the form of *server.domain.category* (sv2.yourserver.net, for instance). If you have a domain name, some servers will let you use it instead of the host name of your server.

3. In the Host Type box, I recommend leaving "Automatically detect" enabled—in most cases, WS_FTP LE should be able to detect your host type. If that doesn't work, try "UNIX (standard)" because the majority of Web servers are still UNIX machines. In most cases, one or the other of these two settings should work. If neither works, you need to find out from your Web space provider the actual host type you should choose here.

4. In the User ID box, type your user name. This is case sensitive, so you should type it exactly, including any uppercase letters.

5. Because you're using a user name and password to log in, you need to disable anonymous login. Click on the Anonymous check box so that it is unchecked (blank). To have WS_FTP LE save your password so that you won't have to type it in every time you log in, click on the Save Pwd check box to check it.

CAUTION ◆◆◆◆◆◆◆◆◆◆◆◆◆◆◆◆◆◆◆◆◆◆◆◆◆◆◆◆◆◆◆◆◆◆◆◆◆

If you are on a network, you should be aware that checking the Save Pwd check box will save your password to your hard drive in an encrypted form. It is, however, not difficult to decode for someone who is determined to do so—a hacker, for instance. If you don't save your password here, you must type it in each time you use FTP to log on to your Web server. It's your pick, in other words—security or convenience. If you are not on a network, however, security shouldn't be as much of an issue because a hacker would have to be sitting at your keyboard to get at your password.

◆◆◆◆◆◆◆◆◆◆◆◆◆◆◆◆◆◆◆◆◆◆◆◆◆◆◆◆◆◆◆◆◆◆◆◆◆

6. Type your password in the Password box. If you enabled Save Password, it appears as a row of asterisks. (Note: Don't type a row of asterisks!)

7. Leave the Account box blank unless your Web host has provided you with an account name.

   Refer back to Figure D.1 for an example of how your filled-out General tab section should look (substituting your own information, of course).

8. Click on the Startup tab.

The Startup Tab

1. At this time, leave the Initial Remote Site Folder box blank. Later, if you want, you can specify a folder or folder path in your site that you would like WS_FTP LE to automatically switch to. Otherwise, WS_FTP LE will connect to the root folder assigned to you by your Web host. Your actual folder for your Web site may be another folder, often named WWW, inside of your root folder, which is the case for my Web site, for instance. For that reason, to have WS_FTP LE switch automatically to that folder when I connect, I've typed **www** in the Initial Remote Site Folder.

2. In the Initial Local Folder box, type the path of your local folder where your Web page files are located, such as **c:\MyPages**, for instance.

3. Click on the Apply button to save your new session profile. (In some earlier versions of WS_FTP LE, this is a Save button.)

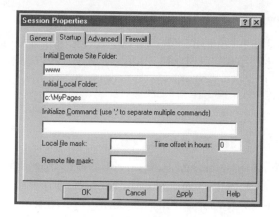

Figure D.2

The Startup tab section of the Session Properties window.

4. Leave the rest of the fields blank. (See Figure D.2.)

5. Click on the Advanced tab section.

The Advanced Tab Section

You need to change the settings here only if the default settings don't work. For instance, if you're having trouble connecting, you might increase the number in the Connection Retry box. You could also increase the Network Timeout entry if you are timing out before you connect. Lastly, a port number other than 21 (which is the standard port number for an FTP server) might need to be set in the Remote Port box, although this is unlikely. (See Figure D.3.)

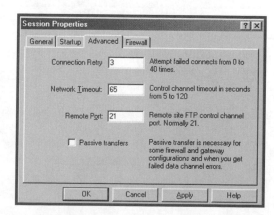

Figure D.3

The Advanced tab section of the Session Properties window should usually be left as is.

The Firewall Tab Section

You don't need to fill out the Firewall tab section unless your Web folders are located behind a firewall, which is unlikely. If you do need to fill out this section, find out from your Web space provider the information you'll need to type in here.

Connecting to Your Server

To connect to your server, just click on the OK button in the Session Properties dialog box. If you haven't already connected to the Internet, you'll be prompted to do so. If your settings are correct, you'll see the root directory on your server displayed in the right-hand window. (See Figure D.4)

If you see a www folder, as shown in Figure D.4, this will be the actual root folder for your Web pages. Some Web hosts may name this folder differently (if so, your Web host should let you know). Other folders might also be present, such as an ftp folder where you could place files that you want to make available via FTP (rather than HTTP).

If this hasn't worked, you'll need to go back to the drawing board. You may need to specify a specific host type (you'll probably have to e-mail your Web host to find out what this is). Make sure that the host name of your Web

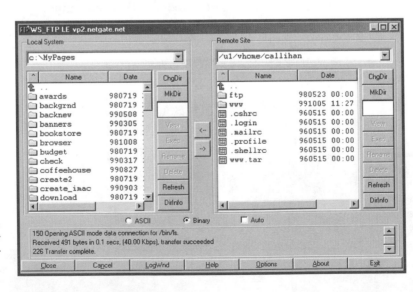

Figure D.4

Once you connect to your server, WS_FTP LE displays your local directories on the left and your directories on your server on the right.

server is correct. You should double-check that your user ID, password, and account name (if you have one) are correct.

If it still doesn't work, under the same Advanced tab, try increasing the Network Timeout amount or the number of connection retries. If none of this works, you'll have to check with your Web host to make sure you're using the correct user name, password, and so on. Also make sure you have the right directory path, if that is required.

 NOTE The whole battle of being able to use FTP to update your Web pages on your server is simply getting these settings correct. So make sure you find out from your Web space provider the *exact* settings you need to provide here. Once you get them right, it is as easy as pie. (But it's pretty much pie in your face if you don't get them right! So be patient if you can't get this to work right off the bat.)

Using WS_FTP LE

Once you connect to your directories on your server, WS_FTP LE's main screen is displayed in the form of two side-by-side windows. The window on the left shows the local folder on your hard drive that you specified in the Initial Local Folder box under the Startup tab. The window on the right shows the directory on your Web server that you specified in the Initial Remote Site Folder box, also under the Startup tab.

As previously shown in Figure D.4, the remote host folder that I log on to on my Web server contains two folders, the ftp and the www folders. My Web pages are actually inside the www folder. If this is also the case on your server, double-click on that folder to open it (or on whatever other folder your Web host has told you should be used to contain your Web page files). (See Figure D.5.)

You'll notice that I have quite a few folders already set up in the right-hand window. That's because I've been a busy chipmunk and have managed to create quite a few Web pages. To keep track of them, I have organized them into separate folders. Because you're just getting started, you might not have any folders or files set up yet, unless your provider has already created some sample folders or files for you.

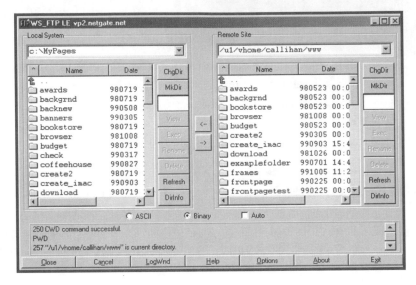

Figure D.5

Your Web page directories may be inside a www folder on your server.

TIP

You'll also notice, as shown in Figure D.5, that my remote folders on my Web server closely match the folders on my local hard drive. When creating Web pages on your local hard drive, you want your folder structure to mirror your folder structure on your remote Web server. So, if you have a `c:\pages\images` folder on your local drive, you'll want to have a corresponding `/www/images` folder, to follow UNIX convention, on your remote server, for instance. That way, if you always use relative URLs to link to other files internal to your own site (strongly recommended), you can fully test the links on your local hard drive and then transfer your Web pages to your Web server without having to reset any of the links.

Navigating WS_FTP LE's Main Window

Navigating WS_FTP LE's main window, you can do the following:

❖ Move up or down the directory structure in either window. Double-clicking on a folder will open a subdirectory. Double-clicking on the two periods (..) will move you up one directory level. You also can use the ChgDir button in either window to change the directory.

○ Use the MkDir button to create a directory in either window. You can use the Delete button to delete a directory.

○ Transfer files from the folder on your local PC to the folder on your Web server (you can also do this the other way around). For instructions for transferring files from your local computer to your server, see "Transferring Your Files to Your Server."

○ Of the remaining buttons, the ones you are most likely to use are the View and Rename buttons, which (unsurprisingly) let you view and rename files, and the DirInfo button, which provides information on the files in a folder (such as size and date).

Transferring Your Files to Your Server

Actually transferring your files onto your server is fairly simple. Just follow these steps:

1. On your local PC (the window on the left), change to the folder that contains the files you want to transfer to your server. Highlight the files you want to transfer.

2. If you're transferring an HTML file or files (or any other kind of text file), click on the ASCII radio button. If you're transferring an image file (or any other binary file, such as a sound file, a zip file, or a program file, for instance), click on the Binary radio button. (Don't check the Auto check box unless you want to transfer a folder and its contents.)

3. To transfer the highlighted files from the local PC directory (the left window) to the currently displayed directory on your Web server (the right window), click on the right-arrow button. (To copy a file the other way, from your Web server to your local PC, you would click on the left-arrow button.)

Be patient. If you are copying several files, or if any of them are large (such as a banner graphic file, for instance), it might take a minute or so before the files have been transferred.

Important: Forcing Lowercase File Names

One gotcha that is easy to trip over when transferring files from your PC to your server is the case sensitivity of file names on UNIX systems. Thus, **Whacko.htm** and **whacko.htm** on a UNIX system represent two *different* files. To avoid this problem (getting the wrong case), I set WS_FTP LE to force lowercase file names when transferring files to my server. I then make sure that all hypertext links in my Web pages are also all lowercase. To set up WS_FTP LE to do this, first log on to your server (or any FTP site). Then, in the WS_FTP LE window, follow these steps:

1. Click on the Options button. Under the Session tab (Session Options in earlier versions of WS_FTP), click the next to last check box, Force Lowercase Remote Names, so that it is checked. (See Figure D.6.)

2. Click on the Set as default button, and then click on OK.

Once you've transferred a Web page and any attendant graphic files to your server, you can run your browser and open your Web page in it by typing your page's URL in your browser's Location (Navigator) or Address (Internet Explorer) box and then pressing Enter. If you've saved your root Web page as index.html, you won't need to include it in your URL (http://www.yourserver.com/yourfolder will do, for instance). (Note: If you've just signed up for your account, it may take twenty-four hours or

Figure D.6

You can force all files transferred to your Web server to be converted to all lowercase letters, which will keep you from tripping over UNIX's case sensitivity.

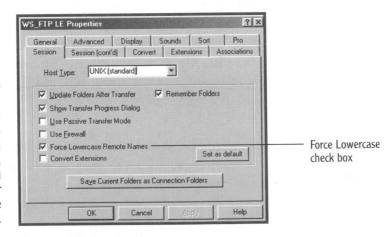

Force Lowercase
check box

more before your URL will be active and available on the Web.) Two errors that are very common when transferring files are transferring files in the wrong mode (ASCII as Binary or vice versa) and not transferring all the graphics that are included in a Web page. The only way you can be sure that everything has been transferred the way you want it is to check out the transferred Web page or pages in your browser. You don't have to exit WS_FTP LE before running your browser to check out your transfer—that way, for instance, if you've sent a file in the wrong mode, you can easily and immediately retransfer it.

Identifying ASCII File Types

If you want to use the Auto check box to transfer whole folders, you should first identify the ASCII file types that might be transferred. Just do the following:

1. Click on the Options button, and then click on the Extensions tab.
2. To add an ASCII file extension, first type the file extension (.HTM, for instance), and then click on the Add button to add it. Figure D.7 shows the .HTM, .HTML, .JS, and .TXT file extensions listed as ASCII file types.

Figure D.7

You can identify any file types of ASCII text files so WS_FTP LE will transfer them as ASCII files when using the Auto check box.

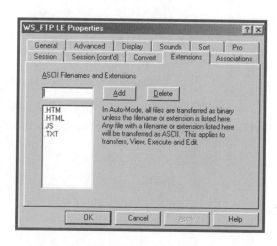

Closing and Exiting WS_FTP LE

When you are through transferring files to or from your server, you should always close your FTP session before exiting WS_FTP LE. To do this, just click on the Close button, wait for the Goodbye message to be displayed in the lower activity window, and then click on the Exit button. After exiting WS_FTP LE, log off the Internet, if you wish.

Using Other FTP Programs to Transfer Your Web Page Files

ON THE

CD

You can use other FTP programs besides WS_FTP LE or HTML editors with FTP capability to transfer your Web page files to your Web site folder on your Web server. Many FTP programs are available on the Web, and any of them will do the trick. Besides WS_FTP LE, the following FTP programs or programs with FTP capability are included on the CD-ROM:

- **WS_FTP Pro.** This is the "professional" version of WS_FTP (those who don't qualify to use the non-commercial version, WS_FTP LE, must use this version).

- **CuteFTP.** This is an excellent shareware program that uses an interface similar to that of Windows Explorer.

- **HTMLed Pro.** This HTML editor also includes the capability of transferring your finished HTML files via FTP.

- **CoffeeCup HTML Editor Express.** This HTML editor also includes the capability of transferring your finished HTML files via FTP.

For links to even more FTP programs and HTML editors with FTP capability, see my Web Tools site at **www.callihan.com/webtools/**.

HTML—Past and Future

To understand where HTML is going, you have to have some idea of where it's been. The following is a brief rundown on what has led to the current state of affairs and what is likely to happen.

Basic HTML: HTML 1.0 and HTML 2.0

HTML 1.0 and 2.0 were the two earliest versions of HTML. In this book, the Basic HTML Tutorial (Saturday Morning) focused exclusively on these versions of HTML. HTML, however, is in many ways like the layers of an onion, with the earlier versions still surviving as the inner layers of later versions. Some features that date back to these first versions of HTML include inline images, bulleted and numbered lists, definition lists (glossaries), and input forms.

Ad Hoc HTML: Netscape and Microsoft Extensions

Both Netscape and Microsoft developed their own special extensions to HTML for use in their browsers. These can be used in any Web document, but they translate into special formatting only when a user views the Web page in the particular browser for which they were created (unless the other browser's manufacturer provides support for the extensions, too).

Most of the extensions to HTML that Netscape pioneered have been incorporated into either HTML 3.2 or 4.0. The only purely Microsoft extension to be included in HTML 4.0 is the FACE attribute for the FONT tag, although Microsoft supported a number of proposed HTML 4.0 elements in its Internet Explorer 3.0 browser prior to the release of HTML 4.0. Some extensions, both old and new, such as Microsoft's MARQUEE tag and Netscape's BLINK tag, can only be displayed in one or the other of these browsers, not both. Unless everybody in your target audience uses the same browser, you should avoid using HTML that will only work in one browser. Preferably, you want your HTML to work in *all* browsers.

Probably the most noteworthy of Netscape's recent innovations is frames (using the FRAMESET and FRAME tags). The use of frames is rapidly proliferating on the Web, compelling other Web browsers to follow suit and incorporate the display of frames in their repertoire. Frames have since been incorporated into HTML 4.0, despite a certain amount of controversy. Although some people hate them, others swear by them. As usual on the Web, what Web publishers use is what matters, and on that score the vote is in: a qualified thumbs-up. The primary objections to frames are a "formal" objection that they violate the spirit of SGML (of which HTML is supposed to be a subset) and a "functional" objection that they make it difficult to link into a subpage within a frameset (meaning that a bookmark, for instance, would return you not to the subpage where you were, but only to the initial "front" page defined in the frameset).

◄◄

A page using frames is defined using the FRAMESET tag, so a collection of Web pages defined by a FRAMESET tag is often referred to as a *frameset*. Every Web page that uses frames starts from an initial frameset, although further framesets may be nested inside of the initial frameset. For HTML templates that can assist you in setting up framed Web sites, see the HTML Templates folder in the Book Examples folder on the CD-ROM.

◄◄

Microsoft has introduced a number of extensions to HTML that have remained unique to its Web browser, Internet Explorer. These include the capability to automatically play background sounds using the BGSOUND tag (you can add background sounds to Navigator, but only by using an entirely different method). Microsoft has introduced scrollable background images (when you scroll down through the text, the background image remains fixed). This same effect, however, can now be done using Cascading Style Sheets. Microsoft's addition of the FACE attribute to the FONT tag, on the other hand, has since been supported in Navigator 4.0 and has been included in HTML 4.0.

A Failed Initiative: HTML 3.0

HTML 3.0 was proposed as the next standard for HTML following HTML 2.0. However, the ambitiousness of HTML 3.0 ultimately proved its downfall—coming to an agreement on how to implement it simply was impossible. Ultimately, the W3C abandoned HTML 3.0 in favor of a much more modest proposal, HTML 3.2.

A number of HTML 3.0 features, however, found support in Web browsers—the most notable of which is tables. Other proposed HTML 3.0 elements that gained the favor of Web browsers to one degree or another include superscripts and subscripts, font-size changing (with the BIG and SMALL tags), and underlining. Many tags and attributes that were first proposed as part of HTML 3.0 have since been incorporated into HTML 3.2 and HTML 4.0.

Current HTML: HTML 3.2 and HTML 4.0

The two latest "official" versions of HTML are HTML 3.2 and HTML 4.0. HTML 3.2 was released in January 1997, and HTML 4.0 was released in December 1997.

HTML 3.2

Here are some of the primary features included in the HTML 3.2 standard:

- Tables
- Applets (for Java and JavaScript)
- Background images
- Background, text, and link colors
- Font sizes and colors
- Flowing of text around images
- Image borders
- Height and width attributes for images
- Alignment (left, center, or right) of paragraphs, headings, and horizontal rules (the CENTER tag)
- Superscripts and subscripts (the SUP and SUB tags)
- Strikethroughs (the STRIKE tag)
- Document divisions (the DIV tag)
- Client-side image maps (the MAP tag)
- Provisions for style sheets (the STYLE tag), left otherwise undefined

A large part of the HTML 3.2 specification is a rubber stamping of what originally were Netscape's unofficial and ad hoc extensions to HTML. The rest of the HTML 3.2 specification covers features of HTML 3.0 that had already gained wide acceptance and implementation (tables, for instance) in Web browsers. HTML 3.2 really offered little that hadn't already been widely implemented.

HTML 3.2 should be fully supported by all current graphical Web browsers. On the other hand, support for many of the new HTML 4.0 features among current graphical browsers is much more spotty. So, if you want to be conservative and make sure that your pages will display the way you want them to in all current graphical browsers, you should stick to using tags and attributes included in HTML 3.2—with the possible exception of the FRAMESET and FRAME tags, new HTML 4.0 tags that have already gained wide support among current browsers. To check out the official specification for HTML 3.2, see **www.w3.org/TR/REC-html32.html**.

FIND IT ON ▶
THE WEB

HTML 4.0

As of December 1997, HTML 4.0 is the officially recommended specification for HTML. Like HTML 3.2, HTML 4.0 is a mix of the old and the new. Included in it are elements that were previously either Netscape or Microsoft extensions (frames and font-face changes), as well as a number of entirely new elements and capabilities. Here are some of HTML 4.0's primary features:

- Frames, including inline frames
- Cascading Style Sheets, level 1 (CSS1)
- New form elements, including the BUTTON element, which allows the creation of graphical form buttons
- New table elements, including the ability to apply formatting to column and row groups
- New text-markup elements, including the INS (insert), DEL (delete), Q (quote), S (strikeout), and SPAN elements
- Microsoft's FACE attribute, which allows you to specify font faces that can be used when displaying text marked by the FONT element

✿ New universal attributes (ID and CLASS) that can be used to apply styles to individual instances of tag elements, as well as additional "intrinsic event" attribute handles that can trigger the activation of scripts from events such as passing the mouse over an element, clicking an element, and so on

At the time of this writing, full browser support for HTML 4.0 had yet to become a reality. Full agreement on how Cascading Style Sheets should be displayed has yet to be achieved—the same style sheet may have radically different results depending on whether it's displayed in Navigator or Internet Explorer. Also, a number of the new tags in HTML 4.0 have yet to be supported by either major browser. Before using a particular HTML element, you should at least check to see if current Web browsers support it. Also, older Web browsers may not support the new elements at all.

Here are some of the current initiatives afoot to expand and extend HTML:

✿ The recommendation for Cascading Style Sheets, level 2 (CSS2) was released in May 1998. These style sheets allow you to specify fonts on the Web that can be downloaded with a Web page, create rectangular regions containing other elements that can overlap and be positioned anywhere on a Web page, and define multiple style sheets for a single Web page that can be used by different media types (such as speech synthesizers, Braille printers, handheld devices, and so on).

✿ The Dynamic Object Model (DOM) is the keystone for the full implementation and development of Dynamic HTML, allowing the dynamic addressing of any "objects" in a Web page via scripts or programs. It allows much more interactivity (that is, the dynamic updating and accessing of Web page content in response to user actions). Right now, Netscape and Microsoft are supporting different versions of the DOM and Dynamic HTML, but they have agreed to standardize on the same DOM in their next generation of browsers.

✿ Mathematical Markup Language (MathML) provides complex formatting capabilities for equations and formulas.

I cover some of the relevant new HTML 4.0 features in The Intermediate HTML Tutorial (Saturday Afternoon) and in The Tables Tutorial (Saturday Evening). Frames is another new HTML 4.0 feature, although it had long been supported by both major Web browsers. While I don't specifically cover creating frames in this book, you can find a couple of frames templates, for creating two-frame and three-frame Web sites, among the HTML Templates that are included on the CD-ROM—just open the index page for the template to see instructions on how to use it.

FIND IT ON ▶
THE WEB

To find out more about HTML 4.0, check out the HTML 4.0 specification at **www.w3.org/TR/REC-html40/**. For other links to where you can find out more about HTML, including links to tutorials, guides, quick references, and style guides, see my Web Links site at **www.callihan.com/weblinks/**.

XML and XHTML

HTML 4.0 is the last version of HTML. Future development of standards for the display of Web-based documents will be focused on XML (Extensible Markup Language) and XHTML (Extensible HyperText Markup Language). XML is not strictly a markup language as much as it is a "meta-language" that allows for the further development of other markup languages (MathML, for instance). HTML 4.0, as such, is just one more markup language residing under the overall umbrella of XML. Conceivably, any interested group could create its own markup language, publish an SGML-conforming DTD (Document Type Definition) on the Web, and then have it instantly recognized by any XML-compatible Web browser. This would allow academic groups, for instance, to create their own markup language for displaying academic and scientific papers and articles, including footnotes, citations, bibliographies, figure captions, and so on. To find out more about XML, see **www.w3.org/XML/**.

FIND IT ON ▶
THE WEB

XHTML 1.0 is intended as a version of HTML that has been brought entirely into conformance with XML (and thus with SGML), as opposed to the "Wild West" variant that has finally evolved into HTML 4.0. Personally, I don't think that individual Web publishers need to be overly concerned with creating Web documents that strictly conform to XHTML. Nobody is going to spank you because you haven't converted all of your Web documents to the new standard. The W3C (World Wide Web Consortium), the organization responsible for HTML and Web development, has committed itself to maintaining the character of HTML as a "language that the ordinary person can use" and its accessibility to individuals who "still find value in writing their own HTML from scratch." Such language is unlikely to be used to describe XHTML. For that reason alone, I cannot help but feel that the future of HTML is quite secure.

With millions of documents currently residing on the Web that have been written as HTML 1.0, 2.0, 3.2, and 4.0 documents, there is little possibility that Web browsers will ever drop support for HTML. The capabilities of HTML 4.0, through the development of Cascading Style Sheets (CSS1 and CSS2) and the Dynamic Object Model (DOM), will continue to evolve and change. These developments alone will ensure that the capabilities of HTML will continue to evolve for many years. It is just unlikely that any new HTML tags or attributes will be added any time soon, which may not be such a bad thing.

The real advantage of XML and XHTML will come into play, I think, when it comes to producing documents that can be displayed across multiple media and for variable audiences, something that straight HTML is not very adept at doing. For instance, you might want to produce a single document to be printed in hard-copy form, displayed on the Web to be browsed, interpolated so someone who is visually impaired could read it using a Braille browser, or spoken through a voice synthesizer so someone who is hard of hearing could listen to it.

A number of changes to long-standing HTML practice will be required to create documents conforming to XHTML. Understandably, most Web publishers will be resistant to recoding HTML documents that have already been created and published to the Web—simply to be in conformance to XHTML—especially when the recoding will have no real impact on how those documents are displayed in current or future Web browsers. To find

FIND IT ON ▶
THE WEB

out more about XHTML, see **www.w3.org/TR/xhtml1/**.

What's on the CD-ROM

The CD-ROM that accompanies this book contains all of the example files that are used in this book's tutorials and work sessions, as well as shareware, freeware, and other software programs that can further enhance your Web publishing efforts.

Running the CD-ROM

To make the CD-ROM more user-friendly and take up less of your disk space, no installation is required. This means that the only files transferred to your hard disk are the ones you choose to copy or install.

◆ ◆

This CD-ROM has been designed to run under Windows 95/98, NT 4, or 2000. Neither the CD nor many of the programs on it will run under earlier versions of Windows. Windows 3.x users can check my Web Tools site at **www.callihan.com/webtools/** to see if 16-bit versions of any of the programs included on this CD-ROM are available for download from the Web.

◆ ◆

Because no install routine is required to use the CD-ROM, running the CD-ROM is a breeze, especially if you have Auto Insert Notification ("autorun") enabled for your CD-ROM drive. Simply insert the CD-ROM in your CD-ROM drive, close the tray, and wait for the Prima User Interface to load.

If you have disabled autorun, with the CD-ROM inserted in your CD-ROM drive, follow these steps:

1. From the Start menu, select Run.
2. Type *d*:\CDInstaller.exe (where *d* is your CD-ROM drive letter) and press the Enter key (or click on OK).

The Prima License

The first window you will see is the Prima License Agreement. Take a moment to read the agreement, and click on the I Agree button to accept the license and proceed to the user interface. If you do not agree with the license, click on the I Decline button to close the user interface and end the session.

The Prima User Interface

Prima's user interface is designed to make viewing and using the CD contents quick and easy. The opening screen contains a two-panel window with three buttons across the bottom. The left panel contains the structure of the programs on the disc. The right panel displays a description page for the selected entry in the left panel. The three buttons across the bottom of the user interface make it possible to install programs, view the contents of the disc using Windows Explorer, and view the contents of a help file for the selected entry. If any of the buttons are "grayed out," it means that button is unavailable. For example, if the Help button is grayed out, it means that no Help file is available.

Resizing and Closing the User Interface

As with any window, you can resize the user interface. To do so, position the mouse over any edge or corner, hold down the left mouse button, and drag the edge or corner to a new position.

To close and exit the user interface, either double-click on the small button in the upper left corner of the window or click on the exit button (marked with a small "x") in the upper right corner of the window.

Using the Left Panel

The left panel of the Prima user interface works very much like Windows Explorer. To view the description of an entry in the left panel, simply click on the entry. For example, to view the general information about Prima Publishing, Inc., click on the entry "Prima Publishing Presents."

Some items have sub-items that are nested below them. Such parent items have a small plus (+) sign next to them. To view the nested sub-items, simply click on the plus sign. When you do, the list expands and the sub-items are listed below the parent item. In addition, the plus (+) sign becomes a minus (-) sign. To hide the sub-items, click on the minus sign to collapse the listing.

NOTE   You can control the position of the line between the left and right panels. To change the position of the dividing line, move the mouse over the line, hold down the left mouse button (the mouse becomes a two-headed arrow), and drag the line to a new position.

Using the Right Panel

The right panel displays a page that describes the entry you chose in the left panel. Use the information provided to give details about your selection—such as what functionality an installable program provides. In addition to a general description, the page may provide the following information:

○ **Web site.** Many program providers have a Web site. If one is available, the description page provides the Web address. To navigate to the Web site using your browser, simply click on the Web address (you must be connected to the Internet). Alternately, you can copy the Web address to the clipboard and paste it into the URL line at the top of your browser window.

○ **E-mail address.** Many program providers are available via e-mail. If available, the description page provides the e-mail address. To use the e-mail address, click on it to open your e-mail program (to send e-mail, you must be connected to the Internet). Alternately, copy the address to the clipboard and paste it into the address line of your e-mail program.

○ **Readme, License, and other text files.** Many programs have additional information available in files with such names as Readme, License, and Order. If such files exist, you can view the contents of the file in the right panel by clicking on the indicated hyperlink (such as the word "here" displayed in blue). When you are done viewing the text file, you can return to the description page by reclicking on the entry in the left panel.

Command Buttons

Install. Use to install the program corresponding to your selection onto your hard drive.

Explore. Use to view the contents of the CD using Windows Explorer.

Help. Click on to display the contents of the Help file provided with the program.

Pop-Up Menu Options

Install. If the selected title contains an install routine, choosing this option begins the installation process.

Explore. Selecting this option allows you to view the folder containing the program files using Windows Explorer.

View Help. Use this menu item to display the contents of the Help file provided with the program.

Accessing the Book Examples

All of the book example files can be easily installed from the CD-ROM. In the Prima User Interface, expand the Book Examples item (click on the "+" button) in the left panel to gain access to these files:

- **Tutorial Example Files**. Select this item and click on the Install button to install all of the example images and other files used in the three Saturday HTML tutorials. These files will be installed to C:\HTML. For further directions, see the Saturday Morning session, "The Basic HTML Tutorial."

- **Example Web Pages**. Select this item and click on the Install button to install the example Web pages and other files used in the Sunday Morning and Sunday Afternoon sessions. These files will be installed to C:\MyPages. For further directions, see the Sunday Morning session, "Planning Your First Web Page."

○ **HTML Templates.** Select this item and click on the Install button to install all of the HTML templates. These files will be installed to C:\MyPages\Template.

You can also individually install any of the HTML templates. Just expand the HTML Templates item in the left panel, select the HTML template you want to install, and click on the Install button. Included are templates for creating an online calendar, two- and three-frame Web sites, your own genealogy Web site, a navigation bar, an online newsletter, and an online résumé. Also included is a set of generic Web page templates that can be used as a basis for creating many kinds of Web sites.

For further directions, see the readme.txt files included in the C:\MyPages\Template folder and in each of the individual template folders.

The Software

This section gives you a brief description of the shareware and evaluation software you'll find on the CD.

The software included with this publication is provided for your evaluation. If you try this software and find it useful, you must register the software if that is a requirement for its continued use (as discussed in its documentation). Prima Publishing has not paid the registration fee for any shareware or evaluation software included on the CD-ROM.

Of the software on the CD-ROM, only Paint Shop Pro 5 and WS_FTP LE are used in this book. Paint Shop Pro 5, used in the Sunday Evening session, "The Graphics Tutorial," has an evaluation period of thirty days, so you should wait to install it until you're ready to do that session. WS_FTP LE, used in Appendix D, "Putting It Up on the Web," is free for qualified non-commercial users—other users must use WS_FTP Pro, also on the CD-ROM, which has a thirty-day evaluation period.

You don't have to install any of the other programs on the CD-ROM to use this book. They are included solely to help enhance your Web publishing efforts. To make full use of the evaluation periods of any programs that require registration for continued use, you should wait to install them until you're ready to try them.

If you previously downloaded and installed from the Web an evaluation program included on the CD-ROM, you may not be able to evaluate it again unless the program on the CD-ROM is a later version than the one you previously evaluated. Check the vendor's Web site to see if a later version than what is included on the CD-ROM has been released.

◆ ◆

1 Cool Button Tool. Lets you create button styles and behaviors.

1-4-All HTML Editor. A tag-based, shareware HTML editor for 32-bit Windows. It will run on Windows 95 and Windows NT4.

3003 Background Images and Sounds. Formerly 505 Backgrounds and then 1001 Backgrounds..., an ever-expanding gallery of backgrounds, watermarks, sounds, and now themes.

Arachnophilia. A robust HTML editor that can import and automatically convert RTF documents, tables, and outlines from any Windows 95-compliant application to HTML.

AscToTab. A freeware program that converts a plain text file containing a table into an HTML file containing a full-fledged HTML table.

Banner*Show. Lets you create slide-show-like presentation of images and text on the Web page.

CGI*StarPro. Enables you to create your own CGI-based Web forms without requiring any programming.

Coffee Cup Image Mapper++. A powerful image map editor that makes adding clickable "hot spots" to your inline images a breeze.

CoffeeCup HTML Editor++. A full-featured HTML editor that includes Expresso FTP for uploading and downloading (now included in the shareware version), an image gallery with quick-linking images, highlighted tags, style sheet help, automatic image sizing, a line reader, and tips.

CoffeeCup HTML Editor Express. A streamlined HTML editor designed to make Web publishing a breeze—even for the novice. Seven preloaded HTML templates (DHTML, too) are included, with the option to create your own templates.

Color Match. This small, free program allows you to select colors and color codes to use in your HTML code.

CompuPic. A great tool for managing, viewing, and enhancing your graphics and other multimedia files.

Cool Edit 96. A shareware digital sound editor for Windows.

CuteFTP. A Windows-based FTP (File Transfer Protocol) client that allows users to utilize the capabilities of FTP without having to know all the details of the protocol itself.

CyberSpyder Link Test. A Web site management program for verifying that the URLs on a site are not broken and for analyzing site content.

DB-HTML Converter. A tool that generates HTML reports from DBase, Paradox, FoxPro, and Clipper databases. Without any additional HTML editor, you can create a set of linked Web pages that can be put immediately on your Web server.

Frame-It. A feature-packed freeware HTML frame generator that allows you to generate complex and impressive HTML frames using only your mouse.

GIF Construction Set. A great shareware GIF animation editor that makes creating your own GIF animations a breeze with its Animation Wizard.

GifArt Clip Art Collection. Includes a wide range of clip art and other graphics and a multitude of links to other graphics Web sites.

GIFmation. An intuitive and powerful application with an extensive feature set to give you the ability to easily create highly optimized GIF animations.

HTML Builder. An HTML 3.2 editor.

HTML Calendar. Automatically generates HTML code for a Web calendar for any month from 1998 through 2002.

HTML Notepad. An excellent shareware Notepad-like HTML editor.

HTML Power Tools. Includes customizable offline HTML validation and link checking; HTML-specific spell-checking; HTML-aware search and replace; site-wide META tag management; automatic HTML file date stamping; IMG tag automatic width, height, and ALT insertion; and HTML-to-text batch conversion.

HTML Table Designer. Aids in building HTML tables with formatted data.

HTMLed and HTMLed Pro. Two excellent HTML editors. HTMLed is true shareware, and HTMLed Pro is trialware with a thirty-day evaluation.

J-Perk. Creates animations and other special effects for Web pages using Java applets.

Link Editor. A nifty utility that helps to speed up the creation of hyperlinks.

LView Pro. A powerful but easy-to-use image editor with handy toolbar icons and extensive options.

Map This! A freeware image editor that can create, edit, and convert clickable image maps. (Unlike with Mapedit, however, you need to manually set the IMG tag's USEMAP attribute in your image map's HTML file.)

Mapedit. A great WYSIWYG editor for creating image maps.

NeoPlanet. Puts diverse interface skins at your fingertips and offers customizable, sharable "content channels." Uses the Internet Explorer engine, so you'll need Internet Explorer 4.0+ installed before installing NeoPlanet.

NeoTrace. Enhanced Traceroute program gives more feedback about failed connections than most other Traceroute programs.

NetSketch. An object-oriented drawing program.

Opera. A Web browser favored by many surfers who prefer their browser to be lean and mean.

Paint Shop Pro 5. An award-winning, image-editing tool that supports more than thirty image formats and several painting and drawing tools.

PicaView 32. An Explorer add-on for viewing images that displays thumbnail, format, and dimensions of selected image in context menu.

PolyView. A high-performance image viewer and format conversion tool that includes support for most of the popular graphics image formats.

Purp's World Graphics Clipart Collection. Includes a wide range of clip art and other graphics.

Template Generator. Helps speed up the process of creating Web pages.

TextPad. A powerful text editor that has many extra features and saves text files in PC, Macintosh, or UNIX formats.

Web Weaver 98. A comprehensive, feature-rich HTML editor.

Webber32. A fast, friendly, and flexible HTML editor that supports long file names and unlimited file sizes and has heaps of other great features.

WebForms. An HTML forms generator that automatically creates HTML forms and reads their responses.

WebPainter. A cel-based paint and animation program for the Web.

WinZip. *The* way to handle compressed ("zipped") files, whether you get them from a friend or download them from the Internet.

WS_FTP LE. A great FTP application for transferring files between your local PC and your Web site folders on a remote server; free for qualified non-commercial users (others should use WS_FTP Pro).

WS_FTP Pro. The "professional" version of WS_FTP. Does everything WS_FTP LE does and more. Includes two user-interface choices: Windows Explorer or Classic.

GLOSSARY

absolute URL. A complete path, or *address*, of a file on the Internet (such as **http://www.someserver.com/somedir/som epage.html**). Also called a *complete URL*. See also *Relative URL*.

adaptive palette. A color palette for an image that has been reduced to only the colors present in the image. Also referred to as a *customized palette* or an *optimized palette*.

alternative text. Text describing an image that is included in an IMG (Image) tag using the ALT attribute and that functions as an aid to surfers who have turned graphics off or who are using a Braille or speech browser.

anti-aliasing. The blending of colors to smooth out the "jaggies" along diagonals and curved edges in bitmap images. Applied most commonly to font characters inserted into a graphic image.

applet. A client-side program, usually Java or ActiveX, that is downloaded from the Internet and executed in a Web browser.

ASCII. American Standard Code for Information Interchange. Defines a standard minimum character set for computer text and data. ASCII files are sometimes called *DOS text* files or *plain text* files.

bandwidth. The transmission capacity of a network, but also the amount of capacity being consumed by a connection. A Web page containing many graphics will consume more bandwidth than one containing only text.

binary file. A non-text file, such as an image or program file.

BinHex. The standard method on the Macintosh of converting a *binary file* into *ASCII* (text) so it can be transferred as an e-mail attachment.

bitmap. An image composed of pixel dots, sort of like a pointillist painting. GIF and JPEG images are bitmap images, for instance.

bookmarks. A means, in Netscape Navigator, for "bookmarking" the URLs of favorite Web sites so they can easily be returned to. Bookmarks are saved by Navigator in an HTML file (`bookmark.htm`). A similar feature in Microsoft Internet Explorer is called *favorites* (but these are saved as separate files rather than in a single file).

Cascading Style Sheets. A means for defining styles, using the STYLE tag, to control the display of HTML elements. A style sheet can reside either inside the HTML file or in a separate file that's downloaded along with the HTML file. Current versions are Cascading Style Sheets, level 1 (CSS1) and Cascading Style Sheets, level 2 (CSS2).

CGI. Common Gateway Interface. An interface to a gateway through which a Web server can run programs and scripts on a host computer.

client. A computer on a network that makes a request to a server.

customized palette. See *adaptive palette*.

definition list. A glossary list in HTML that's created using the DL (definition list) element.

dithering. To create a new color by interspersing pixels of multiple colors so that the human eye "mixes" them and perceives the intended color. This is a technique used by browsers to display colors (or try to display them) that are not included in the default color palette of systems that can only display 256 colors.

domain category. A major grouping of domain names (such as .com, .org, .net, .edu, .mil, and .gov), as well as many national domain categories (.us, .uk, .ca, and so on).

domain name. An alphanumeric alternative to an IP address. Both are registered with InterNIC (Internet Network Information Center).

download. To transfer files from a server to a client. See also *upload*.

Dynamic HTML. Various means of providing dynamic Web content to respond interactively to user actions. Interactive responses may include producing on-the-fly Web pages, starting and stopping animations, and so on.

end tag. The end of a non-empty HTML element (such as </P>). See *start tag*.

extension. A non-standard extension to HTML, implemented by a particular browser (as in *Netscape extension* or *Microsoft extension*), that may or may not be displayable in other browsers.

favorites. A feature in Microsoft Internet Explorer that is similar to Netscape Navigator's bookmarks feature, allowing you to save a list of your favorite sites.

fragment identifier. A string at the end of a URL preceded by a "#" character used to identify a target anchor name. Allows a hypertext link to jump to a specific location in another or the same Web page.

frames. An extension to HTML, pioneered by Netscape, incorporated into HTML 4.0. Allows HTML documents to be presented inside multiple frames in a browser window.

FTP. File Transfer Protocol. The protocol used for downloading or uploading ASCII and binary files on the Internet.

GIF. Graphic Interchange Format. A graphics format developed by CompuServe that has become one of the standard image formats for displaying graphics on the World Wide Web. A GIF can include up to 256 colors, transparency, interlacing, and multiple frames (*GIF animation*). See also *JPEG*.

GIF animation. A GIF image file containing multiple images, usually viewable only in a Web browser.

Gopher. A menu-driven system, predating the World Wide Web, for sharing files over the Internet.

HTML. HyperText Markup Language. A markup language for preparing documents for display on the World Wide Web. The current standard version is HTML 4.0 (previous versions were HTML 1.0, HTML 2.0, and HTML 3.2).

HTML editor. A software program that edits HTML files, usually with the aid of pull-down menus, toolbars, and wizards.

HTML element. May be a stand-alone tag (such as <HR>) or everything between a start tag (such as <P>) and an end tag (such as </P>).

HTML tag. May be a stand-alone tag (such as <HR>) or an HTML start or end tag.

HTTP. HyperText Transfer Protocol. The protocol used to exchange Web pages and other documents across the Internet. A Web server, for instance, may also be called an *HTTP server*, in contrast to an *FTP* (File Transfer Protocol) *server*.

hypermedia. Interlinking of multiple media (text, images, sound, animation, and video).

hypertext. A means of providing for non-sequential linking of information.

hypertext link. A means, using the A (anchor) element in HTML, for jumping from a location in an HTML document to another Web page or object file on the Web, to a location in another Web page, or to a location in the same Web page. Also called a *hyperlink* or *hot link*.

image link. An inline image inserted inside a hypertext link, usually displayed with a blue border to show that it's an active link.

image map. An image displayed in a Web browser that has hidden "hot spots" that can be clicked to link to their designated URLs. Older browsers only supported server-side image maps (image maps executed from a server), but newer browsers also support client-side image maps (image maps executed from the desktop, or *client*).

in-context link. A hypertext link inserted within a paragraph or other text, rather than in a separate list or menu of links.

inline image. An image (GIF, JPEG, or PNG) that's displayed *inline* ("in a line") on a Web page.

interlaced GIF. A GIF image that is displayed in several passes, with only some of the image lines displayed each time, until all of the lines have been displayed. Allows viewers of an image to see what the whole image is going to look like before it has been entirely downloaded and displayed.

Internet. A set of protocols for transmitting and exchanging data among networks.

IP address. Internet Protocol address. A unique number, such as 185.35.117.0, that is assigned to a server on the Internet.

IPP. Internet Presence Provider, also often called a *Web host* or *Web space provider*. A company that rents out Web space.

ISP. Internet Service Provider, also often called an *access provider*. A company that provides dial-up access to the Internet.

Java. A computer language developed by Sun Microsystems for the delivery of cross-platform, client-side *applets* over the Internet.

JavaScript. A scripting language developed by Netscape for the execution by a browser of client-side scripts embedded in a Web page. A close variant, JScript, has been developed by Microsoft.

JPEG. Joint Photographic Expert Group. JPEG and GIF are the most common graphics formats for the display of images on the Web. JPEG images can be created from a palette of up to 16.7 million colors. However, JPEG images (unlike GIF images) cannot be transparent, interlaced, or animated. These are often referred to as *JPG format images* because the file extension for JPEG images under DOS/Windows is ".JPG." See also *GIF*.

keyword. A word used in an Internet or Web search. It is a good idea to include keywords you think others might search for in your Web page's title, level-one heading, introductory paragraph, and alternative text. You can also use the META tag to include a list of keywords in your Web page; this tag will be read by many search engines.

link. A *hypertext link*.

link list. A list of hypertext links, sometimes also called a *hot list*.

link text. The text displayed in a hypertext link, usually in blue and underlined.

MathML. Mathematical Markup Language. The proposed standard for displaying equations and mathematical symbols on the Web.

Microsoft extension. An extension to HTML supported by Microsoft Internet Explorer. The MARQUEE tag, for instance, is a Microsoft extension. Prior to its being incorporated into HTML 4.0, the FONT tag's FACE attribute was also a Microsoft extension. See also *Netscape extension*.

MPEG. Moving Pictures Expert Group. A means of compressing video and audio files.

Netscape extension. An extension to HTML supported by Netscape. The BLINK tag, for instance, is a Netscape extension. Many of the tags included in HTML 3.2 and 4.0 were originally Netscape extensions. See also *Microsoft extension*.

Netscape palette. A color palette composed of the 216 colors utilized by Netscape Navigator to display images on a computer displaying 256 colors. Also called a *safety palette*.

offline browsing. Browsing HTML files on a local hard drive without connecting to the Internet.

optimized palette. See *adaptive palette*.

ordered list. A numbered list in HTML.

plug-in. An application that provides a Web browser with the ability to display or play additional types of media, such as streaming audio or video.

PNG. Portable Network Graphics. The newest standard graphics format for the display of images on the Web. Supports up to 48-bit true color (JPEG supports up to 24-bit true color), as well as transparency and interlacing. So far, PNG is supported only by the latest browsers.

POP3 server. Post Office Protocol, Version 3. An "incoming mail" server (e-mail is received from a POP3 mail server). See also *SMTP server*.

QuickTime. A method developed by Apple Computer for delivering video, animation, and audio files.

refresh. To reload a Web page in Internet Explorer by clicking on the Refresh button. The equivalent action in Netscape Navigator is performed by clicking on the Reload button. In both browsers, Control+R refreshes or reloads a Web page.

relative URL. A Web address stated in relation to the current (or linking) page (as in `<IMG SRC="images/mypic.jpg">` or `<A HREF="../frames/myframe.html">`). Internal links within a Web site should always use relative links. This technique allows the linked files to be uploaded onto a server or moved to another location without the links having to be changed.

search engine. A Web site that has compiled a searchable index of sites on the Web, such as AltaVista or Lycos.

server. A computer on a network that responds to client requests. See also *client*.

SGML. Standard Generalized Markup Language. The parent markup language of HTML.

SMIL. Synchronized Multimedia Integration Language (pronounced "smile"). An HTML-like language for describing multimedia presentations, composed of streaming media (audio/video), images, text, and other media. SMIL, like HTML, can be composed in a text editor.

SMTP server. Simple Mail Transfer Protocol. An "outgoing mail" server (e-mail is sent to an SMTP mail server). See also *POP3 server*.

start tag. The start of a non-empty HTML element (`<P>`..., for instance).

style sheet. A set of descriptions of how elements in a Web page should be displayed by a browser that can display styles. See also *Cascading Style Sheets*.

target anchor. A hypertext anchor that defines the "landing spot" for a link.

TCP/IP. Transmission Control Protocol/Internet Protocol. The standard protocol for transmissions across the Internet.

transparent GIF. A GIF image that has one color designated as transparent. When displayed against a Web page's background color or background image, the color or image will show through the transparent areas of the image.

unordered list. A bulleted list in HTML.

upload. To transfer files from a client to a server.

URL. Uniform Resource Locator. An address on the Web.

vector image. An image where lines, curves, dimensions, and so on are determined by vector equations. Examples of vector images are EPS (Encapsulated PostScript), CDR (Corel Draw), and WMF (Windows Meta File) images. One advantage vector images have over bitmap images is that they are easily scalable. A plug-in is required to display vector images in a Web page.

Web browser. A software program that browses HTML and other files on the World Wide Web.

Webmaster. System operator for a server on the World Wide Web.

World Wide Web. A "wide-area hypermedia information retrieval initiative aiming to give universal access to a large universe of documents," according to Tim Berners-Lee, inventor of the World Wide Web. Also, "the universal space of all network-accessible information" (a more recent definition, also from Berners-Lee).

XHTML. Extensible HyperText Markup Language. A reformulation of HTML as conforming to XML.

XML. Extensible Markup Language. Slated as the next-generation markup language for the display of documents and data on the Web. XML is properly thought of as an SGML-compliant superset for HTML, and not as HTML's replacement. It will facilitate the development of specialized markup languages, as well as multi-modal publishing (Web, print, Braille, and so on) from a single document.

XSL. Extensible Stylesheet Language. The specification for style sheets for XML documents.

INDEX

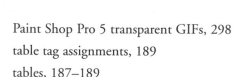

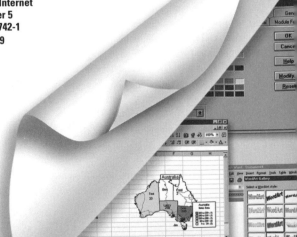

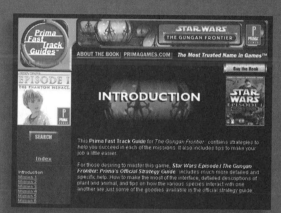

License Agreement/Notice of Limited Warranty